Upasana

With kind regards, ॐ and prem

Swami Niranjan

Upasana

In the Presence of the Divine

From the teachings of Swami Sivananda Saraswati
and Swami Satyananda Saraswati

Yoga Publications Trust, Munger, Bihar, India

Published by Yoga Publications Trust
    First edition 2007

ISBN: 978-81-86336-63-2

Publisher and distributor: Yoga Publications Trust, Ganga Darshan, Munger, Bihar, India.

Website: www.biharyoga.net

Printed at Thomson Press (India) Limited, New Delhi, 110001

Dedication

*In humility we offer this dedication to
Swami Sivananda Saraswati, who initiated
Swami Satyananda Saraswati into the secrets of yoga.*

Contents

Introduction

This text presents the teachings of both Swami Sivananda and Swami Satyananda on the path of upasana: worship of the sacred essence of life, God. Upasana is the path of devotion, adoration and selfless service to God. Upasana is worship of the God, who is everywhere, in everyone and in everything. It is a way that leads us into the proximity of the divine. The path of upasana is essential today, because most of us are unable to relate to the transcendental state of God, and to appreciate the wholeness of life that is God. We may think about these concepts, but for us, God is not a part of everyday life. We cannot feel, hear, see or touch Him. We are trapped and lost in the divine illusion, called maya, avidya or ignorance. This maya has become our reality. We identify with our restricted selves, our fears and pains, likes and dislikes. We have forgotten the awe and wonder of our very existence and we pay it no respect. We have forgotten Him, that priceless gem within.

In this book we learn of the mysterious power of upasana, which turns the mind inwards and eventually brings the devotee face to face with the Lord. Upasana is a method to merge the mind into thoughts of divinity, a means to transmute a person into blessed divinity. Throughout the pages of this book we are reminded that we are the grandeur of God, and that there is a way to turn our mind and see Him, because He is never far from us. We are shown the path, which enables us to feel the nearness of God, to feel His presence, and to be united with Him. Upasana is a method to connect man with God. It is not a sect or a religion; it is a sacred practice that helps us develop a relationship of love with God. And, the basis of God realization is this relationship of love and devotion.

The path of upasana has been preserved for thousands of years in the mystical science of bhakti. It is a spiritual path that has been revealed by the saints and sages of yore, a path which the bhaktas hold as sacrosanct in life. Swami Sivananda and Swami Satyananda are modern day sages; they are bhaktas of the highest calibre, who unfold the sublime essence of upasana in terms most relevant today for the spiritual evolution and upliftment of human kind. The many and varied forms of upasana are illustrated in this book, and any one of them will lead you to the Supreme. Upasana is to get involved in good works and to start benefiting others as well as yourself. Singing God's name, visiting pilgrimage places, temples and places of worship are good acts. Worship God by dedicating yourself to His service, by serving your country or community, by building hospitals, schools and orphanages, by uplifting the state of women, or by caring for your natural environment.

You may worship God in an idol, or you may chant His glories. Find any means of worship that attracts you. His worship also includes listening to His stories, meditating upon Him, describing His incarnations, teaching His name or inspiring others to love Him. Celebrating His birth, offering Him flowers, sandal paste and food in simple or elaborate rituals and yajnas, is worship, upasana. On the other hand, if you prefer, you can earn and donate money to help worthy people in one form or another. Whether you worship with music or dance, or with mantra japa in anushthana and purascharana, upasana is to be practised with deep faith. It is not necessary that you have a one-pointed mind when you worship God, but have faith. It is faith that takes you into the lap of God.

This book captures the sense of reverence and faith that these two great masters have for the ancient scriptural teachings. Their teachings will bestow a divine perspective upon your entire existence and will inspire you to walk with God. They will give you a means to transform your life into a heaven on earth. When you read what they have offered, you are certain to be left with a feeling of inexpressible gratitude.

In the words of Swami Satyananda: "God is wherever you are. Always remember there is a priceless gem in each and everyone. People know Him by different names, but nobody knows just what His reality is. You may call Him God, Atman, Paramatman, or anything else. There is a very great prize within you, but it is so deep. You won't have to search for Him anywhere else, although He is elsewhere also. God is not far from you. He is closer than your own breath, closer than your own prana, closer than your own mind. He is your closest companion, much closer than your husband or wife. God is your friend, your prana, your life, your eyes and your ears. All your energy is His. He is so close to you, just turn your mind within and you will see Him."

Upasana

From the teachings of Swami Sivananda Saraswati

1

Defining Upasana

The term *upasana* literally means 'sitting near the Lord'. Upasana is approaching the chosen ideal or object of worship by meditating on it in accordance with the teachings of the *shastras* (scriptures) and the guru, and dwelling steadily in the current of that one thought, like a thread of oil being poured from one vessel to another. The practice consists of those observances and methods, both physical and mental, by which the aspirant makes steady progress on the path of spirituality and finally realizes the presence of God within himself. *Upasya* means that which is the object of upasana, namely, God.

Upasana or worship is the expression of devotion, reverence and love for the Lord. It is the expression of a keen yearning to be united with Him, and of a deep spiritual thirst to hold conscious communion with Him. Worship God. Praise Him. Seek enlightenment and realize serenity, truthfulness, compassion and love. Man can never get full satisfaction from sensual pleasures. He will always feel that he is lacking something. He remains restless and discontented. Then he longs to come into conscious communion with the Lord of the universe and to attain immortality and everlasting peace. This ultimate craving finds its satisfaction in worship. The individual soul desires to unite with his father, the Supreme soul.

Upasana is a broad term that includes many forms of worship, such as: *pooja* (rituals), daily morning ablutions, prayer, repeating verses in praise of God, kirtan, japa, meditation, etc. Worship is again either gross or subtle according to the nature of the seeker, his degree of competency or advancement on the path. One who worships the Lord in the form of a *murti* or image, rings a bell and offers sandal paste, flowers, etc. practises an exoteric form of worship, whereas one who visualizes the image of their *ishta* or personal deity internally, meditates on it and makes mental offerings practises an esoteric form of worship.

No matter the form of worship, the devotee longs for the benign grace of the Lord to grant him devotion and remove the veil of ignorance. The devotee constantly remembers His name, he repeats His mantra, he sings His praise, he does kirtan, he hears and recites His stories, he lives in the company of His devotees, he meditates on His form, nature, attributes and pastimes. The devotee visualizes the form of the Lord with closed eyes and enjoys supreme peace and bliss. Love and devotion naturally arise in his heart when he hears the glory and greatness of the Lord. The devotee's worship helps his spiritual evolution.

Hearing stories of the Lord, singing kirtan and bhajan, constant remembrance of the Lord, service of His feet, offering flowers, prostration, prayer, chanting of mantras, self-surrender, service of devotees, service of humanity and country with *Narayana bhava* (attitude of serving all), etc. constitute worship of a form, *saguna upasana*. Here, an object of worship is necessary for man to pour forth his love and devotion. Service to humanity and country with atma bhava, mental japa of Om, chanting of Om with atma bhava, meditation on the mantras Soham or Shivoham, or on the *mahavakyas* (great sayings of the Upanishads), such as *Aham Brahma Asmi* or *Tat Tvam Asi*, and contemplation of the doctrine *Neti-neti* ('Not this, not this'), constitute examples of worship without form *(nirguna upasana)*.

The fundamental aim of the worshipper, or upasaka, is union with the Lord, who pervades or permeates all these names and forms. The Supreme has many different aspects or forms, such as Brahma, Vishnu, Shiva, Rama, Krishna, Ganapati, Kartikeya, Durga, Lakshmi, Saraswati, Indra, Agni, but whatever the name or form, it is the one God who is adored. In whatever form the Lord is worshipped, the devotion goes to the same Lord. All are worshipping the one basic reality, *Ishwara*. The differences are only differences in names and forms on account of differences in the worshippers. Worship of the form of Lord Jesus, Prophet Mohammed, Sri Guru Nanak, Lord Buddha or Lord Mahavira is really worship of Ishwara. Similarly, in the *Bhagavad Gita* (4:2) it says: "However men approach Me, even so I welcome them, for the paths men take from every side are mine, O Partha."

There is another classification of worship according to the nature and capacity of the individual. Some worship elementals and lower spirits. Some worship forefathers, rishis and celestials. Some worship avataras, such as Krishna and Rama. Some worship the *saguna Brahman*, God with attributes. Some worship *nirguna Brahman*, the formless, attributeless, unmanifest. There is also nature worship. Parsis worship the element fire. Hindus worship the river Ganga, cows, the peepal tree, etc. There is hero worship in which the individual imbibes the virtues of the person whom he worships. Birthday celebrations of great persons are forms of worship.

There is relic worship, where hairs and bones of departed souls are worshipped. There is worship of gurus, *rishis* (seers) and *devatas* (gods). Meditation is mental worship of the Lord. Singing the Lord's names or *kirtan* is vocal worship. Service of living beings with love and a divine attitude is physical worship. As a person evolves, he passes from one stage of worship to another. The lower stages drop away by themselves. A person of a higher stage should not condemn one who is in a lower stage. One should not forget the underlying, indwelling, interpenetrating, one essence or intelligence when doing worship of any kind.

9

Upasana in the Bhagavad Gita

The *Bhagavad Gita* is a most popular scripture in which Lord Krishna delivers many discourses to his disciple Arjuna on how to obtain self-realization by *karma* (action), *jnana* (wisdom), *dhyana* (meditation) and *bhakti* (devotion). As Sri Krishna speaks to Arjuna about these four paths to moksha, he describes many types of upasanas, such as meditating on the forms of God, on the divine qualities of a devotee, on the yoga practices of asana and pranayama, on devotion and surrender to God's will, and on satsang. All of these upasanas are to be performed selflessly, without attachment to the results.

In the *Bhagavad Gita* (4:24–30), the upasanas performed through karma yoga are described. These include different forms of *yajna* or worship through sacrifice:

- Ritual sacrifice to the gods or deities, such as *devi yajna*.
- Sacrifice of self, *atma yajna*, understanding that the *atma*, or individual Self, is a part of *Paramatman*, the Supreme Self, but conditioned by body, intellect and ego.
- Sacrifice of the senses, restraint of the senses (*indra yajna*).
- Sacrifice of prana through the actions and breath, *yoga yajna* refers to the sadhana of asana and pranayama, etc. For example, *pranopasana* is the practice of pranayama, controlling the prana through regulated inhalation, retention and exhalation, by restricting the diet and offering the five pranas: *prana, apana, samana, vyana* and *udana*, into controlled breathing. *Prana* is the vital life force of all creatures; it is the essence of God.
- Sacrifice of wealth, offering of wealth to the downtrodden and needy without any expectation of return or benefits. (*dravya yajna*).
- Sacrifice by reading and study of the scriptures (*swadhyaya yajna*)
- Sacrifice by following austerities and observing a life of austerities (*tapo yajna*).

10

- Sacrifice by accepting the rigid vows of an ascetic, *vrata yajna*: observing vows prescribed by the scriptures, and spiritual preceptors.
- Sacrifice by *seva*: selfless service to mankind.

Upasana performed as karma yoga has two different aspects: one is *sakama* (with desire) and the other is *nishkama* (without desire). In sakama upasana the upasaka worships the deities for worldly gain, such as wellbeing, wealth sons, and victory, etc. Yajna is a type of sakama upasana. In the yajna the devotee offers the deity different objects as sacrifice. In the *Srimad Bhagavat*, we are told that Paramatman fulfils all the desires of the upasaka. Therefore, in sakama upasana, God confers *preyas* on the devotee, i.e. whatever he wishes. In nishkama upasana there is no request for any worldly desires. The nishkama upasaka aims only to possess *nishshreyas*, ultimate knowledge and unification in Brahman.

Upasanas performed through meditation or dhyana yoga are described in the *Bhagavad Gita* (6:11–15). These include the nirguna upasanas, worship of the soul, seeking unification with the Paramatman.

Upasana through bhakti yoga is described in the *Bhagavad Gita* (6:17). The four classes of bhaktas are: *arta*, one who is distressed; *artharathi*, one who seeks wealth, possessions, children, etc.; *jignasu*, one who worships for knowledge of the Supreme; and *jnani*, the real upasaka, whose worship is divine and unites him with the Supreme. Lord Krishna says that the bhaktas who worship with expectation will obtain the fruits that disappear after some time, but the bhaktas who require only unification with Him will succeed in their worship and never again return to the worldly realms.

Symbols used in worship
There are people in different stages of evolution towards God, so there are simple and concrete forms of worship as well as the higher, abstract forms. All the different forms of worship are merely so many ways of fixing the mind on God

and making it one-pointed in worship. External symbols have a strong power that can affect our thoughts and feelings. A particular object, which may be different for each person, will draw feelings of kindness from the heart and stir within us feelings of love and devotion to God. This type of object must be chosen as the image or symbol for daily worship. This symbol will stand for God and be a constant reminder of God. In whatever form you may choose to worship God, bear in mind that God is One. All the different forms are different aspects of the one God. No one form is better than another. All are one and the same.

Benefits of worship

Worship enables us to feel the nearness of God and to feel His presence. Worship is the means to be united with God. It is our prayer to Him to give us more devotion, to remove our ignorance, to show us the right and proper method of getting rid of our impurities, defects, pains and sufferings. It is our effort to actually feel the gracious presence of God in our hearts, knowing that it is He alone who is working through us. Worship is a way of showing love for God as well as a means by which we can develop love for Him. Through regular worship we gradually feel a stronger and stronger love for God. We become in tune with the divine will of the Lord, which grants us peace, prosperity and protection in our daily lives.

There are many benefits of worship, some of which are enumerated below:
- It purifies the heart and fills it with pure love for the Lord.
- It turns the mind inward and allows us to look at ourselves honestly.
- It steadies the mind and develops effortless concentration.
- It destroys evil qualities such as anger, lust, jealousy, hatred, egoism and greed.
- It fills the heart with the divine virtues of honesty, understanding, forgiveness and cheerfulness.

- It slowly changes man into a divine being, like a holy saint.
- In the end it leads to union with the Lord, which is the goal of human life. Krishna says, "O Arjuna, by devotion to Me alone, I may be perceived, and known and seen in essence, and entered."

The mysterious power of upasana

Upasana transmutes a person into blessed divinity. One who leads a mere sensual life without doing any worship is only an animal, although he appears outwardly in the form of a human being. Eating, drinking, sleeping, fear and copulation, etc. are common in brutes and human beings, but that which makes one a real man or a god-man is upasana. Of all the things that are conducive to spiritual advancement and the acquisition of virtues, upasana is not only an indispensable requisite, but is also eminently beneficial to all classes of people. It is easy, too. All gifts that are inspired by the fever of upasana and the love of God are *sattwic* (truly pure). If the giver does not have faith, charity will not attain its fullness, and he will not get the maximum benefits. In austerity, yajna and kirtan, the cumulative powers of faith, love of God and keen longing for divine illumination produce sattwic benefits or fruits. Patanjali Maharishi emphasizes the importance of worship in various places in his *Yoga Sutras*. Worship is necessary even for a raja yogi; he must have his own *Ishta*, or guiding deity.

Man sows an action or thought and reaps a habit of doing or thinking. He sows a habit and reaps a character. He sows a character and reaps a destiny. Habit is second nature – or rather first nature itself. Man creates his own destiny by thinking and acting. He can change his destiny also. He is master of his own destiny; there is no doubt of this. By right thinking, enquiry and strong self-effort, he can become master of his destiny. Markandeya changed his destiny through austerity and worship of Lord Shiva. Vishwamitra became a Brahmarishi (realized sage) through vigorous austerities. You can also do so if you have a strong will and iron determination. Vashishtha preaches self-effort to Sri Rama. This yoga element is predominant in Vashishtha. Savitri changed the destiny of her husband, Satyavan, through the power she obtained following the rules of a *pativrata dharma* (a chaste wife).

Upasana destroys subtle desires, cravings, egoism, lust, hatred, anger, etc. It changes the mental substance, destroys *rajas* (restlessness), removes *tamas* (dullness), and fills the mind with *sattwa* (purity). Upasana turns the mind inward and eventually brings the devotee face to face with the Lord, thus freeing him from the wheel of birth and death and conferring on him immortality, *moksha* (freedom). The mind becomes that on which it meditates. There is a mysterious power in upasana which makes the meditator and the meditated upon identical.

Understanding the method of worship

Worship is the expression of love and devotion to the Lord, of extreme reverence towards Him, of keen longing to be in conscious communion with Him, of eager aspiration to be always at His feet and of intense craving to be united with Him. During worship the devotee feels the pangs of his separation from the Lord, sheds profuse tears and sings his praises, glories, splendour and greatness. In order to attain this level of worship, you should have a proper understanding of the method of worship, the meaning of the verses you recite, the significance of the mantras and rites, the benefits of japa and worship.

You should cultivate *shraddha* (faith), *bhava* (feeling) and devotion. You should have *ruchi*, a taste for God's name. You should have knowledge of the science of upasana, japa yoga, mantra yoga, and bhakti yoga. You should have a clear idea of the goal and nature of God. You should have *vairagya*, non-attachment to the sensory experiences. You should know how mantra japa produces its purifying effects on the mind, destroys rajas and tamas, fills the mind with sattwa, and changes human nature into divine nature. Only then will you be highly benefited and have quick progress in the spiritual path. Enquire, think, and cogitate.

Parents should also lead a religious and pious life. They should be well versed in the science of upasana, mantra yoga, japa yoga and bhakti yoga. They should train their children in the spiritual path from their very infancy in the proper manner. Then only will their home be a *vaikuntha* (heaven) on earth. Then alone will harmony, peace, plenty, prosperity fill the home. A life without worship is a dreary waste.

15

2

Nine Modes of Worship

Upasana is supreme attachment to God with intense inner feeling. Intense and exclusive love is the common factor expressed through all the nine modes of worship. All bhaktas of this type are above the formalities of the world. They are untouched by the laws of human rules of right and wrong, and are out and out concerned with God. Maharishi Sandilya tells of this in *Srimad Bhagavat*. Good conduct that is in accordance with moral law is an auxiliary to upasana and it follows the upasaka wherever he goes. One cannot practise true worship of God if he is crooked in his heart, if he has objects of love in the world, if he is tempted by charming things, if he wants to feed his body well, if he wishes to take care of his wife, children and relatives, and if he wishes to earn great name and fame.

Perfect detachment from all objects is a preliminary to real devotion and worship. Vairagya is the product of real love for God. One who has love for the world cannot have love for God. Where there is *kama* (desire), there cannot be Rama (God), and where there is Rama, there cannot be kama. Love for the world and love for God are diametrically opposite. One has to renounce one for the attainment of the other. This renunciation can be acquired through the nine forms of worship. A devotee can worship by any method that suits him best, and through that he will attain divine illumination.

16

The *Bhagavad Gita* is an authority on the nine modes of worship. Lord Krishna illustrates that the various modes of devotion all lead to the Supreme. In the *Uddhava Gita* also Lord Krishna tells Uddhava about these nine forms of upasana. Lord Krishna says that to worship an idol as his *pratika* (symbol), to serve, to eulogize Him and to chant of His glories is his upasana. His worship also includes listening to His stories with faith and devotion, meditating upon Him, dedicating oneself to His service, reciting and describing His incarnations, celebrating His birth, going on pilgrimage, offering Him flowers, sandal paste and food.

In the *Srimad Bhagavat* and the *Vishnu Purana*, the nine forms of worship are given as follows:
1. *Shravana* – hearing of God's *lilas* (divine plays) and stories
2. *Kirtan* – singing His glories
3. *Smarana* – constant remembrance of His name and presence
4. *Padasevana* – service to His feet
5. *Archana* – ritual worship of God with or without form
6. *Vandana* – prostration, prayer to the Lord
7. *Dasya* – cultivating the inner attitude of a servant of God
8. *Sakhya* – cultivating the attitude of friendship with God
9. *Atma nivedana* – complete surrender of the self.

Shravana or satsang

Shravana is listening to the stories of the Lord that are connected with His divine name and form. It includes hearing about His virtues, glories and sports. The devotee becomes absorbed in the hearing of divine stories. When the mind merges in the thought of divinity, it is no longer charmed by the world and cannot think of non-divine things. In this way, the devotee remembers God only, even when dreaming. The upasaka should sit before a learned teacher, who is saintly, and hear the stories. He should hear them with a sincere heart, devoid of criticism and fault-finding. He should try his best to live by the ideals preached in the scriptures. In the *Bhagavad Gita* (4:34), Lord Krishna says:

"Know that by long prostration, service and enquiry, the wise who know the Truth shall instruct thee in that wisdom."

One cannot attain shravana bhakti without satsang, being in the company of saints or the wise. Mere reading for oneself can only give a partial experience. Doubts will come up, and they cannot be resolved by oneself. An experienced worshipper is necessary to instruct the devotee in the right path. Shankaracharya says: "The company of the wise, even for a moment, becomes the boat to cross the ocean of *samsara* (the illusory world)." Without satsang, *sadhana* (spiritual practice) does not become perfect and strong. The fort of sadhana should be built on the foundation of satsang.

Mere austerities are not the end of sadhana. Satsang illumines the devotee and removes his impurities. It is only then that subtle truths are grasped. Lord Krishna says to Uddhava that nothing but satsang can put an end to all worldly attachments. In the *Bhagavat* it is said that the best dharma in this world is to hear the Lord's glories, for thereby one attains to the divine abode. King Parikshit attained liberation through shravana and satsang. He heard about the glories of God from Maharishi Suka and his heart was purified. He became liberated and attained the abode of Lord Vishnu at Vaikuntha. He enjoyed supreme bliss.

Kirtan

Kirtan is singing the Lord's name and glories, and is the easiest of all the modes of worship. The upasaka is thrilled with divine emotion and loses himself in the love of God. His voice becomes choked with emotion; tears of joy fill his eyes, and he flies into a state of divine ecstasy. He is ever engaged in singing the Lord's name and describing His glories to one and all. Wherever he goes he sings and praises God. He requests all to join his kirtan. He sings and dances in ecstasy. He inspires others to dance with him. Such practices should be the outcome of a pure heart, and not merely a show. God knows the inner heart of all and none can cheat Him.

In the *kali yuga* (the fourth and present aeon of the world), kirtan alone is the best yoga, and is the prescribed method of upasana. The mind that is ever intent upon singing the Lord's names and glories has no occasion to take interest in things of the world. Day and night the upasaka feels the presence of God and thins out his ego. He becomes pure at heart. Great divine personalities like Narada, Valmiki and Sukadeva in ancient times, and Gouranga, Nanak, Tulsidas, Surdas and Chaitanya in comparatively recent times, have all attained perfection through kirtan alone. Even the great sinner Ajamila crossed the ocean of worldly existence by repetition of the Lord's name in kirtan. If even sinners can cross over samsara through kirtan, what to speak of good persons, who have a pure heart, who have served their guru and country?

Kirtan is sweet and pleasant, and easily changes the heart. It is also a very effective method of worship for another reason. Man is an erotic being; he loves and loves. He cannot but love the things of the world, but this is passion and not pure divine love. Man wants to see beautiful objects, hear sweet music and dance. Music melts the heart of even the stone-hearted man. If there is anything in this world that can change the heart of a man very quickly it is music and dance. Through kirtan, this aspect of man's nature is directed towards divinity instead of towards sensual enjoyments. Kirtan provides a means of expression for man's love of music so that it need not be suppressed or destroyed.

Maharishi Suka is an example of a shravana and kirtan bhakta. He narrated the *Srimad Bhagavat* and was completely immersed in the state of superconsciousness attained by bhaktas through the intense emotion derived from this form of worship. When Sri Suka was singing the glories of the Lord, the *devas* (gods) themselves came down from heaven and took part in this worship with various musical instruments. Narada played his vina and Indra played the mridanga. Prahlada danced with his cymbals and Lord Shiva himself began to dance. Lord Vishnu was present, and all those assembled there were thrilled by the occasional dance of Sri Suka himself in ecstasy.

Kirtan is the most suitable method for all, especially for householders. It gives pleasure to the mind and at the same time purifies the heart. Kirtan is the easiest, best and cheapest method of worshipping God for all people, without distinction.

Smarana

Smarana is constant remembrance of the name and form of the Lord at all times. The mind does not think of any object of the world, but is ever engrossed in thinking of the Lord alone. The mind meditates on what is heard about the glorious Lord. The mind meditates on His virtues and names, etc. and forgets even the body. Japa also comes under this category of upasana. Remembrance includes stories pertaining to God, talking of God, teaching others about God, meditation on the attributes of God, etc.

Worship of the Divine through smarana has no time limit as God is to be consciously remembered at all times without a break. The worship begins from the moment the devotee awakes from sleep in the morning until he is completely overpowered by sleep in the night. He has no other duty in this world. Remembrance of God alone can destroy all worldly tendencies. It can turn the mind away from sense objects. Generally the mind runs outward to the sensual world, but remembrance of God makes it introverted.

Smarana is a very difficult method of upasana, equal to concentration or meditation. All the qualities that a raja yogi needs to perfect the practice of meditation are also required for the practice of smarana. It is not possible to remember God at all times, and the mind will cheat the upasaka. He may think that he is meditating on God, but actually he is dreaming of some worldly concept. Practising smarana is like swimming against the forceful current of the river of maya. However, when mastered, it leads to exclusive meditation on God, as is attained in raja yoga.

20

The company of real devotees and service of *mahatmas* (great souls) are necessary auxiliaries to the remembrance of God. The mind cannot but remember divine things when in the company of divine people. Therefore, one should have satsang and serve a saint or a great bhakta regularly. While practising smarana, the upasaka should not be perturbed by censure or ridicule from the world. He should rely on God and rest assured that God will help him in all troubles and will give him final emancipation. Constant remembrance is the fruit of almost all the other methods of sadhana.

In the *Bhagavad Gita* (8:4), Lord Krishna says: "O Arjuna! He who, fixing his mind on me, constantly remembers Me, I am easily attained by that yogi, ever united with Me." Prahlada practised such remembrance of God. He never forgot the Lord at any time. His cruel father punished him in all possible ways, but the devoted Prahlada crossed over all troubles and obtained the supreme grace of the Lord. He was lost in God consciousness. The seventh section of the *Bhagavat* gives a beautiful description of how Prahlada practised bhakti even amidst trying conditions.

The miser does not forget his wealth even when he is engaged in other duties. The passionate man does not forget his beloved, and the cow does not forget its calf even while grazing. Even so a worldly man should remember God although he may be engaged in other duties. Remembrance of the Lord has given liberation even to those who remembered Him through hatred, like Kamsa and Sisupala. Hatred of the Lord leads to the state of liberation through *vaira bhava* (feeling of enmity). This is the most potent method of upasana, and the most difficult also.

Padasevana

Padaseva is serving at the feet of the Lord. Actually, no mortal being has the good fortune to practise this method of upasana because the Lord is not visible to the physical eye. Only Lakshmi or Parvati can really perform this worship. However, it is possible to serve the image of God and, better still, to serve the whole of humanity as God. So, padaseva is service to the sick and the poor. The whole manifest universe is only the form of the Lord. Service to the citizens of the whole world is worship of the Lord. This form of worship can be started in your own neighbourhood; there are endless opportunities to serve your fellow beings.

Service to the Lord's feet can be done through formal worship to one's guru, to images of God in temples or one's home, or to a mental image of God. There are many ritual forms of padaseva, such as: (i) observing the sacred feet of the Lord again and again with a devotional gaze, (ii) worshipping and serving them, (iii) sipping the sacred water in which the Lord's feet have been washed, (iv) worshipping the sandals of the Lord, (v) meditating on them and praying to them, (vi) taking the dust of the Lord's feet and applying it to the forehead, (vii) serving in holy shrines and places of pilgrimage and places where the Lord incarnated for the good of humanity, (viii) regarding the Ganges as directly flowing from the feet of the Lord, and (ix) worshipping, bathing in and drinking of such divine water. This kind of upasana destroys all worldly attachments and allows the mind to think exclusively of God.

Bharata served the sandals of Sri Rama throughout the period of his forest exile. What devotion! He kept them on the throne and worshipped them as representing Sri Rama Himself. He ruled the kingdom in the name of Sri Rama's sandals, himself acting only as the servant of Rama. This is worship through padasevana.

Archana

Archana is upasana through worship of an image of God in whatever form attracts the devotee. Serving the poor and sick and worshipping saints is also archana of the Lord in His manifest and living forms. The Lord appears in all forms. He is everywhere and in everything. The scriptures declare that the Lord appears in every sentient and insentient being. The upasaka should consider all creatures, even down to a worm, as forms of God. This is the highest form of worship. Archana is generally practised through tantric or vedic methods. It can be performed in a temple, in one's own home, or at any place.

The object of archana is sincere devotion and real surrender for the sake of union with the Lord. During worship, the mind of the devotee should always be concentrated on the form of the Lord. The upasaka should think of His infinite attributes, nature, bliss, immortality, etc, and not of earthly things. The food offered to the Lord during worship is actually taken away by Him when it is offered with sincere feeling. There are cases where devotees with burning love for God offered food to God and He actually appeared before them in his supreme form and partook of the food offered to Him. These are rare cases, but it must be known that true devotees are very rare in this world.

Vandana

Vandana is worship through prayer and prostration. This form of upasana includes: humble prostration, touching the earth with the eight limbs of the body *(sashtang namaskara)*, bowing down with faith and reverence before a form of God, bowing to all beings as forms of the one God, and getting absorbed in the divine love of the Lord. The *Bhagavat* says: "The sky, air, fire, water, earth, stars, planets, the cardinal points (direction), trees, rivers, seas and all living beings constitute the body of Sri Hari. The devotee should bow before everything in absolute devotion, thinking that he is bowing before God Himself."

In the *Uddhava Gita*, Lord Krishna says to Uddhava: "One should prostrate and bow down to all beings, even to the dog, the ass, the pariah and the cow, giving no attention to those who laugh in ridicule, forgetting the body and insensible to shame. All is Myself; nothing is but Myself." Similarly, in the *Bhagavad Gita* (11:40), Arjuna says to Krishna in a most beautiful manner: "Salutations to You from the front, salutations to You from behind, salutation to You from every side! O All! Immeasurable in strength, You pervade all. You are all."

The aim of this form of worship is to realize God through exclusive love. The *Mahabharata* says: "There is nothing more auspicious than the Lord, Vasudeva; there is nothing more purifying than Vasudeva, and there is no higher deva worthy of being worshipped than Vasudeva. One who offers his salutations to Vasudeva suffers no afflictions." The ego is completely effaced through devout prayer and prostration to God. Divine grace descends upon the devotee and man becomes God.

Again, the *Mahabharata* describes how the great warrior Bhishma offered his salutations to the Lord: "Having thus offered his prayer to the Lord, Bhishma, whose mind was wholly absorbed in the Supreme, said: 'Salutations to Krishna' and bowed his head to Him. Learning the depth of Bhishma's devotion through His power of yoga, Sri Krishna bestowed upon Bhishma the light of divine knowledge which illumines the three worlds."

Sincere prayer has a tremendous influence. If the prayer proceeds from the bottom of your heart, it will at once melt the heart of the Lord. Sri Krishna had to run barefoot from Dwaraka on hearing the heartfelt prayer of Draupadi. Lord Hari, the mighty ruler of this universe, apologized to Prahlada for coming to his rescue a little late. How merciful and loving is God! Prayer can work miracles and move mountains.

Say even once from the depths of your heart: "O Lord, I am Thine. Thy Will be done. Have mercy on me. I am Thy servant. Forgive. Guide. Protect. Enlighten." While praying, have a meek, receptive attitude of mind. Feel the prayer in your heart. Such prayer is at once heard by the Lord and responded to. Do this in the daily battle of life and realize the high efficacy of prayer for yourself. You must have strong conviction in the existence of God to practise this form of upasana.

Christians have different prayers for asking for various gifts and bounties from God. Mohammedans have daily prayers at sunrise, noon, sunset, just before eating and just before retiring to bed. Prayer is at the beginning of yoga. Prayer is the first limb of yoga and the preliminary spiritual sadhana. Prayer can be addressed to a deity or to God through a song of devotion which seeks blessings. In the *Rig Veda*, the prayers offered to the deities are in the form of hymns, called *suktas*. These hymns are addressed to different deities such as: Agni, Indra, Mitra, Yama, Marut and others, All of these deities represent the various aspects of the same Paramatman, the almighty Supreme Self.

The worship of any deity through prayer is upasana of the one and same God. In prayer the upasaka remembers his deity, praises Him, offers milk, fruits, honey, nuts, etc. and asks Him for blessings of goodness, wealth or self-realization. When chanting prayers, remember the divinity of God repeatedly, and gradually uplift your mind towards the Divine. If you pray to God for purity, devotion, light and knowledge, you will get these things.

Get up early in the morning and say a prayer for physical, mental and spiritual wellbeing. Pray in any way you like. While praying, become as simple as a child. Open the chambers of your heart freely. Pray without cunningness or crookedness. You will get everything. Sincere devotees know well about the high efficacy of prayers. Remember how Mirabai prayed and Lord Krishna served her as a servant. Pray fervently right now, from this very second. Do not delay, because 'tomorrow' never comes.

Dasya

Dasya bhakti is the worship of God through the servant sentiment. To realize God's wishes and carry them out, considering oneself as a servant of God, the supreme master, is dasya worship. Serving the saints and sages, the gurus and the wise men, serving those who serve society, the sick, the poor, the downtrodden, serving the devotees of God, sweeping the temples, meditating on God and serving Him like a slave is dasya worship. To follow the words of the scriptures, to act according to the injunctions of the Vedas, considering them to be direct words of God is dasya worship. Association with love-intoxicated devotees and service to those who have knowledge of God is dasya worship.

The purpose behind this form of worship is to be ever with God in order to offer service to Him, earn His divine grace and thereby attain immortality. Arjuna prays to Lord Krishna with this sentiment in order to receive His grace: "O Lord! I am your disciple; I have taken refuge in You. Teach me." This should be the feeling of a servant of God. He should completely give himself up to the Lord through His worship, and not retain any personal reservations with Him. Dasya upasana is total relinquishment of the self to God.

Lakshman, Hanuman and Angada cultivated dasya bhava. At times, Lakshman could not even speak to Rama in his extreme love and humility before him. Hanuman is a towering example of divine service to the Lord. He spent his whole life worshipping Rama through service. Hanuman was an exceptional type of devotee, and it is very difficult to develop a passion such as that which possessed him. The heart has to be purified, the mind and ego thinned out, and the desires annihilated. Only then can the devotee feel real love for God; otherwise, the love of God is coloured with worldliness and does not bear fruit. Total surrender is the ideal of the dasya upasaka. The servant loses nothing, but gains everything through the service of God, either in His transcendental or immanent aspect.

Sakhya

The sakhya upasaka considers himself a friend of the Lord. Sakhya worship is practised by being with the Lord, treating Him as one's own dear relative or closest friend, being in His company at all times, and loving Him as one's own self. The sakhya takes up any work of the Lord with eagerness, leaving aside even the most important and urgently pressing personal work. He assumes the attitude of neglect towards personal work and concerns himself totally with service of the Lord. How do friends, real friends, love one another in this world? What amount of love do they possess for one another? Such is the adoration developed towards God instead of towards man in this form of upasana. There is a transformation of mundane physical love into eternal, spiritual love.

In sakhya upasana, the devotee considers all his actions as 'merely nothing', even if he has performed a superhuman act. He always does what may serve God in all respects. He considers all as God. He treats every being of the world as his own dearest friend. There is no feeling of selfishness, hatred or separateness in him. He becomes one with all in feeling. All is God, and God is the supreme friend. He is always satisfied with what is ordained by God and is immensely joyful if anything of his own becomes useful in the service of God. He moves with God and relates to Him, not as a dignified, overbearing, hard taskmaster, but as a sweet and loving friend. He longs to see God and considers himself and whatever belongs to him as useful only if it is in the service of the Lord, for he cannot live without Him.

God is the innermost and dearest friend of His devotee. In life, all friends may desert a person, but God will never desert His devotee. He loves and sustains His devotee, even if the devotee does not love Him. The devotee feels himself merged in an ocean of joy on seeing, touching or thinking of His beloved Lord. Merely hearing His name kindles the devotee's love. He lives in ecstasy, ever expecting to meet Him. In order to practise this form of upasana, one needs to first find out where his love lies, whom he loves most in the world. Love for friends and relations is *moha*, or deluded attachment, which binds one fast to the wheel of samsara. It is fleeting and fraught with all sorts of consequences. Love of God is liberating and leads to perennial bliss and immortality. Sakhya upasana leads to eternal union with the Lord.

Atma nivedana

Atma nivedana is self-surrender. The upasaka starts with hearing the stories of the Lord and slowly ascends the different rungs on the ladder of upasana, until ultimately the highest rung, atma nivedan, is reached. Here, the devotee offers everything to God, including body, mind and soul, and keeps nothing for himself. He gives himself up to God and has no personal or independent existence. God takes care of him and treats him as Himself. This devotee treats happiness and sorrow, pleasure and pain as gifts sent by God, and does not become attached to them. He considers himself as a puppet of God and an instrument in His hands. He gives his ego over to God, and God takes care of everything for him. In this form of upasana, the will of the devotee becomes one with the Lord, and he enjoys all the divine splendour of the Lord.

The Lord speaks and works directly through the different organs of this upasaka as his egoism is totally destroyed. The obstacles that stand in the way of self-surrender are desires and egoism. The self-surrender must be totally unreserved, ungrudging and unconditioned. Sometimes the devotee keeps certain desires for his own gratification. That is why he is not able to perfect self-surrender and have the *darshan* (inner vision) of his deity. The ego is very stiff and obstinate, like hard granite. It has to be split by constant hammering with the chisel of bhakti. When a necklace is made, the hard diamond must be pierced and a slender wire passed through the hole. Even so, this hard heart must be pierced through self-surrender and the slender thread of bhakti must be passed through the hole. Only then will the Lord take His seat in the heart of His devotee.

Self-surrender destroys the five afflictions of the mind and prepares it for union with the Lord. In the *Yoga Sutras* of Patanjali there is an aphorism (1:23) *Ishwara pranidhanava*, which means 'or by surrendering to Ishwara'. Samadhi can be attained by surrendering the little self and the fruits of one's actions at the feet of the Lord. Self-surrender is one of the five *niyamas*, or personal observances, defined by Patanjali (2:1) and he also mentions it as one of the three limbs of kriya yoga: '*Tapas swadhyaya Ishwara pranidhanani kriyayogaha*': austerity, self-study and self-surrender constitute kriya yoga."

Lord Krishna says in the *Bhagavad Gita*, "Abandoning all duties, come to me alone for shelter. Fear not. I will liberate thee from all sins." This is a powerful mantra that will help the upasaka in effecting self-surrender if he holds the feeling of this *sloka* (verse) constantly before his mind. The heart, mind, intellect and soul should all combine harmoniously in affecting self-surrender, only then will it be true, complete and perfect. In order to practise this form of upasana, one must constantly ask oneself: Am I a hypocrite? Have I made any kind of self-surrender? Beware of moral and spiritual pride! Maya assumes various subtle forms. The moral and spiritual pride of an upasaka is more dangerous than wealth, power and position of worldly people.

Often in spiritual life, tamas or inertia is mistaken for self-surrender. However, self-surrender is not attained by sitting idly, craving for God to help you. Rather, be up and doing, as God helps those who help themselves. Do the best you can and leave the rest to God. This is the highest form of upasana. There are many devotees who even expect God to do the surrendering for them. This is mere foolishness. The upasaka will need to do the work of self-surrender himself, and this point should be remembered well.

There is no loss in total self-surrender. It is not at all a bad bargain; rather it is a mighty gain indeed. You give your possessions, body, mind and soul unto Him and then the Lord gives Himself unto you. The whole wealth of the Lord belongs to you. The Lord Himself becomes your own, but He wants your whole heart, fully charged with pure love in return. Even if you have the slightest tinge of selfishness, you cannot attain Him. So, purify your heart by serving humanity with nishkama bhava, the feeling of freedom from attachment to the fruits of your labour. Be kind to all.

29

Restrain the senses. Speak the truth. Develop humility, patience and the spirit of self-sacrifice.

The Lord is quite close to you in your heart. Live in Him. Feel yourself merge with Him. You can practise surrender by remembering and singing His name always. Feel His presence everywhere. See Him in every face. Realize Him. That is your highest duty. The *gopis* (milkmaids) practised this mode of upasana with Krishna. They lost themselves in Krishna, and lost themselves in God consciousness. In this way, these village girls attained the Supreme. Self-surrender leads to the highest stage of spiritual life and can be practised by observing the following stages:

- *Satsanga*, company of saints
- *Swadhaya*, self-study and study of devotional books
- *Shraddha*, faith
- *Sadhana bhakti*, devotion to sadhana, mantra repetition, constant remembrance, kirtan
- *Nishtha*, devoutness
- *Ruchi*, taste for hearing and chanting the names and glories of the Lord
- *Rati*, intense attachment to the Lord that softens the heart
- *Sthayi bhava*, steadfastness
- *Jivanmukta*, liberation while living
- *Maha bhava*, living in the Lord

Lord Krishna teaches Arjuna that total and exclusive self-surrender alone can give him peace and relieve him of all anxieties and concerns. One who studies the *Bhagavad Gita* and the *Srimad Bhagavat* will come to know what great importance is given to total self-surrender; for self-surrender is the annihilation of individual consciousness and the attainment of absolute consciousness, which is equal to *nirvikalpa samadhi* or direct realization. The devotee flies to the state of supreme devotion and merges himself in God. Worldly consciousness vanishes into universal consciousness. Man becomes God, and the mortal becomes immortal.

3

Divine Bhava

Bhava means nature, feeling or attitude. Divine bhava is spiritual nature or attitude. Bhava is what counts most in meditation and upasana. There is a delay in the vision of God when one does not have an intensity of bhava. God does not want golden temples and rich presents. He only wants your bhava, your devoted heart. He is immensely pleased with a little flower, fruit or water if it is offered with intense devotion, faith and love. Therefore, worship God with all your love. Praise Him. Seek enlightenment through Him and realize divine bliss. Worship for worship's sake. Do not put any conditions on God. Worship God with the flowers of sacrifice, equal vision, serenity, truthfulness, compassion and love.

People go here and there in thick forests, mountain summits, lakes and gardens in search of flowers and other items for offering to the Lord, and yet fail to attain the bliss supreme. They could easily get eternal bliss if they would offer the single stainless flower of their heart to the Lord. God does not want precious or expensive gifts. Many people spend millions of rupees opening hospitals and rest houses for pilgrims, but they do not give their hearts. It is necessary to cultivate the divine bhava again and again through love, faith, devotion, japa, prayer, enquiry, meditation and service to the Lord. The friendly communion between the worshipper and God is necessary for real happiness. Cultivate

31

the nine modes of worship and you will be rich in divine bhava. All troubles and miseries will come to an end.

There are four indispensable requisites for cultivating divine bhava:
1. The upasaka should yearn for the vision of God.
2. He should be a nishkama karma yogi, wanting nothing from God.
3. He must be regular and earnest in his devotional practices.
4. His awareness of God should be continuous and unbroken, like the flow of oil.

Four stages of bhava

In upasana there are four stages of bhava corresponding to the four different states and dispositions of the seeker himself:
1. *Pooja bhava* is external worship, which arises out of the dualistic notions of the worshipper and the worshipped, the servant and the Lord. This duality necessarily exists to a greater or lesser degree until the experience of oneness is attained.
2. *Japa bhava* is higher than pooja bhava, and is the expression of mantra repetition and hymns of praise.
3. *Dhyana bhava* is the expression of constant meditation upon the form of the Lord in the heart, and is higher still.
4. *Brahma bhava* or *atma bhava* is the highest state of realization that the supreme spirit, Paramatma, and the individual spirit, atma, are one, that everything is Brahman and nothing but Brahman. One who experiences Brahma bhava knows that all is Brahman. For this type of devotee there is neither worshipper nor worshipped, neither yoga nor pooja, neither meditation nor japa, neither vows nor rituals. He is a *siddha*, a perfect sage in its fullest sense. He is one who has attained *siddhi*, perfection, which is the aim of sadhana.

Brahma bhava cannot be attained all at once. One has to slowly ascend the ladder of bhava, from pooja bhava to japa bhava to dhyana bhava to Brahma bhava. The heart must be

32

purified thoroughly through pooja, japa, hymns, prayer and meditation. There are rituals in the path of upasana for beginners. But, when the upasaka advances and the mind is totally absorbed in the object of worship, there is no use in waving lights, offering sandal paste and ringing bells. The whole cosmos is Vrindavan for him. What a glorious state of devotion it is! The devotee attains *para bhakti* (supreme devotion) or divine bhava. All rituals drop away by themselves for such an exalted devotee. However, rituals are of great help for beginners in developing upasana, and they should not be ignored on any score.

The upasaka should pass through the various initial stages of upasana, just as an academic student goes through matriculation and BA before sitting in the MA class. He should make garlands of flowers for the Lord and sweep the floors of the place of worship. He should light lamps and ring bells. All these should be done with faith, devotion and intense feeling. If the aspirant falsely and foolishly imagines that he has attained the highest state of para bhakti and neglects to practise upasana, his little devotion will also evaporate quickly. He will soon fall into the deep abyss of worldliness.

When an ignorant neophyte in the path of upasana says, "I practise para bhakti, so there is no need for me to go to temples or places of worship. What is there in worshipping idols, offering flowers and waving lights?" He is labouring under a serious delusion. This is the state of those who proceed on the spiritual path without the advice or aid of a spiritual preceptor. They do whatever they like. They follow the prompting of the lower mind, and do not make any spiritual progress.

The upasaka who has developed the supreme attitude to his worship and sadhana is not a slave of forms, formalities and dogmas. There is no outward show. He does not care for the sarcastic remarks of the world. He simply pours forth his devotion into his upasana. His love is spontaneous. The flow of his devotion is like a continuous stream of oil.

There is no break and nothing can obstruct its flow. Although his path is beset with difficulties, this type of upasaka is adamant in his resolve. He has dedicated everything to the Lord and he crosses over all difficulties through divine grace at every step. He always lives in God.

This degree of upasana is very difficult to develop. The internal enemies: lust, greed, anger, hatred, egoism and jealousy, are very powerful. They stand in the way of cultivating devotion. One who has reached the stage of para bhakti will be absolutely fear-less, desire-less, anger-less, I-less, mine-less. He will be extremely humble and have no attachment for anything. He will be above body consciousness. If someone does not possess all these characteristics, but simply says, "I am a para bhakta," put no value on his words. Such people even shed false tears, which are not the sincere teardrops of divine love.

Be aware, dear upasakas, that every aspirant on the spiritual path becomes a victim to the mood of depression in the beginning stages of the sadhana period. You will overcome this state of mind through discrimination, reflection, enquiry, prayer and singing the Lord's name. Singing is an easy method to drive away this low energy state. Depression is like a passing cloud and you should not be unnecessarily concerned. It will pass off quickly if you are vigilant. Allow the tears of divine ecstasy to trickle down on those occasions when you are in a profound prayerful mood or meditative state. Shed the precious tears of divine love when you are in communion with the Lord.

It is very important for the upasaka to have simplicity and purity of heart. Think that you are only a very small student in the bhakti yoga class. Open the doors of your heart. Let the lightning spark of love arise in your heart. Let the heart sing to heart. Let the tears flow and divine ecstasy fill your whole being. Only then can you grow in upasana and only then will divine grace descend. Upasakas bold! The Lord loves you even when you turn away from Him. How much more will He love you if you turn to Him again

34

sincerely with faith and devotion! Very great is His love, greater than the greatest mountain. Very deep is His affection, deeper than the unfathomable depth of the ocean.

Five bhavas

Upasana is a near and dear relationship with the Lord. In upasana the devotee strives to establish such a relationship with the Lord. He cultivates any one of the five bhavas according to his temperament, taste and capacity. The five bhavas of the upasaka are:

1. *Santa bhava* – attitude of the saintly disciple's relationship with the Lord
2. *Dasya bhava* – attitude of the servant towards the master in one's relationship with the Lord
3. *Sakhya bhava* – attitude of friendship with the Lord
4. *Vatsalya bhava* – attitude of parent and child in one's relationship with the Lord
5. *Madhurya bhava* – attitude of lover and beloved, the highest culmination of worship, merging or absorption in the Lord.

Classification of upasakas

There are four general classifications for upsakas: arta, artharthi, jignasu and jnani.

1. The *arta* upasaka is the distressed devotee, who is suffering on account of disease, disaster, failure, loss or harassment. He performs different upasanas, hoping to receive God's grace in order to relieve the pain and sorrow in his life.
2. The *artharthi* upasaka is not satisfied with what he already has in this world. He practises different upasanas in order to gain additional comforts, worldly possessions, assets, property, position and progeny. He propitiates God so that he can amass wealth and enjoy a happy life.
3. The *jignasu* is the enquirer, the intellectual upasaka. He is dissatisfied with the world and feels a void in his life. He regards sensual pleasure as the lower form of happiness, and thinks there is an eternal bliss untainted

by pain and suffering to be found within. The jignasu seeks knowledge because he feels ignorant in regard to spiritual matters. He performs upasana to attain the highest wisdom.

4. The *jnani* is the wise upasaka who seeks God without any expectations and ultimately attains para bhakti. The jnani realizes that the Lord is within his own Self. He is satisfied with the Self and is free from desires. He worships God in praise of the Self. The jnani is an upasaka of the imperishable atman. He is a *para bhakta* (supreme devotee) and performs upasana by constant renunciation of all karmas and actions, with awareness constantly fixed upon the Supreme. He is ever united in bliss with the Lord. This upasana of the jnani is the most difficult. He does not see, hear, speak or meditate on anything other than Ishwara. A jnani works in society, knowing that his deeds do not bind him. A jnani is firm in his vow of realization of the Supreme. He loves God and constantly remembers Him. He sings His glories and tells His stories to all. The jnani is the enlightened soul who constantly worships the Lord as the one essence in all forms

The first three types of upasaka described above, arti, artharathi and jignasu, do not worship for the attainment of para bhakti and supreme bliss. Until the upasaka attains jnana and worships as a para bhakta, he will return again and again to worldly life to purify his soul.

The best upasaka

The ultimate aim of upasana is to remain forever in the state of unification with God. Through love of God the devotee attains moksha, for example, the adoration of Arjuna for Sri Krishna in the *Bhagavad Gita*, the gratitude of Ikshvaku towards God in the *Bhagavat*, and the love of Hanuman for Lord Rama in the *Ramayana*. Hanuman lived only to serve Rama; Bali surrendered everything to God; Prahlada saw God in each and every speck of creation. You can hear of the bhakti of Vidura in his darshan of God, and the love of the gopis towards Lord Krishna during the Rasa Lila. Worship all the incarnations of God because all are forms of the Paramatman. This is the ultimate upasana of the *bhakti marga* (path of devotion) which leads to the experience of para bhakti. The love of God for fulfilment of worldly desires is not the ultimate form of upasana.

The best upasaka lives only through the love of God. O upasakas, worship God through kirtan, yajna, *vrata* (vows), *daana* (giving), dhyana, and attain the highest goal of life, para bhakti. Read the scriptures which talk exclusively on bhakti, written by Narada, Sandilya, Garg and Vyasa. Read the *Bhakti Sutras* by Lord Narada, the *Bhagavat Purana* by Rishi Sandilya and the *Devi Bhagavat*. These scriptures are important for the upasaka. Worship of the mind as Brahman will turn the intellect towards the Self and allow it to merge into the Paramatman. Surrender every action to God; thereby, your work is transformed into worship. This is the upasana of God which will create the highest love in your mind.

Preparation for upasana

Bhakti also implies the knowledge of God. If the gopis did not know the real nature of Krishna, how could they have loved Him as God? Sri Krishna tells Uddhava that the devotee like Narada, who sees Him as the inner soul abiding in all, is dearest to Him. The *Narada Bhakti Sutras* say that upasana through bhakti is liberation itself. There is no place for worldly desires in this type of worship, which teaches you to become one with Ishwara. There are different levels of upasana in bhakti. You perform upasana in your worship of the gods. You perform upasana when you extol the different stories of God; this is meditation on the Self! Upasana is the highest, the most intense worship and love of God. It is total attachment to God with distaste towards everything else.

The upasaka takes refuge in Him alone. Upasana gives *amrita bhava*, the sense of absolute fulfilment. Then one knows everything and becomes calm and quiet. Jnana yoga, raja yoga and karma yoga are simply the means to prepare the aspirant for real upasana. Bhakti is the reward for the sadhaka's efforts in yoga sadhana. Bhakti is the means as well as the goal. To prepare for real upasana you must relinquish all interest in sensual life and practise detachment to everything except God. By keeping the company of saints and sages, you will naturally imbibe real love towards God. This is important; the saints and God are not different from each other.

You should avoid association with worldly-minded people who have no faith in God because you may lose interest in attaining the highest state of bhakti in this type of company. Never boast of your knowledge of the scriptures. Avoid egoism. Avoid debate. Renounce the passions of your personality like pride, anger, greed, etc. Practise the upasana of yama and niyama, and help others who walk this path. Do not display your siddhis or accomplishments. Siddhis attained by upasana are not to be flaunted, and if they are, all the experiences and merits gained thereby are lost. Siddhis are merely signposts to help you along the way.

In the days when Ramakrishna crossed the Houghly river from Dakshineshwar to Kolkata by ferryboat, he would pay a fraction of a rupee as the fee. Once he was crossing along with a siddha who had the ability to walk on water. The siddha asked Ramakrishna, "You're a great mystic; why don't you walk on water?" Ramakrishna asked him, "How many years of sadhana have you spent to attain this siddhi of walking on water?" He answered, "About sixty to sixty-five years." Ramakrishna said, "You must have struggled a lot to accomplish that siddhi." The siddha replied, "Yes, I gave up everything I had just for that." Then Ramakrishna said, "Well, I can cross over the water on the ferry for a fraction of a rupee, so why would I spend sixty-five years of my life doing sadhana for something so silly?" That is the value of psychic powers, even though they appear to be very impressive.

Different paths of upasana

According to the inherent predominance of sattwic, rajasic and tamasic qualities, people have different types of nature and abilities to understand and relate in life. Therefore, different modes of upasana are undertaken to achieve self-realization. The karmas of past lives also play a major part in determining human temperament. For this reason, Lord Krishna describes upasana according to the attitude of the worshipper. Performance of sacrifices prescribed by the Vedas is an upasana that leads to moksha for people living in the world. Similarly, to work hard for social welfare and to enjoy name and fame is the highest goal for those who are immersed in active life. Yogis give importance to self-restraint, discrimination, detachment, etc. which lead to moksha. Intellectuals and politicians give importance to wealth, prestige and power as the highest goal.

Some regard the worship of deities as a means to attain God. For others, the observances of yama and niyama are important to attain moksha. Lord Krishna teaches that all these inclinations towards upasana lead only to temporary satisfaction if performed without dedication to Him. All the impurities of the mind, all the wandering tendencies and extraneous desires vanish when the upasaka performs worship with intense devotion to the Lord. In the *Srimad Bhagavat,* Lord Krishna teaches Uddhava that whatever action is performed should be done to please God only, with faith, devotion and love towards God. By following this way of life and worship, one can definitely attain moksha and supreme bliss. Sri Krishna gives the same teaching to Arjuna in the *Bhagavad Gita* when He tells him that unification with God is achieved by giving one's mind to Him only. One should act with a pure mind and try to surrender to God. After the state of complete surrender, the real upasana begins.

4

Saguna and Nirguna Upasana

Nirguna Brahman is pure consciousness without any limiting adjunct and *saguna Brahman* is pure consciousness with limiting adjuncts. Just as vapour, water and ice are one and the same in essence; similarly, saguna Brahman and nirguna Brahman are also one. Worshippers of saguna and nirguna Brahman reach the same goal. But the latter path is very hard because the aspirant has to give up all attachment from the very beginning. It is very difficult for those with attachments to reach the imperishable Brahman, which is unmanifest, incomprehensible to the senses and devoid of all attributes. The nirguna Brahman is beyond time, space and causation; it is eternal and indefinable.

Therefore, in the early stages of sadhana it is extremely difficult to fix the mind on nirguna Brahman, which is formless and without attribute. Saguna Brahman has form and attribute, yet is still omniscient, omnipotent, and omnipresent. Saguna Brahman is Ishwara. One who realizes saguna Brahman attains *kaivalya*, separation from the wheel of life and death, without any effort, through the grace of the Lord. In this way he experiences the same state attained by jnanis through the practices of *shravana* (hearing the scriptures), *manana* (reflection on their meaning) and *nididhyasana* (deep meditation). *Avidya* or ignorance is destroyed in the saguna worshipper through knowledge of the Self.

Saguna upasana relates to the practices of bhakti yoga, the yoga of devotion, and nirguna upasana to the practices of jnana yoga, the yoga of knowledge. In nirguna upasana the aspirant aspires to attain realization by imbibing the four means of liberation:

1. *Viveka* (discrimination)
2. *Vairagya* (indifference to sensual enjoyments)
3. *Shatsampat* (sixfold wealth): *sama* (tranquillity), *dama* (restraint), *uparati* (renunciation), *titiksha* (endurance), *shraddha* (faith) and *samadhana* (balance of mind)
4. *Mumukshuttva* (keen longing for liberation or deliverance from the round of births and deaths).

Then he approaches a guru who has realized the Supreme Self and hears the scriptures from him. Afterwards he reflects and meditates on the Atman, and eventually attains direct realization of the Self. Contemplation on nirguna Brahman demands a very sharp, one-pointed and subtle intellect. The scriptures say: "The Atman is hidden in all things and does not shine forth, but is seen by seers through their sharp and subtle intellect." One who realizes the nirguna Brahman attains eternal bliss, self-realization or kaivalya, liberation, which is preceded by the destruction of avidya.

Methods of upasana

Pooja is an important form of upasana which involves the ritual worship of the Lord. Pooja transforms the upasaka into a divine being by bringing him into the proximity of the Lord and enabling him to commune with Him. Pooja purifies the heart and steadies the mind, filling it with *shuddha bhava* (pure feelings) and *prem* (love) for the Lord. The upasaka performs worship according to his choice, but with faith and devotion. The object of worship is the *ishta devata*, personal form of the deity that the devotee worships. For example, Vaishnavites worship Vishnu in any of His ten forms, such as Rama and Krishna. Shaivites worship Shiva in one of His eight forms. Shaktas worship Devi in one of Her many forms. The method of pooja is chosen in

41

accordance with the requirements and preferences of the devotee, and may be vedic, tantric or mixed.

In external pooja an object is used, which can be a three-dimensional image, a picture or a symbol, such as a *shaligram* (fossilized shell taken as a symbol of Lord Vishnu) in the case of Vishnu worship, or a *lingam* (smooth, oval, black stone) in the case of Shiva worship. During a simple pooja specific mantras are recited, water is poured over the image, flowers are offered, sandal-paste is applied, food and water are offered, and camphor and incense are burned. While performing these rituals, the devotee pours his love and devotion upon the Lord, who is represented by the image, picture or symbol. In this way, the devotee superimposes the Lord and His attributes on the concrete symbol and ultimately it becomes God for him. Traditionally, there are eight kinds of images of God: stone, metal, earth, sandal paste, painting, precious stone and mental image. The image can be moveable or fixed.

Performance of pooja

You should take a bath in the morning before performing pooja and daily prayer. An image of the devata may be used for the pooja; otherwise the worship can be done on the floor itself after cleaning the place and drawing a *mandala* (spherically based pattern) there. Keep the following items ready beforehand: flowers, incense sticks, sandal paste, oil lamp, camphor, fresh water, food offerings for the Lord, a clean seat to sit on, a small bell, conch and cymbals, if available. You should not need to get up in the middle of the pooja to find anything. Repeat the mantras and prayers which you have decided upon to kindle your divine emotion. You should decorate the Lord with fresh clothes and garlands made of flowers. Adore him with ornaments, flowers, scent, sandal paste, etc. Perform the offerings with intense love and devotion.

Offer the Lord sweet cooked rice or some other appropriate food that can be offered with love or bhava. Foods specially prepared with ghee, milk and curd, or vegetables and butter are traditionally recommended. Offer prayers with the feeling of devotion. Offer flowers or rice soaked in water with *kumkum* (vermillion powder) to the Lord as you chant his one hundred and eight names or his *beeja mantra* repeated 108 times. Offer *abhisheka*, bathing of the Lord, with fresh water, milk, ghee, honey or *panchamrit* (five nectars of banana, ghee, honey, brown sugar and milk) as is convenient. If possible, offer flowers with the thousand names of the Lord. Offer water and burn camphor, etc. Mentally always think of the form of the Lord; although you worship the image, keep the all-pervading Lord before your mental eye. Sing the Lord's glories and chant his names.

Offer prayers and surrender yourself to the Lord. Hear the stories of the Lord as recorded in the *Bhagavat* and *Ramayana*. Say, "O, Lord! Have mercy on me. Be gracious unto me." Place your head on the Lord's feet and pray, "O Lord! Protect me from the ocean of samsara with the shark of death in it. I am terribly afraid of it. I have taken shelter in Thee." Do everything with the feeling that you are an instrument in the hands of the Lord. There should be no selfish desires behind your worship. While performing pooja, you must abandon the idea of ownership of the articles of worship and think that you are only the caretaker, because all the articles and wealth actually belong to Ishwara. Only then will His worship bring the desired result. Prostrations, offering, etc. are outer forms of worship; meditation is the inner worship.

Distribution of prasad

Pooja is done with flowers, leaves from the *bel* (a tree sacred to Lord Siva), leaves from the *tulsi* (a sacred medicinal plant), and *vibhooti* (sacred ash), which are given as prasad from the Lord at the end of the worship. During pooja, *havan* (ceremonial worship with fire), kirtan, *arati* (waving of lights before a deity), and on important occasions, almonds, sultanas, milk, sweets and fruits are offered to the Lord and then distributed as *prasad* (consecrated items) to everyone. All forms of prasad are charged with mysterious powers by the chanting of mantras during the worship. Vibhooti is the prasad of Lord Shiva, which is applied to the forehead; a small portion can also be ingested. Kumkum is the prasad of Sri Devi or Shakti, which is applied at *bhrumadhya*, the space between the eyebrows. Tulsi leaves are the prasad of Lord Vishnu, Rama and Krishna, which are to be ingested.

Prasad gives peace of mind and is a great purifier, panacea and spiritual elixir. Prasad is the grace of the Lord and an embodiment of His *shakti* (power); it is divinity in manifestation. Many sincere devotees get wonderful experiences from prasad alone. Many incurable diseases are cured. Prasad energizes, invigorates and infuses devotion; it should be taken with great faith. Those who are brought up with modern education and culture have forgotten about the glory of prasad. But, if you live for a week in Vrindavan, Benares or other places of pilgrimage that are filled with the divine energy of saints and sages, you will realize the glory and miraculous effects of prasad.

Prasad bestows good health, long life, peace and prosperity to all. Glory to the Lord of prasad, who is the giver of immortality and undying happiness, the bestower of peace and bliss. Offer prasad to all. If possible, feed some poor people every day and give them clothing. Worship the poor, as the Lord, through service and offer them prasad.

Shodasopachara pooja

This pooja is a traditional form of worship with sixteen types of offerings. The materials used or services offered in the pooja are known as *upacharas*, so this elaborate form of pooja has *shodasa* (sixteen) upacharas. The image is first rubbed with oil, cleaned, adorned and given such loving treatment, which one would offer to one's dearest and most beloved. During the shodasopachara pooja, the following sixteen upacharas are offered before the image to pay respect to the Lord:

1. Offering a seat for the image (*asana*)
2. Welcoming the Lord (*swagata*)
3. Water for washing the feet (*padya*)

4. Water offering made in a vessel *(arghya)*
5. Water for sipping *(achamana)*
6. A mixture of honey, ghee, milk and curd *(madhuparka)*
7. Water for bathing *(snanam)*
8. Cloth or garment *(vastra)*
9. Jewels *(abhushana)*
10. Perfume *(gandha)*
11. Flowers *(puspha)*
12. Incense *(dhoopa)*
13. Lights *(deepa)*
14. Food *(naivedya)*
15. Betel nuts, etc. *(tambulam)*
16. Prayer *(vandana)*

The devotee invokes the deity into the image by what is called the *avahana* (welcoming) and *prana pratishtha* (life-giving) ceremonies. When the worship is over, he performs *visarjana* (bidding the deity to depart). The *Purusha Sukta* (an ancient hymn from the Vedas) is chanted throughout the shodasopachara pooja to all the deities being worshipped.

Manasic pooja

In *manasic* (mental) pooja, the worship of the Lord is performed without any external materials. Here the same services or upachara offered in the outer pooja are mentally offered to the deity. There is no difference regarding the items and the sequence of offerings. Before starting, all the materials necessary for the pooja must be imagined in the mind, and during the pooja you should mentally feel that you are offering each item to the Lord, as in formal worship. In the mind the worship takes place; in the mind the incense, sandal paste, flowers, etc. are offered to the Lord. In manasic pooja you must generate the feeling of what is otherwise offered with the hands. Feeling is more powerful than action, so concentration is better in manasic pooja than in external pooja.

Mental pooja belongs to the interiorized forms of ritual, like mental bath, mental fire sacrifice or mental repetition of a mantra. Mental pooja cannot be thought of without the idea of the external pooja on which it is modelled. But as imagination is unrestricted, more offerings, and among them rare and expensive ones of best quality and in any season, may be given. The image that receives these offerings is also mental. When you perform this pooja, mentally enthrone the Lord on a beautiful seat of honour set with diamonds, pearls and emeralds, etc. Mentally apply sandal paste to His forehead and body. Mentally offer water, madhuparka, various sorts of exotic flowers, and magnificent clothes, etc. Mentally burn the most fragrant incense, wave lights and burn camphor. Mentally offer various kinds of fruits and sumptuous sweetmeats. Be extremely generous in manasic pooja, and in no way miserly.

In tantric pooja, the mental worship usually comes first, followed by the outer pooja. After being worshipped mentally in the devotee's heart, the deity also enters the image or *yantra* (geometric symbol of divinity) and is worshipped outwardly. So, for the entire duration of the outer pooja, the deity is ever present in the devotee's heart. In mental pooja offerings can be symbolic. For example, the lotus of the devotee's heart is offered as the deity's seat (asana); the nectar flowing from sahasrara chakra is the water for washing the feet (padya); the mind is the arghya offering; the functions of the senses and the restlessness of the mind are *nritya* dance.

Mental pooja demands full concentration of one's mind and cannot be done absentmindedly. Therefore, when performed correctly, mental worship is said to be far superior to outer worship. While outer pooja requires the use of utensils and materials to be offered, mental pooja can be done independently. Purification rites, bathing, cleaning one's teeth, etc., similar to those preceding the outer worship, are performed mentally first. In the end repeat mentally, "Whatever action I perform with the body, speech, mind, senses, intellect or my own nature, I offer all to the supreme Lord." And finally repeat, "I offer everything to the Absolute"

(Om Tat Sat Brahmarpanamastu). This will purify your heart and remove the taint of expectation of reward.

Para pooja

Uddhava asked Lord Krishna for the method of worshipping Paramatman. Lord Krishna replied that the upasaka should sit on a level seat in a comfortable posture. He should commence with the practice of pranayama, followed by *pratyahara* (sense control), and then repetition of the mantra *Aum*. He should perform this worship three times daily for one month to acquire breath control. He should then fix his mind in the heart centre and contemplate upon the sun, the moon, and fire. In that fire, he should visualize the sacred form of the Lord of dark blue hue, with the goddess Lakshmi, sitting beside Him. He should see the Lord with four arms, graceful poise and a charming smile, adorned with ornaments, a garland of flowers and the precious jewel. In his hands he should see the conch, chakra and mace. Contemplating in this way upon the form of the Divine, the upasaka becomes one with Him. By performing this para pooja intensely, and abandoning all else, the upasaka experiences the Paramatman, or Supreme Soul.

In the traditional para pooja attributed to Adi Shankar-acharya, the jnani devotee mentally worships the Supreme without attributes. This form of pooja is beautifually described in the following poem:

> *Why summon by invocation that which fills all?*
> *Where is the seat for the indweller of all?*
> *Why give water for feet washing or oblation to one*
> *who is transparently clear?*
> *Why offer water for rinsing the mouth to one who is*
> *absolutely pure?*
> *Why bathe one who is free of all blemish and stain?*
> *Why offer clothing to one who encompasses all?*
> *Why give a sacred thread for one who needs no support?*
> *Why adorn with ornaments one who is intrinsically*
> *beautiful?*

Why offer perfume to one without odour?
Why offer flowers to one without vasanas?
Why offer incense to one free of all scent?
Why wave lamps before one who is self-luminous?
Why make a food offering to one who is ever satisfied?
*Why offer the after meal betel nut to one who is
all-pervading?*
What fruit offering can there be for the giver of fruits?
What gift can be offered to the Lord of Lakshmi?
*What circumambulation is done of one whose extent
is without end?*
How can there be bowing before the One who has no second?
*What leave-taking can there be of that which is full within
and without?*

This para pooja of jnanis is considered to be the highest
kind of worship in all conditions and at all times. Immersed in
this worship, the devotee feels that he can do nothing but
experience God. He thinks, "O Lord, how can I worship you,
who is without parts, who is Existence itself? How can I pray to
you, when you are my very being itself? How can I offer water
to you, when you are ever pure?" This form of para pooja leads
to direct realization of the Self.

5

Significance of Symbols

During pooja, bells are rung in temples to shut out the external sounds and to draw the mind inward. The waving of lights before the deity denotes that the Lord is light, the self-effulgent light of the universe. Light also signifies the illumination of the devotee, the removal of darkness and the bestowing of divine light within. The burning of camphor denotes that the individual ego melts like the camphor, and the individual soul becomes one with the supreme light of lights. The incense burnt before the deity spreads throughout the room, which denotes that the Lord is all pervading. He fills the whole universe with His living presence. It also signifies the purity of the devotee, the disappearance of desires and dormant tendencies. When sandalwood is ground into paste, a sweet odour emanates, which reminds the devotee that he should see beyond the difficulties and pain that arise in life, and trust that by coping with the hard times, the sweetness, the spiritual fruits, will be realized.

Upasana is sublime and does not end with the pooja and worship of an image. The upasaka is taken step by step to higher stages of devotion, samadhi and communion with God through worship. After doing pooja with flowers and other articles of worship for some time, he can take up mental worship, an advanced form of worship. The upasaka has to feel His presence in the heart as well as in all objects everywhere.

49

Even in worshipping a small image, he has to repeat the *Purusha Sukta* and think of the *Virat Purusha* (universal body of God), who extends beyond the universe with countless heads, eyes, hands, and also of the Lord or Atman, who dwells in the hearts of all beings. The upasaka gradually feels that the Lord he worships in the pooja is in the hearts of all creatures and in all the names and forms of this universe.

In this way, the upasaka begins to feel His presence everywhere. During worship, as he repeats the mantra of the Lord and touches his heart, head, tuft, arms and hands, he feels the divine consciousness in every letter of the mantra. Through the touching of the body with repetition of the mantra, the upasaka gradually transforms himself into an instrument of the Divine. Spiritual currents are generated and there is an awakening. Tamas and rajas are destroyed and he is filled with pure sattwa. In this way, the upasaka becomes identical with the object of his worship. He actually beholds the Lord in his worship and is absorbed into the Lord. There are many instances when the Lord manifested Himself to the devotee. The sacred bull Nandi, which sits before Shiva's image, took the food offered by Tulsidas. The image of Krishna played with Mirabai, and manifested full of life and consciousness for her.

Pooja vidhi, the ways, rules and secrets of worship with form described in the ancient scriptures is scientifically accurate and highly rational. Those who denigrate the worship of *murtis* (images) have not studied the scriptures or associated with devotees and great souls. The Sanatan Dharma upholds that the various images and symbols are required to prepare the initiate's mind for concentration. There are thousands of images and symbols to select from, and the beginner chooses one according to his spiritual ideals and convictions. At the same time, the use of an image or symbol is not compulsory, and for some advanced *sadhakas* (spiritual practitioners), yogis or sages, it may not be necessary at all.

A symbol is like the slate used by a child in first standard to learn his letters. However, those who do not need the symbol have no right to say that it is wrong to use one. There is nothing wrong in superimposing God and His attributes on an image in the beginning. However, you must think of the *antar atma*, or inner spirit, that is hidden in the image. Worship of an image is only the beginning of religion; it is certainly not the end. The same Hindu scriptures which prescribe worship of an image for beginners speak of meditation on the Absolute or contemplation on the significance of the mahavakya: *Tat Tvam Asi*, Thou art That, for advanced aspirants. There are different grades of worship, each marking a stage of progress.

The first stage is the performance of ritual worship and pilgrimages to holy places. The next is recitation of mantras and offering of prayers. The third is worship of symbols. The fourth is meditation on the Supreme Self, the Absolute or the attributeless, *nirguna Brahman*. The final state is self-realization, or *Brahma sakshatkara*. In this process, the shastras and gurus are like kind mothers. They take hold of the upasakas and lead them step by step until they are established in *nirvikalpa samadhi*, the superconscious state. For gross-minded beginners they prescribe external forms of worship, and for advanced upasakas endowed with pure, subtle and sharp intellect, they give lessons on abstract meditation.

The upasaka makes different attempts to grasp and realize the Infinite or the Absolute according to his degree of evolution. He soars higher and higher, gathers more and more strength, and eventually merges in the Supreme and attains oneness with Him. Glory to the tradition of the rishis and the scriptures of Sanatana Dharma! Glory to those who take the upasakas from the lower to the higher forms of worship stage by stage, and ultimately help them in their quest to realize the attributeless, all-pervading, formless, timeless, spaceless Brahman, the infinite and the uncon-ditional Brahman of the Upanishads.

Beloved upasakas! Enshrine unshakeable, living faith in your heart this very moment. Recall to mind the glorious

51

worship performed by Mirabai, Sri Ramakrishna Parama-hamsa and the South Indian Alwars and Nayanars, who reaped the rich spiritual harvests. You too can enjoy great peace, happiness and prosperity and attain Him here and now if you have faith in worship. Though you may perform external worship at regular intervals, let the internal worship of the Lord in your heart be constant and unbroken. In this way worship attains completeness. All aspects of life are parts and paths of divine worship. Through upasana may you realize the significance of the universal worship of the *Virata* (cosmic form of God) in your daily life.

Symbols of the subconscious mind

Symbols are very important in the evolution of man. Primitive man thought in symbols as he had no vocabulary to express abstract ideas and qualities. Before the alphabet was invented, there was only picture reading and writing. The ancient Egyptian *Book of the Dead* is written entirely in picture-symbols. Modern psychology has revealed the significance of symbols in relation to the subconscious mind, that man has two minds, conscious and subconscious. The sub-conscious mind stores all the memories right back to childhood, along with all the racial memories since the dawn of history.

The subconscious is the seat of deep feelings and emotions; it is also the seat of telepathy, clairvoyance, hypnotism and other occult powers. In man, the activity of the subconscious mind is seen in dreams. For example, if some feeling of ambition is aroused in the mind, we dream that we are flying in the air; if there is fear in our mind, we dream of demons and frightful animals, and so on. The suggestion or repetition of the same idea again and again also influences the subconscious mind. It can also be influenced by loud sounds like ringing of bells or music. But the subconscious mind is hardly influenced by intellectual ideas; it thinks entirely in symbols.

52

Purpose of the symbol

The image of God is a support for the neophyte, a prop during his spiritual childhood. A form or image is necessary in the beginning as an external reminder of God. The worshipper associates the ideas of infinity, omnipotence, omniscience, omnipresence, purity, perfection, freedom, holiness and truth with the form of worship he chooses. The material image calls up the mental idea. Steadiness of mind is obtained by the worship of an image. For a beginner, concentration or meditation is not possible without a symbol. The mind requires a symbol because it cannot hold a concept of the absolute in the initial stages. To behold God everywhere and to feel His presence every moment is not possible for the ordinary person. The mind cannot be centralized and fixed on the Absolute without the help of some external aid.

Therefore, a symbol is absolutely indispensable for a beginner. The mind is disciplined in the beginning by fixing it on a concrete object or symbol. The image or murti of the deity, sun, fire, water, shaligram, lingam, swastika, cross, Om, Tao, circle, triangle are all symbols that help the upasaka to attain one-pointedness of mind and purity of heart. When the mind is rendered steady and subtle, it can be fixed on an abstract idea such as *Aham Brahma Asmi,* I am Brahman. As the upasaka advances in meditation, the form melts into the formless, and he becomes absorbed in the formless essence. The worship of form is not contrary to the view of *Vedanta* (the final teaching of the Vedas); even the vedantin has the symbol of *Aum* on which to fix his wandering mind. Images of God are considered an aid to the highest vedantic realization.

Symbols may be concrete or subtle. Pictures and drawings are pictorial forms of images. The gross mind needs a concrete symbol as a base, and the subtle mind requires an abstract symbol. Dialectics and great leaders also become symbols, not only the pictures or images in stone or wood. The *Puranas* (ancient mythological scriptures) and the *Agamas* (esoteric scriptures) describe how form is to be worshipped both in the home and in the temple. Worship of form is not peculiar to any one religion. Every Hindu worships an image of his choice. Christians worship the cross and have the image of it in their mind when they pray. Muslims hold the direction of the Kaaba in their mind when they kneel and do prayers. Most people throughout the world, save for a few yogis and vedantins, are all worshippers of form. They keep some image or the other in their mind.

Every deity is identified with a separate universal power. For example, the Sun is a divinity representing the spirit of all sentient and insentient beings. It is given different names like Aditya, Vishnu and Mitra. Indra is described as the god of warfare who bestows victory. Usha is the deity of the dawn. The Maruts are the deities of power. Agni symbolizes fire or the light of the Sun on Earth. Agni is worshipped for gaining food and nourishment, wealth, cattle, progeny, and so on. The mental image is also a form; the difference is not of kind, but of degree. All worshippers, however intellectual they may be, generate a form in the mind and make the mind dwell on that image.

There is one class of symbol which represents the images of avataras such as Jesus Christ, Buddha, Krishna or Rama, whom the devotee believes are incarnations of God. Another class represents the different aspects of God; for example; the image of Saraswati represents knowledge or learning, and Lakshmi represents wealth or beauty. There is no philosophical difficulty in regard to the former class of symbols. If the devotee believes they were divine incarnations, he worships their images exactly as he would have idolized them had they still lived. Some Semitic religions, such as Islam and Judaism, forbid idol worship because their prophets felt that worship of the idea of God as an abstract entity was sufficient. But generally, the use of symbols is common to all religions.

In Islam and Judaism, the sacrifice of animals on certain occasions is permitted to bring to mind the necessity of sacrificing our lower instinctive nature to God. Even metaphysical ideas of God are in fact symbols, because the conception of God is not possible for the human mind without some kind of association. Indeed, symbols are much more powerful and effective in arousing the emotions of the subconscious mind than merely abstract, intellectual ideas. This is now a well-established truth of modern psychology.

There is another mystic reason for idol worship. Thoughts are potential entities; they continue to remain in the subconscious mind and influence our conscious thoughts and attitudes. A devotee who worships Krishna or Rama is helped by the thought forces of millions of devotees who have meditated upon and worshipped these divine symbols through the centuries.

Here the racial, traditional mind is touched, but if I invent a new name for God for myself, such as AQB or P239, I shall not feel much religious emotion while uttering these names. On the other hand, if I use a symbolic name that has been used by mankind for a long time, such as Allah, God, Narayana or some sacred personality, I shall be easily inspired. So the name of God is also a symbol, but there must be some sort of association with it to capture our attention. *Sankirtan* (singing God's name), *namaz* (prayer), church hymns, or simple repetitions of the Lord's name arouse the emotions of the subconscious mind. Religious music, the ringing of bells in temples, or the resonant chanting of psalms are definitely useful and almost universally necessary for the same purpose.

Communion with God

A symbol is a medium for establishing communion with God. Images are not the idle fancies of sculptors, but shining channels through which the heart of the devotee is attracted to God and flows towards him. Altough the devotee seems to be worshipping an image of God he is actually feeling the presence of the Lord within that image and pours his devotion upon it. The ignorance of the modern sensual man clouds his vision and prevents him from seeing the Divine in the lovely and enchanting images of His forms.

The scientific advances of this century ought to convince one of the glories of symbolic worship. Are the singers and orators confined to a small box called a radio or a television? The box is a lifeless mechanical structure, which would break into a thousand pieces if thrown. Yet, if you know how to use it, you can hear music and see pictures through it, which are occurring hundreds or thousands of kilometres away.

Even as you catch the sound waves of people all over the globe through the radio and TV, it is possible to commune with the all-pervading Lord through the medium of an image. The divinity of the all-pervading God is vibrant in every atom of creation; there is not a speck of space where He is not. So, who can say that He is not in His images as well? There are many who say. "Oh, God is an all-pervading formless being. How can He be confined to this image?" But are such people really conscious of His omnipresence? Do they see Him and Him alone in everything? No, it is the ego that prevents one from bowing down to the image of God. The bhakta beholds the Lord in the symbol or image. For him, there is no such thing as insentient matter; everything is God or consciousness, so his worship of an image is worship of God.

All images, such as, pictures, drawings, photos, icons and idols are symbolic forms. They represent the cosmic body of the Lord, and the Lord is pleased when His body is worshipped. A reputed businessman once said, "Swamiji, I have no faith in the worship of images; it is all foolishness." This man had a photo of his guru in his pocket, and I asked him to take it out and spit on it. He was aghast and replied, "Swamiji, this is a photo of my mentor. I serve him, I have great respect for him, and he has made me a success in life. How can I spit on this picture of him?" I said, "Look here, my friend, you love your master and this paper image reminds you of the respect you have for him. The picture is not the man in person, nor can it eat or move; it is just a piece of paper! You associate his presence with the photo. Is this not image worship?"

A practical person, who worships and meditates, who is full of knowledge and real devotion, always keeps silent. He alone knows whether or not an image is necessary in the beginning of one's search for God. However intellectual one may be, one cannot concentrate without the help of some symbol. An intellectual person may say, "I do not like idols; I do not wish to concentrate on a form." Yet, he cannot concentrate on the formless One either, so because of his ego he fails to progress in his worship. The idol is a concrete, physical image or symbol, a representation of God, which is an abstract concept. The image in a temple, though it may be made of stone, wood or metal, is precious for a devotee as it bears the mark of his Lord, and represents something that he holds holy and eternal.

The devotee superimposes all the attributes of the Lord on the image, and when his devotion and meditation becomes intense and deep, he does not see the form as a stone image. He beholds it as the Lord, who is pure consciousness. Therefore, worship of form is very necessary for beginners on the path of spiritual awakening. The idol may remain an idol, but the worship goes to the Lord. The inner love of the devotee finds expression through external forms of worship. The wandering mind is fixed in this form of worship and the aspirant gradually feels the nearness of the Lord. He attains purity of heart and slowly annihilates his egoism. All matter is a manifestation of God. God is present in everything. Everything is an object of worship.

Awakened image
Worship of form develops devotion and makes concentration simple and easy. For example, you can bring before your mind's eye the great pastimes of the Lord in whichever incarnation you view Him. This is one of the easiest modes of self-realization that suits the majority of people today. Just as the picture of your beloved evokes a feeling of love in your heart, so also the picture of God elevates your mind to divine heights. Just as the child develops the maternal feeling

by caressing, nursing and protecting its doll made of rags, and suckles it in an imaginary manner, so also the devotee develops the feeling of devotion by worshipping the image and concentrating upon it.

Regular worship and other modes of recognizing the divinity in the form unveil the Divine latent within it. Then the devotee is able to visualize the indwelling presence in the idol. The power of God in the devotee can awaken the latent divinity in the form, and thus God becomes enshrined in the image. This is truly a wonder and a miracle. The idol or image actually comes to life. From this moment the idol will protect the devotee in a special manner. The image can become a mass of consciousness through which the devotee can draw inspiration. It can answer the devotee's questions and solve his problems. The idol can speak to the devotee and guide him. It can help him in a variety of ways that only the devotee understands.

When the image comes alive, it can perform miracles. The place where the living image is installed is transformed at once into a temple. Those who live in such a place are freed from misery, disease, failure and worldliness itself. The awakened divinity in the image acts as a guardian angel, blessing all, conferring the highest good on those who bow to it. For a devotee or a sage, there is no such thing as insentient matter. Everything is consciousness. The idol is the same as the Lord, for it is the vehicle of the expression of the deity. The devotee should regard the idol in the temple with the same attitude of respect and reverence that he would evince should the Lord Himself appear before him in person and speak to him in articulate sound.

The worship of form is not in any way a hindrance to the attainment of God-realization. Study the lives of reputed Tamil saints, such as Appar, Sundarar, Samnbandhar and others. They all had the highest adwaitic realization. They saw Lord Shiva everywhere, yet they visited all the temples of Shiva, prostrated before the image and sang hymns which are still remembered today. Madhusudana Swami had adwaitic realization and beheld the oneness of the Self in all creation, but was intensely attached to the form of Lord Krishna with a flute in His hands. The sixty-three Nayanar saints practised worship of Lord Shiva's images solely and attained God-consciousness thereby. They swept the floor of the temple, collected flowers, made garlands for the Lord and put lights there. Although illiterate, they attained the highest realization. They were embodiments of karma yoga and their hearts were saturated with pure devotion.

Selection of a symbol

The whole world worships symbols and images in one form or another. The very act of worship implies that the object of worship is superior and conscious, for all is a manifestation of God, who is therein worshipped. This is the way a devotee looks at things used as objects of worship. The untutored mind does not view the symbol in this manner. For the average person of weak or impure mind, the object chosen for worship must be pure. It must help to uplift the personality, inspire purity of heart, and encourage one-pointedness of mind. Those objects that excite passion or dislike are to be avoided. Although the rare and advanced seeker, who has purified his mind and sees the divine presence everywhere and in everything, can worship any kind of object.

While all things may be used as objects of worship, the choice of object is naturally made for the effect it will have on the mind. An image of any archetypal emblem easily induces concentration of mind and is likely to raise the thought of the devata in the mind of the worshipper. Every person has a predilection for a particular symbol, image or emblem, according to their personal inclination and belief in its special efficacy. Psychologically, this means that a particular mind finds a specific symbol or image that works best as a means to direct it to its goal. A symbol is absolutely indispensable for fixing the mind in the direction the worshipper wishes to move. Christians use the cross. A gross mind needs a concrete symbol as a prop, whereas an abstract symbol is more appealing to the subtle mind. In the beginning stages of spiritual practice, one cannot concentrate on the formless. The help of some kind of symbol is a necessity.

Therefore, worship of the Lord's form is a great aid to the eventual realization of the Lord in his all-pervading formless aspect. The form is essential for the purpose of introducing the practices of concentration and meditation. The upasaka who worships the image of the Lord from the beginning beholds the Lord everywhere and develops para bhakti. Later he beholds the whole world as the Lord. The form melts into the formless and becomes one with the formless essence. The ideas of good and bad, right and wrong vanish. He sees the Lord in all things and feels His presence in his heart as well as in all objects: dacoit, cobra, scorpion, ant, dog, tree, log of wood, block of stone, the planets, fire, earth, etc. This vision or experience baffles description!

Story about evoking the living presence

Puran Chand's guru had initiated him into the Narayana mantra and given him a small image of Lord Narayana for worship. Puran was regular in his worship and did not omit repetition of the sacred mantra, but there was no sign of the image blessing him. So he went to his guru and asked him the reason. The guru smiled at Puran and said, "Well son, take this image of Lord Shiva. I shall initiate you into the Shiva mantra. Worship Lord Shiva with faith and devotion; he is considered as Bholenath who is easily propitiated. He will bless you soon."

The next six months saw Puran Chand immersed in japa and worship of Lord Shiva. The idol of Lord Narayana was placed on a dusty shelf in the pooja room. Again Puran Chand went to his guru and complained that his worship of Shiva had brought him no result. He begged for the image and mantra of a devata that would bless him. The guru smiled and said, "Good son, in this yuga, Mother Kali is *pratyaksha devata*, the manifest deity. Worship this image of her and repeat the *Navarna* (nine syllable) mantra, and you will obtain her grace."

This time, Puran Chand had no misgivings whatsoever and commenced Kali worship with full faith. Shiva joined Narayana on the shelf. With devotion, Puran waved incense before the image of Mother Kali, but the fumes rose up to the shelf where the other two images were kept. Puran was enraged, thinking what right had Shiva to smell the incense intended for Mother Kali? Shiva had refused to be propitiated when he had tirelessly worshipped Him; it was Mother Kali whom he now worshipped. With great anger he took down the image of Shiva and began stuffing cotton wool into his nostrils to stop him from smelling the incense.

However, before he could accomplish this task, the statue disappeared and before him stood the Lord, smiling in all his mercy and compassion. Speechless with wonder and amazement, Puran prostrated himself before the Lord, who told him to ask for any boon, as he was immensely pleased with his devotion. Puran answered, "My Lord, I am very much perplexed. You did not deign to bless me when I devoutly repeated the *Panchakshara* (five syllable) mantra for six months. But you suddenly chose to reveal yourself to me, when I had discarded your image and given up your worship. What is this mystery, O Lord?"

The Lord answered, "My child, there is no mystery to be explained. How could I reveal myself when you treated me as a mere image, a mere piece of metal, to be worshipped or thrown away according to your whim? Today you treated my image as a living presence, when you wanted to plug the nostrils with cotton wool. Thus you revealed that you recognized my living presence in the image and I could no longer withhold myself from you." Speechless and enlightened, Puran bowed once more and was immersed in His love. He could ask for no greater boon, for in His love he found total fulfilment.

6

Devi Upasana

Worshippers of *Devi*, or *Shakti*, are called *shaktas*. The Agama literature details the upasana for shaktas. The concepts behind Shaktism play an important role in the esoteric aspect of yoga. The worship of God as Mother is a very old concept and images of the mother goddess are found amongst the relics of many ancient civilizations. In one of the hymns of the *Rig Veda*, Shakti is described as residing in heaven and supporting the earth. In another passage the goddess *Aditi* (meaning the 'boundless') is identified with all gods and all men, with 'whatever has been and whatever shall be'. In the *Taittireya Upanishad* the teacher says as his final instruction to the pupil: "Regard your mother as a god." There are many minor Upanishads in which Shakti is worshipped as the absolute Brahman, the One without a second.

Shaktas believe that the Supreme Mother transcends the divine trinity of Brahma, Vishnu and Shiva. She is Durga or *kriya* (power as action), She is Lakshmi or *iccha* (power as will), and She is Saraswati or *jnana* (power as knowledge). For the first three days during *Navaratri* (nine nights auspicious for sadhana), She is worshipped as Durga, for the second three days as Lakshmi, and for the last three days as Saraswati. On the tenth day She is adored as *Rajarajeshwari*, the empress, transcending the triple aspects that constitute the changing world.

Sir John Woodroffe has said: "Ritual is an art, the art of religion. Art is the outward material expression of ideas which are intellectually held and emotionally felt. Ritual art is concerned with the expression of these ideas and feelings that are specifically called religious. It is a mode by which religious truth is presented and made intelligible to the mind in material forms and symbols. It appeals to all natures passionately sensible to that beauty in which God most manifests Himself. But it is more than this, for it is the means by which the mind is transformed and purified. The shakta is thus taught that he is one with Shiva and His power of Shakti. This is not a matter of mere argument; it is a matter of experience. It is ritual yoga practice that secures that experience for them."

In tantric philosophy, God is worshipped in the form of the Divine Mother, or Devi. She is invoked by various names such as Lakshmi, Saraswati, Maha Kali, Durga or Tripura Sundari. In the Semitic religions, such as Islam, Judaism, or Christianity, God is worshipped as father. Mother worship appears to the followers of these religions as pagan and strange, but in fact worship of God the Mother is older than worship of God, the father. Essentially, God is neither male nor female. God is the absolute Reality, but human language is bound to express its ideas about this in relative terms. Naturally, in a society where the father is the head of the family, and the child is accustomed to treating the father as the person in authority, people can easily imagine God in the form of a father.

However, this patriarchal concept developed later. Anthropological research shows that primitive man lived in matriarchal societies on every continent around the globe. In matriarchal society, the wife did not go to her husband's family after marriage, but the husband lived with the family of the wife. Such types of society still exist in South India and are common in Tibet. The renowned Sanskrit scholar and the erstwhile Sanskrit professor of Leningrad University, Rahul Sankrityayan, proved that the matriarchal society did certainly exist among the Aryans. Worship of the Divine

Mother was developed in such societies. This kind of worship was very popular and soothing to the mind as no other relationship could exceed the feeling of the mother for her child. This concept of mother goddess was a great help to the devotee. Just as a child feels more at ease with the mother than the father, the devotee is also more comfortable with the God as mother than with God as father.

Absolute surrender is the main feature of Devi upasana, as in other forms of worship. Mother-worship may also be synthesized with the worship of God as father, as when Sita and Rama or Radha and Krishna are worshipped together. Devi-worship is a potent means for the removal of passion. The aspirant sees the Divine Mother in every female form and tries to maintain this attitude in life. Carnal emotions cannot thrive in this case, for anyone can imagine how sacred is the person of one's own mother. The sacred word 'Om' is also a remnant of ancient Aryan mother worship. In every language of the world, the sound 'Ma' expresses the idea of mother: in English, 'mother'; in Latin 'mater'; in Sanskrit 'matri'; in French 'mammon'; in Persian 'madar; in Arabic 'umm' and so on. The sacred mantra 'Om' occurs in every religion of the world as well. In Christianity it occurs as Amen, in Islam as Amin. The Buddhists chant Om Mani Padme Hum. Om is really a universal name for God.

Sri Vidya upasana

The main tantric upasana of Devi is *Sri Vidya* which has two aspects, exoteric and esoteric. It involves external meditation on the *Sri Chakra yantra* (the most respected geometric symbol of Devi) and internal meditation on the mental form of the Devi or Shiva/Shakti. This upasana leads to the identification with the Divine Mother within oneself. The internal form of worship is for more advanced sadhakas, while the external worship is for the less advanced.

In the external form of Sri Vidya upasana, the Sri Chakra yantra is inscribed upon a gold or metallic plate. During the worship, mantras are repeated with gestures, postures, waving

64

of lights, incense, and various food offerings. The internal form of worship has neither rituals nor ceremonies. Shiva united with Shakti is worshipped mentally at the various chakras or centres of energy. Those who perform the internal mode of worship believe in the identity of Shiva/Shakti and the awakening of *kundalini* (the evolutionary consciousness and energy in man). By mental worship and mantra japa, they take the awakened kundalini up through the various *chakras* (psychic and energy centres) to *sahasrara*, the thousand-petalled lotus at the crown of the head, where the individual soul unites with the Supreme soul.

Each verse of the Sri Vidya text also has a particular yantra with *beeja aksharas*, or seed syllables, and a prescribed course of worship. The beeja aksharas and yantra are inscribed on a gold or copper plate. The food offerings to the Devi vary, according to the mode and purpose of worship. There is a definite distinct aim to be achieved by a particular mode of worship with a particular yantra and a particular offering. The days of worship also vary from four to 180 days.

Many results can be attained by this worship of Devi such as: wealth, learning, lordship, success in enterprise, mastery over the elements, eloquence, poetic talents, conquest over the enemy, eradication of incurable ailments, and so on. Generally, people perform this upasana for the fulfilment of worldly desires. Success depends upon the faith and devotion of the upasaka. If there is any delay in the attainment of the specific result, the worship will have to be continued for some more days with intense devotion. The verses can be used for internal worship also and will result in the attainment of final beatitude if the upasaka seeks that alone from the Divine Mother.

An upasaka who has been initiated into the worship of Sri Vidya should meditate on the Devi and identify with her, and then he will become one with the Devi. Sri Chakra is the residence or the temple of Devi and is important in Sri Vidya upasana. Adi Shankaracharya describes Sri Chakra in *Saundarya Lahari* (v.11): "O Mother, the four triangles with downward apex are called *srikantha*, because they belong to Shiva, and the central point is Shiva himself. The five triangles, starting from the central point, belong to Shakti. These nine triangles together are called *shivayuvati*. By interlacing these nine triangles, forty-three triangles are created, the main point, housing the *bindu* (central point), is itself the forty-fourth triangle. Surrounding all of these triangles are two circles: the first is an eight-petalled lotus, and the second a sixteen-petalled lotus. Three concentric circles surround these lotuses. A triple lined square with four gates, called *bhupura*, encloses the whole diagram.

The upasaka meditates on this Sri Chakra yantra, step by step. First, he meditates on the four gates located in the four directions of bhupura. The three lines of the bhupura are said to be white, red and yellow respectively. The ten siddhis reside in the ten directions. Different shaktis, called yoginis, protect the different parts of the chakra, and the upasaka must please them by his upasana. The eight *matrikas*, the 'little mothers' of the Sanskrit letters, reside at the right and left side of the doors of the second line. The yoginis reside on the third line.

The lines of the three *mekhala traya* (concentric circles) are said to be the forms of sattwa, rajas and tamas; the moon, sun and fire; or iccha, jnana and kriya shakti. The circle of the sixteen-petalled lotus is said to represent the moon, with sixteen yoginis in their unmanifest forms, residing within it. The circle of the eight-petalled lotus is the residence of Shiva. The eight petals are symbolic of his attributes: the five elements, sun, moon and atman. The portion nearest these lotuses is referred to as *kshira sagara*, milk ocean.

The fourteen triangles are called *saubhagya chakra* in which the fourteen yoginis of the fourteen *sampradayas,* or traditions, reside. The ten triangles are called the residence of the ten incarnations of Sri Vishnu. The *kulottirna* and *nigarbha yoginis* are the residing deities of these triangles. Then there are the eight *vag devatas* known as the *rahasya yoginis*. Through this step-by-step meditation, the upasaka now enters the main triangle where the deities of sattwa, rajas and tamas reside. The *nada*, or sound, starts from this point, where the three consecutive circles represent the seats of Brahma, Vishnu and Mahesh and their consorts. *Jagriti* (waking consciousness), *swapna* (dream consciousness), and *sushupti* (unconsciousness) are the three deities of these seats. In the main triangle Maha Tripura Sundari in the form of a girl is united with Shiva, and here she is called Parabhattarika. This Devi has the Sri mantra or *panchadas sakari* (fifteen syllable) mantra. Each letter of this mantra is an attribute of the Devi. The upasaka is to meditate on this mantra. The mantra, the Devi and the world are the same.

The kundalini is identified with Tripura Sundari, who represents the universal energy, or *prakriti*. She is the primal energy, and in the human body resides in the form of kundalini, lying dormant at mooladhara chakra. The six main chakras: *mooladhara, swadhisthana, manipura, anahata, vishuddhi* and *ajna*, are similar to the diagram of Sri Chakra, where the Devi resides unified with Shiva. In *Saundarya Lahari* (v. 42 & 74) the form of Tripura Sundari is described as follows: Sri Devi is in the form of the female. She has three lines on her throat. She sings beautifully. She wears red garments and a necklace of pearls. She looks in the eightfold directions at her devotees. Her complexion is red. She has besmeared her forehead with saffron paste. She wears a garland of red flowers. She holds the flower arrows, a bow of sugarcane, noose, and goad in her hands.

Along with Shiva/Shakti, various manifestations of Mahashakti or Parashakti are also worshipped in this upasana. The body of Parashakti is formed of pure and concentrated sattwa, without any admixture of rajas and tamas. The other shaktis merely have a preponderance of sattwa over rajas and tamas, and are not of pure sattwa. Therefore, She is the highest prototype of Parabrahman. The different Shaktis are: Adi Shakti, Iccha Shakti, Kriya Shakti, Jnana Shakti, Bala, Tripura Sundari, Rajarajeswari, Annapurna, Gayatri, Savitri, Kundalini and many others.

The worship of each Shakti produces a specific result, but may produce a general result also. Any name of the Devi may be repeated; however, the goddess must be invoked by the corresponding name to obtain a particular result.

Just as the fruit is hidden in the seed, butter in the milk and virility in boyhood, so various Shaktis remain latent in man, veiled by ignorance. If you purify your mind and practise concentration and meditation, all these latent powers will shine forth. The best fruit of upasana or meditation is identity with the object meditated upon. The meditator and the meditated become one. The devotee of Devi attains realization of oneness with Her through intense upasana or worship. The *Kurma Purana* says: "Water is able to quench the fire, the presence of the Sun to dispel darkness, and the repetition of the name of Devi to destroy the multitude of sins in the Kali age." The *Brahma Purana* says: "Those who worship the Supreme Shakti, whether regularly or irregularly, are not entangled in samskara. There is no doubt they are liberated souls."

Ananda Lahari/Saundarya Lahari

Ananda Lahari, meaning 'waves of bliss' is a devotional poem of forty-one stanzas by Sri Shankaracharya, containing beautiful hymns in praise of Devi, the goddess Tripura Sundari. The stanzas contain various mantras along with yantras for the worship of Devi and the attainment of various siddhis or powers. Ananda Lahari is universally recognized as an ancient and authoritative tantric work, and many commentaries have been written on it. *Saundarya Lahari* is a carry over of Ananda Lahari and means 'waves of beauty', because it gives a description of the beauty or perfection of the Devi's form. The first forty-one stanzas of Saundarya Lahari encompass Ananda Lahari, and the remaining sixty-two verses constitute Saundarya Lahari. The complete text is generally called Saundarya Lahari.

Among the hymns addressed to Devi, Saundarya Lahari occupies a unique position as one of the most inspiring

68

devotional poems. Being an important work on Tantra Shastra, it deals with kundalini yoga, the chakras and other tantric subjects. Saundarya Lahari describes the worship of the Supreme Being in its feminine aspect of Shakti or cosmic power, which is the same creative energy known as Sri Vidya. It contains the essence of Sri Vidya in a nutshell and includes beautiful hymns in praise of the Devi or the goddess Tripura Sundari, such as the following:

O Tripura Sundari! O Adorable Mother! I bow to you.
Without your grace, no one can succeed in spiritual sadhana
and attain salvation at the end.

O Compassionate Mother! You are an ocean of mercy.
Bless me. If I receive a drop from that ocean, will it ever dry up?
O my sweet Mother! Guide me. Protect me. Save me.
I am your child. Jaya Tripura Sundari! Salutations to you.

May all my idle talk be your japa, sound divine,
May all my gestures be your mudra,
May all my steps be around your seat,
May all my lying down be your pranam,
May your oblations be my only food,
And, may all acts of mine be in joy for you.

69

Upasana

From the teachings of Swami Satyananda Saraswati

7

Importance of Worship

Mankind has a natural urge for light, bliss, freedom, immortality and knowledge, which leads him towards the path of worship and god-realization. Continuous and repeated thoughts about God make a person pure. This type of worship is called upasana. To sit near God and think about Him again and again is worship. Upasana means being in the proximity of God. Upasana or worship is such a profound subject that it cannot be explained in a few words. It is very difficult to define upasana with a synonym, like the terms technology or medical science use. Upasana is a vast, deep subject that comprises a number of aspects. In the vedic and upanishadic texts the word upasana has many associations, such as: archana, aradhana, pooja, seva, yajna, vandana, dhyana, *chintan* (inner reflection), japa, *upasthana* (being close), sravana, kirtana, smarana, bhajana, yoga and samsharayana, all of which relate with the concept of worship.

The shastras teach that the path of worship is the simplest and easiest path to experience God in the kali yuga. A rational understanding is not required, because worship transcends the logical level of mind. The first important act of worship is to bow down before the deity, who is greater than any other power of the world. Upasana starts from this act and progresses gradually towards bliss, and love. It is necessary to begin with the deity one loves and adores, but the upasaka should progressively rise beyond the gross form of that deity and reach the all-pervading dimension, finally merging into the supreme Atman. In this way, all names and forms, *nama* and *roopa*, are ultimately transcended. The upasaka thus becomes one with Brahman and is called a *jivanmukta* (one who is liberated in this life).

Presence of God

The divine is ultimately worshipped in the form of eternal presence. God in the form of omnipresence is everywhere, but why don't we feel Him? I know a lot about the subject. I've written books and spoken about it at length. I have done a lot of japa, lakhs and crores of japa. I have done a lot of mantra writing. I have visited all the pilgrimage places, but I did not know how to have the divine presence. I was aware that there is something called the divine presence, but I did not know how to have the experience of it. Even today, I don't know how to have it – but I have it! I was aware of the fact that God's presence can be experienced in the same way that we experience the spirit, or the presence of fear, animosity or lust.

I knew that God's presence is throughout, and I tried to experience Him in different ways, just as a woman thinks and feels about a man or a man about a woman. For that experience, I moved straight and also obliquely, spoke for hours about Him, wrote book after book, but the path leading to Him remained far away from me. I used to ponder over which way to go to Him. Whichever path I trod I found His door locked and barred. But now I experience Him, although I can't explain why I have this experience now. When I experience His presence, only He remains in my vision. Then I recall the words of Kabir, "When I was present, He was not. Now, He is present and I am not", because in His presence this differentiation between Him and me is completely obliterated.

How to experience the presence of God has been the eternal question. In answer to this, the sages and saints developed upasana, which means nearness or proximity to

God. If nothing else, even nearness will do. It doesn't even matter if we can't see God; at least we will have Him near us or amongst us. We will enjoy proximity to Him. He could be sitting next to us even now, but in what form we do not know. We cannot say whether He will come in the four-armed human form or in another form.

Shabari was a tribal lady. Her guru told her that Lord Rama would come to her doorstep one day. Hearing this, she was initially so overwhelmed with joy and happiness that she could not say anything. But after recovering, she asked certain questions: "I am by caste one of the down-trodden. How can I touch and worship the feet of Sri Rama? I have never performed any acts of charity. I have never taken a bath in the river Ganga to purify myself. I have never had darshan of any god or goddess. I have never been to a temple or on a pilgrimage. How can I, a down-trodden one, deserve to have darshan of the Lord?"

These were the questions that Shabari put to her guru, and this was the answer she received: God's feet touch everything. God is present everywhere. You don't have to be born into a high caste; you don't have to be a *sannyasin* (renunciate) or a good person. To reach God you need neither a certificate nor virtue. Whatever you are, whether thief, robber, dacoit, rascal, drunkard, Hindu or Muslim, virtuous or debauched, the Lord's feet are available to everybody. Only one thing is necessary, and that is intense love for God, who is the dearest thing in this world. By what means can you forget yourself? That love is the only way.

The Atman, the Self, and the feelings all reside in the heart. The experience of God, therefore, takes place through the heart. If only you could awaken this intense love for God in your heart, that would be enough. The most important thing that you have to understand is that God is the centre of the universe, and the heart is the eye through which you can see Him. You will never be able to see Him without heart. You may study all the scriptures, the Puranas, the *Koran* and the *Bible*, but it will be to no avail. You can only see God through the eyes of your heart. The same God that you experience through your heart is the centre, the soul and the totality of the universe. God and the universe are identical; there is absolutely no difference.

Purpose of human existence

There are 8,400,000 species in this world and the four instincts: desire for food, desire for sex, desire for sleep, and fear of death, exist in all of them, right from the smallest bacteria or insect to the largest elephant. However, one special quality is found in man: only he can worship God, sing God's name, do japa and meditate on God. Does the cow or the dog ever think about God? Do they ever go to the temple to sing *Jai Jagdish Hare*? Apart from human beings, no other species can ever think about God. We can experience God. We are aware of God. We are searching for Him. We have questions about Him. Only human beings are capable of talking about God, listening to stories about God, and offering their lives to God. This is the highest aim of human existence.

Therefore, the first duty of man is to worship God, to establish a relationship with the Supreme Being, to unite with God. That is the purpose of human birth; everything else is secondary. So, why has man considered everything else as more important and neglected his primary goal? The *jiva* (living being) passes through 8,400,000 *yonis* (wombs) to obtain the human form, which has only that one aim, to attain God. The living beings in this world are not different from Paramatman, the transcendental God. They are all part of God, part of the one form in which God has manifested Himself. The happy ones, the unhappy ones, the trees, the animals, all are a part of Him. If you want to realize God, then try to know, not only the transcendental God, but also the God who lives in each and every living being, and also in non-living things. Only then can you know Him fully. Just knowing a part of Him is not enough. You should know Him in totality and in all His forms.

Your inner awakening will really take place someday. God is always with you. Nothing is difficult for Him; only He should be convinced that you are totally honest in whatever you are thinking and doing. If you have a knife to cut vegetables and you cut somebody's throat with it, that is a misuse of the knife. Similarly, God gave you this life for the purpose of chanting His name and you have misused it for sensory pleasures. You have misused the body, so you have to bear the fruits of your actions. The day you realize this, all your attachments, hatred, sin and crookedness will slowly diminish like the waning of the moon during the dark fortnight. The negative qualities will automatically subside with this realization, but nothing will help before that. You may go to priests, psychologists, and psychotherapists, drink potions, eat herbs and take drugs, but nothing will work.

Why is there human incarnation? Why is a donkey or a dog born? Why does a snake incarnate? Why does a human incarnate? What is nature's purpose in creating and evolving the human body? It is precisely for manifesting the unmanifest God. Man has been given this body to realize the invisible God as a visible power. Understand this clearly, because man is the only creature who can think about God and proceed towards Him. The rest of the 8,400,000 species of creation simply eat, sleep and procreate, so what is the difference between a man and an animal? There is only one difference, animals cannot discuss or understand God, although they live by the grace of God. A man can talk about God and wonder about Him, and this is a very big difference.

All the saints, such as Mohammed, Christ, Guru Nanak, have said the same thing. If a man wants to improve himself, then let him behave as a man and not as an animal. A man who casts off his body without worshipping God, without attaining God, without devotion, without singing devotional songs in His praise, has to undergo the cycles of rebirth again. He has to come back again, because he leaves this life with an unfinished task. If you cannot live in accordance with the laws of God and the Divine, then you are inviting problems in life. Life has to be lived in accordance with the laws of dharma.

Dharma is not religion in the sense that we generally understand it. Dharma is not just ethics or morality; it is true religion. It is that kind of expression, or behaviour, which is related with humanity, with the people around you, but always through God. Religion should relate to humanity through God.

You do not understand that your real obligation is not social, it is spiritual, it is to yourself and to God. So why misuse the body, why waste this incarnation? Once it is realized that the main purpose, the main agenda of life is divinity, the whole code changes; the entire direction of the clock changes automatically. But nobody wants to realize this for themselves. Everyone thinks, "If I worry about God, then what will happen to my children?" The maximum concern is for the children and family, not for realizing God. Therefore, man is unable to deal with the mind or to make positive use of his life.

Easiest way to God

God is the centre of life. Worshipping Him and loving Him are the main duties of every human being. Man alone can investigate God. Man alone can dedicate his whole life to God, no other life form can do it. Only man can worship God. If that is the Truth, and if that is the law of nature, then the prime duty of everyone is worship of the Divine. Worship and devotion pave the way to oneness with God. Upasana or worship is the first duty; family is the next. The two main aspects of worship are repetition of God's name and helping others. God's name can be repeated for a short period of time with a mala, either verbally or mentally. You can use any name of God: "Om Namah Shivaya," "Sri Rama," "Lord Jesus," or "Hail Mary"; it is up to you.

All keen travellers on the spiritual path seek a higher, divine and infinite experience. They wish to know about divinity, which is beyond name and form, beyond the senses and intellect. The easiest path to divinity is to think about others. To think about others is to think about God; to serve another is to worship God. Have at least some corner in your heart for the suffering and misery of others. If you can help your fellow beings even a little, God will most certainly shower his grace upon you. Helping one another is worship, upasana, therefore, do not underrate this act. This is sadhana, a spiritual practice in itself. By doing good to others, your mirror will become clean. One day you will see yourself very clearly and exclaim in realization, "Oh, I am Brahman."

This is the truth based on my own experience. I have lived a spiritual life for more than half a century. I have practised every form of yoga, from the Himalayas to Rameshwaram. But ultimately I found that when I began to think about others, God began to think about me. God sent me to Rikhia and one day I heard Him say to me, "Take care of your neighbours, just as I have taken care of you." I began to reflect on these words and asked myself, Satyananda, are you really so selfish? Will you eat all the sweets by yourself? Will you have the darshan of God all by yourself? What is the use of the *atmajnana* (spiritual knowledge) that you attain? How can the world benefit by your self-realization and spiritual gain? You are very selfish; give up selfishness. Then and there I said to God, "Show me the path. I am blind. Tell me what to do." Henceforth, God began to show me the path. He said, "Give blankets to those who are fighting the cold." In this way, slowly the guidance came in clear terms.

Many paths of worship
In India, most people worship the embodied deity. We are not monotheistic, because worship of God in only one form brings disaster to society. All the world's terrorists are monotheists. Monotheistic philosophy breeds intolerance, which ultimately reflects in the political system. The impact of monotheism on the political system will be felt in times to come. A polytheistic society in which God can be worshipped in any form according to the choice of each citizen is a

better society, a non-violent society, and a society with greater understanding and tolerance. Polytheism always has a positive impact on a nation's politics, culture and civilization. On the other hand, the impact of monotheism has an adverse impact. In Indian philosophy, although the Upanishads speak of one God, they add that this God has various forms: *Ekam sat viprah bahudha vadanti* – "Although the truth of the supreme spirit is One, the wise identify Him by various names."

Therefore, it is not necessary to worship one God alone. As there are various forms of God, it is foolish to say that God is without form. God is both with form, *sakara*, and without form, *nirakara*. It is up to you to make a choice about how to worship Him, adore Him, and ask a boon from Him. You will have to make a choice between the embodied God and the formless God, and then offer your obeisance to Him. You are absolutely free to exercise your preference for any form of God. Hanuman is not greater than Sri Rama and Sri Rama is not superior to Hanuman. Even so, Devi is not superior to Sri Krishna and likewise Sri Krishna is not greater than Devi. Previously I had one name, now I have another name, but I remain the same person. Can you say which of my two names is greater? Similarly, the names of God may be different, but the ultimate Truth is the same.

Whatever your country or culture, your forefathers were polytheists. Two thousand years ago they were forced to accept monotheism. The Anglo Saxons had a polytheistic culture. The forefathers of the Americans, English and Australians were polytheistic and worshipped various deities. Two thousand years ago they were forced to accept monotheism or be burnt alive. Christianity is one way to salvation, but it is wrong to say that Christianity is the only way. My house has more than one door. If you are coming to Deoghar, it is not essential to go via Bhagalpur. You can come via Kolkata. You are free to take the route through Kathmandu or Mumbai to reach Deoghar. There are many doors to my house. You may enter through any of them. I have hammered this idea into people's minds; that God is not one form only, God is infinite; God is an integral whole.

Upasana is worship of God by chanting His name, singing His glory, performing pooja to Him with ritualistic precision, or by mental absorption in Him. Ritualistic precision means with articles of pooja, like the conch, bell, flowers and leaves, lights and incense. Worship of God can be done at the mental level also, without these external means. Chanting *Hanuman Chalisa, Ramacharitamanas* or singing kirtan are also forms of worship. Whenever you remember God, whenever you worship Him with any of the aforesaid attitudes, it becomes upasana. You may cry out to Him in your adversity to remove your sorrows and sufferings, you may ask His favour for wish fulfilment, you may turn to Him for knowledge about Himself, or you may love Him just for the sake of love. All these types of worship are called upasana.

The tradition of bhakti does not insist on the necessity of ceremonial worship, as much as other traditions. In fact, ceremonial worship is usually recommended only to the wealthy householders, who can thereby utilize their riches in an appropriate manner. The *Bhavagat Purana* emphasizes that worship with little means, but offered in a spirit of devotion, exceeds an elaborate ritual carried out in a purely mechanical way. The Lord once asked his childhood friend Sudama: "Oh Brahmana, what present have you brought for me from your house?" When Sudama hesitated to offer his meager gift, the Lord said, "Even the slightest offering, given with affection by my devotees, is considered by me as very great. But lavish offerings given by one who is not my votary bring me no joy or satisfaction."

Another form of upasana is to engage in every action as a form of worship. The *Bhagavat Purana* narrates the story of King Ambarisa, an ideal bhakta of Vishnu, who dedicated all his actions to the Lord's service. "He engaged his mind in meditation on the lotus feet of Lord Krishna, his speech in singing of the excellences of Lord Vishnu, his hands in services such as cleaning the temple of Hari and other duties, and his ears in listening to excellent stories of the imperishable Lord. He employed his eyes in beholding the images and shrines of Vishnu, his touch in embracing those who served the gods, his nose in smelling the fragrance of the Tulsi leaves dedicated to His feet, and his tongue to what he offered to the Lord. King Ambarisa used his feet in walking to the holy places, hallowed with Lord Hari's feet, his head to bow down to the feet of Lord Vishnu. He employed his own desire in the humble service of the Lord, and not for the fulfilment of worldly desires. In this way the king dedicated all his daily activities and duties to the glories of the Lord, so that his whole life became a form of worship.

8

Love of God

B hakti means pure love, true love. What the world calls love is not true love. Love for your children, your mother, your brother, your wife is not true love; it is attachment, *asakti*. There may be an element of love there, a minute amount, but it is not true love. There is no true love in this world. Bhakti is true love and it is not associated with the body, mind or soul. Bhakti is concerned with the heart and pure feeling. The feelings of fear, passion, hatred, jealousy, anger, worry, love and devotion all come under the category of bhavana or feeling. When you hate someone, you think about him day and night. When someone who is dear to you dies, the memory haunts you and you cannot forget it, even if you want to. That feeling is bhavana, which is the chief ingredient, the basic cause of love.

When you speak of love, it is a very vague idea. True love is the feeling of oneness with another, to feel for another as you feel for yourself, to feel the difficulties of another as you feel your own. Duality fused into unity is one expression of love, where the two become one. Sometimes emotion takes the form of love, but there is a clear cut distinction between love and emotion. They are two different substances completely; they belong to two totally different castes, but they look almost alike. What most people call love is really emotion. The feeling for a girl or a boy is passion. The feeling for money is greed. The feeling of a mother towards her child is affection. When the feeling is directed towards a peer, it is friendship. Whether paternal, maternal or fraternal, these are all feelings. When the feeling is directed towards God, it is called bhakti.

Passion is a mutilated form of bhakti. When the emotions go the wrong way, the feeling is eros. When the feelings go the right way, it is bhakti. Yoga is easy, but bhakti is not easy, because it is related to your inner, personal feelings, not the mind. Bhakti has nothing to do with mind or intellect. Bhakti is concerned with the heart and feeling. To direct this feeling to God is a very big job; it is not an ordinary job. Therefore, you may start by directing the feeling towards that form of God which you love. You must understand that true love is not easy; it is a river of fire and you have to dive into it. You have to purify your mind and undergo a lot of experiences in life to attain this caliber of love. Love requires a lot of sacrifices from you: your comforts, your idio-syncrasies, your ego, your money, your life, everything.

You have to develop love of God within you, but love does not grow without facing hatred, jealousy, greed, selfishness and mean-mindedness. You have to confront these negative aspects if you are going to climb up towards love. At different points, you will encounter these rascals, these *rakshasas* (demons): Miss Jealousy, Mr Arrogance, and Mrs Selfishness. They have their quarters, and when you go there, they talk to you very nicely. You are going in search of love, but you may stay with jealousy for a lifetime. Suddenly, one day, you realize, 'Oh God! I was going for love, but I am with jealousy!' By then, however, you are too old and cannot climb any more.

Feeling and intellect

The intellect is discerning, but feeling is blind. Emotions and feelings make you religious or spiritual. The intellect can only make you learned, a great scholar or mathematician, but it cannot make you religious or spiritual. Intellect can make you an Einstein or Newton, but not a devotee. For upasana, it is essential to develop your emotions and keep them healthy and positive. Blind faith and experiential faith are both manifestations of emotion and feeling. Blind faith is a label given to certain feelings. I have obtained a lot of enlightenment from this so-called blind faith. Actually, I have a lot of blind faith. I have just married a *tulsi* plant to a *shaligram*. I made all the arrangements with loving care. I got jewelry and finery and distributed sweets. What would you call an educated man, marrying a tulsi plant to a stone? I do not know about the meaning of this, but I enjoyed doing it. I liked decorating the plant with flowers and putting candles all around.

The greatest intellectual giant can become like a child. For example, Vivekananda did not understand the significance of what Ramakrishna was saying to him in the beginning, because he was an intellectual. Finally, when Vivekananda surrendered to Ramakrishna, he became the medium. Therefore, it is the feeling which you have to develop, not the intellect or reason. Aurobindo said that reason is the barrier to spiritual life. At some point you must transcend reason. There is a time when intellect is necessary, but the time also comes when your life must be steered by positive feelings. What are those feelings? They are not the feelings of jealousy and fear, but of devotion and love. When these feelings come into play, then God takes a form, He is seen and He begins to speak.

You may say that all this is psychosis or neurosis. Well, it is better to suffer from God psychosis and neurosis than from this worldly psychosis and neurosis. I prefer to be called a spiritual psychotic. The intellectuals of Bengal used to call Ramakrishna Paramahamsa a psychotic. The western psychologists call this Christ neurosis. It is better to have Christ neurosis than worldly neurosis. The simple person, who does not use his head too much, finds God very soon. God gives darshan easily to people who have the heart of a child. Those who are adult at heart, who are very intellectual and talk about philosophy and knowledge, do not reach

God. It is not even essential to be a good person to reach God. It is essential to be good for social reasons; otherwise there would be riots and terrorism. To reach God, it is simply necessary to learn to love; that is all.

The ultimate love is union, when the jivatman and paramatman become one. The essential thing is love, merging of the mind, and awareness of God all the time, not thinking of anybody else, not thinking of friends, not thinking of disciples. Once you begin to experience real devotion, your only concern is with God. You are not bothered in the least even if the whole world is against you, because the all-encompassing love of God is such that it engulfs your body, mind and entire being. You may think that only saints can experience such love for God, but ordinary people living in the world can develop it also through the practice of upasana. The practice of bhakti, which refines the bhava, the feelings, and transforms you into a bhakta, is upasana.

Quality of feelings
The ultimate point of fusion is when you split the atom and explode the nucleus. The ultimate point of bhakti is devotion, love. Real devotion comes from the heart, it is an expression of bhavana, feeling, not a product of intellect. Bhavana is internal, not external. Upasana is a process that limits the flow of thoughts and feelings to the object of emotion, thereby intensifying and uniting the feeling. In order to develop devotion, you have to streamline your bhavana. Instead of directing it towards fear, anger, animosity, hatred, maya and moha, you have to direct it towards God through the practice of upasana. Bhavana is fully developed in every being; you do not have to develop it. When you can love Him as you would love your boyfriend or girlfriend, then God will be there. He will come immediately.

When you worship God, you have some feeling for Him. When you go to the temple or holy place, you have some feeling, but the depth of feeling and awareness for God has to be much deeper. You do not have to be told how to develop feelings. You only have to be taught how to channel your feelings, how to change the direction of the flow. The same feeling that was running towards jealousy, anger, greed and passion has to be redirected, and then it becomes bhakti. Throughout history there have been many people who were wretched, passionate and debauched, but something happened in their lives, and within the twinkling of an eye, they became great bhaktas. They did not have to develop that love, because it was already in them; it was only misdirected and misguided.

Through the practice of upasana, you can bring more devotion into your life; there is no other remedy. If the feelings are channeled towards God, life will be full of bliss and wonder, and the journey of life will be completed successfully. The goal is difficult, but the practice is easy. Go on with regular practice and see the difference; the goal will be achieved. Doesn't a schoolchild eventually obtain an MA degree? First he goes to primary school, then high school, then college, and finally university. In spiritual life the course is also graded. Everybody wishes to attain the love of God in this body, in this lifetime, but it does not happen like that, because people are at different levels. If all the people leave Ayodhya, the place will become desolate and forlorn. There must be someone ahead and someone lagging behind.

In spiritual life it is essential to refine the quality of feeling, just as you try to improve the quality of the dal. You have divided your love in many directions and, therefore, you are not able to refine your feelings and love God with intensity. The problem is that your feelings are confused, preoccupied with the tangles of the world, so your bhavana is not free. You have to free your feelings, one way or another. Sometimes something happens in life, which frees the bhavana for a while, say five to six months, but the feelings should be constantly free. When a young man and woman fall in love, their bhavana withdraws spontaneously from all other avenues and becomes concentrated in the partner. Laila could only see Majnu and Majnu could only see Laila, nothing else. Similarly, Hanuman's awareness was constantly focused on Sri Rama; this is the oneness of bhavana.

Faith and trust

In upasana, the important feelings that you need to cultivate are faith and trust. The main purpose of faith and trust is to develop love for God, even while living in the external transient world. It is not a matter of surrender to God and then everything becomes okay; that is not the purpose of faith and trust. Faith and trust are necessary in order to experience God, to have darshan, and to merge in Him. This should be the aim, if not today then tomorrow, if not tomorrow then in the next life. The path of faith and trust is the best path for a spiritual aspirant. It does not matter what clothes you wear, what food you eat, or how you live. Nothing matters as long as you have faith and trust.

You may study and attend satsang, but you will not experience anything, you will not receive any grace, until your faith and trust become stable and powerful. Without faith, there is no point in coming to the spiritual path. In fact, one cannot survive without faith and trust, they are man's greatest assets. Faith and trust are not worldly virtues; they are spiritual qualities. You should aim to develop these qualities by attending good satsang, not the satsang where politics and social problems are discussed. The word *satsang* means 'association with truth', from the roots *sat* and *sanga*. The truth here is God. In the *Bhagavad Gita*, Lord Krishna has declared: "Men devoid of faith do not attain Me, but return to the path of the mortal world."

Faith in God is a glorious, wish-fulfilling jewel. Knowledge of God does not bring you closer or guarantee communion, but faith in God does. Through knowledge alone you may or may not develop communion; it is never a certainty. Therefore, faith is a valuable gem, like a rare diamond, pearl

88

or ruby. The most precious and valuable jewel is faith. If you can attain this jewel then your path becomes clear. If your heart is full of faith, you will always be radiant. Throughout the day and night there will be no darkness. This illumination does not depend on any lamp or candle. Even if you are poor, it doesn't matter. In fact, poverty never approaches one with faith. Remember that poverty has nothing to do with money. There are people without money who are very rich. There are very wealthly people who, in fact, are poor; that is real poverty.

Poverty means ignorance, *avidya*. Faith dispels the overpowering gloom of ignorance like sunlight dispels the clouds. Vanity and ignorance automatically go away with the gem of faith. When faith and trust develop, illumination arises from within, just as the sun rises and illumines the darkness. You will travel at the highest speed. All the obstacles that arise on this journey will disappear and that is the highest path. You will discover that faith brings spontaneity into your life. Even if you do not want to love God, you will love Him. Even if you don't want to surrender, you will do so. Even if you don't want anything from Him, He will give you everything. Faith in God brings spontaneous blessings. You don't have to ask God for anything in a church, temple or prayer hall.

Christians know what faith means; faith is the basis of Christianity. Faith is the basis of the teachings of the *Bible* and of the *Ramayana*. Faith is the basis of spiritual life, and the only thing you have to cultivate in life is faith. Even propensities like lust, anger and greed will never approach if that gem resides in your heart. Poison is transformed into nectar and enemies become friends. Those who are suffering from mental afflictions will find that their pain disappears. When the jewel of faith in God lives in the heart, one cannot have suffering, even in dreams. Those who strive for that jewel are the wisest of people.

Shraddha, or faith, is the *brahmastra*, the ultimate weapon of spirituality. It is the ultimate armour, the ultimate power of spiritual life. In the *Ramacharitamanas*, it is said: "Without shraddha and *vishvas*, faith and deep conviction, even great siddhas cannot achieve spiritual attainment." Again in the *Bhagavad Gita* (12:2), Sri Krishna has said: "I consider those to be perfect in yoga, who fix their mind on Me and worship Me, ever steadfast and endowed with supreme faith." In modern times Mother Theresa has said: 'We are called upon not to be successful, but to be faithful.'

Research into faith

Faith and trust belong to your psychological personality, and their effects can be measured in terms of electromagnetic radiations. What is the effect of faith, trust and belief on the blood pressure and metabolism? Faith and trust are personal things. How can I know how much faith and trust you have? Can they be measured if I cannot see them? We cannot see faith or belief, but we can feel them. However, that is not enough. It has to be proved that I have faith and belief, and this is the result, in black and white. Objective data should be produced. Trust and faith are the basis of bhakti, but they cannot be seen with the eyes. Sometimes you think that you believe, but you do not. Many times your beliefs are broken, shattered and impotent. But sometimes belief is so powerful that it can restore life to the dead.

Sometimes faith works miracles and sometimes it fails. What is it that fails? What is that faith? Is it a blood flow or a current of electromagnetic radiation? What is the form of bhavana, of feeling? Has it got weight? Does it have some impulse or is it some sort of light or vibration? Is bhavana a vibration or a flow? Bhavana is what you call a feeling and it exists for sure, because when we are angry, we hate. We feel like killing that person because of this feeling and we cannot sleep at night. The feeling of anger disturbs the heart and blood pressure, doesn't it? When you have enmity towards someone, you lose your appetite. The liver also functions improperly. In many people worries and anxieties cause the eyesight to become weak. This means that the effect of bhavana or feeling on the human body is tangible. Although you cannot see faith or belief, its effects can be felt on the body. Therefore, you can know the cause through the effect.

Many times you may not know the cause, but you can come to know it by the effect. In this case you know the effect first and then postulate a cause. Faith in God can be the next topic of scientific research. Until now scientists have only conducted research on matter. They have not researched the soul or atma, because they say it does not exist. What research will they do into the spirit? But certainly they can research the feelings of faith and trust.

Something transcendental has to become a focus for the mind. In the last part of the twentieth century, God was not something to be talked about, but now you can talk about Him. Faith in God will be *the* subject of the next century. God has to be established very systematically and scientifically, not as someone mysterious. I never spoke about God before in my life, but suddenly I am not able to speak of anything else. There is nothing you can do for the present generation, but you can try to inspire the future generation to take a new direction. Set your children on the path of bhakti. You do not have to tell them to get married and become householders, because this is a natural drive. You do not have to tell your children to eat, they will eat because it is a natural drive. You have to teach them how to fast, how to devote more time to God, how to be spiritual, how to make some time in the morning and evening for sadhana and upasana.

Yoga of the new millennium

I have had a glimpse of the future. Yoga as we know it now will go backstage, and bhakti will take its place. Faith, devotion and pure love will become prominent, not as a religion or belief, but as a science. Those scientists who have been working in the fields of biology, physiology, physics and so on will work on bhakti. What is the impact of faith in God on human behaviour, on the human body, on the human mind and consciousness? Scientists have been working within the dimension of matter, now they will work on human emotions, because emotions are more powerful than matter. In the twentieth century, we suffered because of the emphasis on materialism, pleasure and enjoyment. That century did not support bhakti; it supported politics, materialism and the fulfilment of petty desires. You wanted to own a bicycle, a motorcycle or a car, and that was all you thought about.

International peace can only be achieved if every individual and every family is peaceful. In the twenty-first century, bhakti will be supported by society and by the scientists. The same scientists who have been experimenting on matter, physics, nuclear physics and other sciences will conduct experiments on bhakti and kirtan. Your children will sing even against your wishes, because the times are changing. The winter of materialism is going and the spring of bhakti is coming. When the winter goes and summer comes, you take off your sweaters. Similarly, the season of materialism is going. People are tired, frustrated and disappointed with this culture. The whole of life is based on materialism. Wouldn't you prefer a simple life with peace of mind? What kind of life do people experience in Indian cities? They experience slum life. What facilities do they have there? They live in one room with an open drain in front.

What has this present civilization given to you? It has given you filth, crowds and mistrust. It has given you broken families, anxiety, confusion and irritation. You are experiencing distress, just as your children do when they have to sit for their first examination. You experience worry in applying for an interview, you even worry while playing sports. Anxiety has become your culture and later, when this anxiety increases, it turns into neurosis. Now, only God's name, bhajan and kirtan are left for this century, because no one can perform yajna, not even saints and sages.

Saints and sages of this era also belong to society; they have not come from heaven. You must understand that the saints and sages of today cannot do penance, as they did in the times of old. After just one day of fasting, they start complaining of gastric acidity! If their head aches even a little, they call for the doctor. The qualities of asceticism are not present. In this age, renunciation, penance, fasting and yoga are not suitable paths to reach God; only faith in God and remembering His name can help you. If you lack faith and belief, you cannot approach God. Faith in God has to become a living force in our personal lives and in our society; it should not be confined to churches, pagodas or temples.

9

Relationship with God

Establishment of the relationship with God is tantamount to the attainment of God. It is easy to worship God, to sing His praise, to hear His praise, to read about Him in books like the *Ramayana* and *Bhagavad Gita*, but to link oneself with God in a definite relationship, and to actually feel that relationship in your heart is not easy. Relationship depends upon the depth of your faith and trust. Without faith and trust there can be no relationship. If there is no faith and trust between husband and wife, between father and son, between brother and sister, there can be no relationship. Thus faith and trust are the basis, the very foundation of all relationships. Faith is impossible until the hard crust of the ego breaks. To break your hard-hearted ego, you have to bow down before the God of stone. You have to worship God in His visible form, the *sakara ishwara*.

God is infinite, in myriads of forms. If you say God is only One in the numerical sense, then there is a problem. But if by that One, you mean infinite, then it is all right. All the jivatmas, all the beings in this cosmos have a relationship with God; there is a connection. Everything that exists in the world, be it a flower, a leaf, a tree or whatever, is part of God. There is nothing in the universe that is not related to God. We worship God as something apart from ourselves, but one thing we forget is that we are related to Him. Everyone is connected to God, just as all the light bulbs, fridges, air conditioners, machinery plants, and everything electrical is connected to the main powerhouse. It doesn't matter that one appliance gives light, another heat and another cold. Everything is connected to the powerhouse, but the relationship is different. The relationship between the powerhouse and a fridge, bulb or cooler is different in each case.

Everyone can interact together in harmony when they relate to God, rather than to each other. But everyone wants to establish a relationship with others, be it occupational, professional, social or academic. Wherever people go, they try to establish a relationship with others, but the most important need is to establish a relationship with God. Once that relationship is known, the feelings automatically arise and the ego-identification, the feeling that 'I am doing', becomes less and less prominent. There is only one truth in the world, God. It does not matter whether you call it Ishwara, Atman, Paramatman, Shiva or Rama. There is one God and every person has to find a personal relationship with Him.

There are many types of relationships in the world, but for every person there is one specific relationship with God. The relationship between you and God is very personal. My relationship with God cannot be the same as yours, because my relationship is purely personal and yours should also be. My relationship with God is with Him alone. It is a direct relationship and has nothing to do with my relationship with friends, disciples and devotees. Your relationship with God is absolutely private; there is only you and Him. Your mother, father, husband or wife, children, in-laws, none of them come into the picture. The love between Radha and Krishna was like that of the individual soul and the cosmic soul, like *prakriti* (cosmic energy) and *purusha* (consciousness).

Role of guru

The relationship between two lovers is unique; nobody else can come in between. It is something from inside, which is very secret. You should not even talk about it. For a brief period there is guru between you and your God. This is necessary because you need a guide, but it is not right to become attached to your guide. There is a very limited role for the guru on this path. Gurus are not of one type; they are like teachers. One teacher teaches one subject, another teaches another subject. Every teacher has his own area. Hence the guru or teacher, who shows you the spiritual path, has a restricted role. To remain attached to the guru is like a Brahmin and his follower drowning together. The guru and disciple will both go down if they remain attached.

When you talk with the guru about God, you are ultimately connected with God. Your real relationship is with God, not with the person in between. God makes you His disciple through the guru, but in your ignorance you do not know that you are God's disciple. You do not know God, so you never think about it in this way. If you send somebody a letter through the post office, the postman delivers that letter. Now is that letter connected with you and the receiver, or with you and the postman? You send the letter and the postman only deliverers it. You must remember that the guru is only an agent. He just comes in between for some time. Ultimately there should be no attachment, no dependence, no thought of relationships like those we have in the world. You get obsessed, you get caught up. The guru is somebody who comes and wakes you up, that's all.

You have to establish a relationship with your master, who is your inner self, who is within you, who is the breath of your breath, who is the life force in you, who is the essence of your life, and on whom your life depends. The first step is to find out how you are related to God. Who is He to you and who are you to Him? God cannot be explained; He can only be experienced. But sometimes it is inspiring to hear about Him, it gives you courage and strength to face life squarely. Whatever you think about God becomes relevant only when you have established a relationship with Him. You may have a particular feeling for God, because you like

Him, but that is not enough. Whatever feeling, whatever sentiment you have for Him must be expressed through you in its real form.

What is your relationship with God? That is what you have to discover. To discover your relationship with God takes time. But once you have discovered it, your journey will be nearly complete, for then you will be very close to Him. You have already discovered relationships with men and women, young and old, with your father, father-in-law, brother, brother-in-law, son, with your wife, sister, daughter, mother or mother-in-law. Similarly, discover a relationship with God. This is the most difficult task, but once you do it, life becomes much easier. It is true that God is eternal, without name and form, omnipotent, omniscient and omnipresent. It is well and good to know this, but there has to be a very tangible relationship between myself and Him. I must feel who I am to Him.

Discovery of my relationship with God

I pondered over this for many years in order to establish my relationship with God, but it did not work. Sometimes I believed Him to be this and sometimes that. None of these relationships worked. I did not do any work, instead I used to enjoy singing the bhajan, "Oh God, the giver of bliss, reveal the knowledge to me." I sang for hours on end. I sang Sanskrit stotras, including the whole of *Ganga Stotram*, and tears would roll down my cheeks. However, this served no purpose; it was just like feeding a donkey, neither sin nor blessing came. Then one day I realized that I am God's servant, His bonded labourer. I must live, think, eat, sleep and do sadhana with this feeling only.

So, the idea came to me of my relationship with God, and I am now settled in that idea. It gives me enlightenment, it shows me the way and it has set my mind at rest. I am not anxious, whereas previously I was always anxiety-ridden, always asking, "God, when shall I meet you?" But now that anxiety is over. Now I say, "If it is your wish, give me your darshan. And if you do not wish it, that is also okay." My guru had told me, "You will see Him in the form of Shankara." That is fine, come in whatever form you like.

I realized after coming to Rikhia that I am a servant of God. Before that, I thought I was a bhakta, a devotee of God. Before that, I thought I was a jignasu sadhaka, a spiritual seeker, and before that, a moksha sadhaka, a seeker of liberation. I thought I had many other relationships with God, but everything changed after coming here. I found out how wrong I had been all along. Now, my relationship with God is confirmed. You are my boss and I am your slave. You tell me what I have to do. I have no choice, no priorities, no right of selection, no philosophy, and no tradition. A slave has no tradition; the master's religion is the slave's religion. The master's order is supreme to a slave. A slave cannot decide anything for himself; it is the master who decides everything.

While searching for some relationship with God, I found the Radha-Krishna relationship too difficult; I could not manage it. It is not possible for me to feel that I am God's wife or that He is my wife and I am His husband! Then I thought, is God my Father? No, I do not understand these father, mother, brother, sister, uncle, aunt relationships at all, because I have never lived a family life. I understand only one relationship, because I lived with my guru, Swami Sivananda, and served him for many years. So this relation-ship of master and servant is easy for me, because it is my training. In relation to God, I always feel that I am a servant and I will do whatever He says. I have full faith in Him, because twice I have heard the voice. The voice is not the voice of my mind; it is a voice from outside which I have heard inside, and what I heard came true – that is the proof.

What is your relationship?
The purpose of life is not to know this man from Greece or that man from Canada, England or Deoghar. Of what use is it to recognize all and sundry, if we do not recognize God?

To know all about someone by name, place and profession is incidental. We are all fellow travellers, meeting on a railway platform, and nobody has any real relationship with anybody else. We only have one link and that is with God. This is true for everyone. The relationships of mother and father, brother and sister, friend and associate, are for the dealings of the world. The real relationship is only with God.

What will be your relationship with God? To decide this, you have several relationships to draw upon. You are familiar with these three relationships, which are very powerful, because they draw on the feelings from inside. The first relationship, the closest relationship in the world, is between husband and wife or lover and beloved. This relationship is very powerful and can influence your bhavana totally. It is directed by *madhurya bhava*. The word *madhu* means 'honey' or 'sweetness'. That is why the beloved is called sweetheart.

The second relationship is directed by the feeling of affection, called *sneha bhava*, between brother and sister; it is also very strong. The third relationship is directed by the feeling of parental love, called *vatsalya bhava*, which is the love of the mother or father and child.

There is another relationship, which is not usually considered, called vaira bhava, the feeling of enmity. This feeling is said to be more powerful than any other bhava and that is why Ravana resorted to it. He thought that the love of Dasharath, Lakshman or Hanuman for Rama was not possible for him, so the best way would be to adopt veera bhava. He decided to create enmity with the Lord by abducting Sita, thinking the Lord would, therefore, kill him and he would attain liberation. It was easy for Ravana to practise veera bhakti, because he had that inimical nature, but it is not so simple for everyone.

You can mobilize your *bhavana* through certain relationships, but if you consider God as your personal deity only, you will not be able to activate the feeling for Him. Similarly, if you consider God as your in-law, it will not work. If you think of God as your father-in-law, mother-in-law or sister-

99

in-law, He will become the object of your worry. These relationships will not work; they are cold relationships. How did Chaitanya Mahaprabhu, Mirabai and many other saints mobilize their bhavana? They made their feelings active in a very powerful, dynamic way that influenced, infused and took over their minds. Mirabai considered God as her husband. You can have two husbands, one external and the other internal; I do not see any difficulty in that.

So, first, you have to discover your relationship with God; that is your first priority in life. You may ask, 'But how can I consider God as my husband?' Yes, He is my husband. Why? Because I am female and you are also female. We are all prakriti; we are not purusha. We are all prakriti and we have all the feminine qualities in us. *Mamta* – attachment and *irshya* – jealousy, are both feminine qualities. All the qualities born of prakriti are feminine qualities, and the qualities born of purusha are masculine qualities. *Tyaga* – renunciation, *tapasya* – austerity, *titiksha* – endurance, and *vairagya* – non-attachment, are all masculine qualities, born of purusha. *Karuna* – compassion, *daya* – mercy, *sneha* – affection, are all feminine qualities, and they are all in us.

FIVE BHAVAS

Traditionally, there are five bhavas, or relationships with God. You may cultivate any one of them, according to your personality:
1. *Santa bhava* – attitude of the saint and devotee
2. *Dasya bhava* – attitude of the servant and master
3. *Sakhya bhava* – attitude of the friend
4. *Vatsalya bhava* – attitude of the parent and child
5. *Madhurya bhava* – attitude of the lover and beloved.

Santa bhava

Santa bhava is the attitude of peace, self-control, serenity and good will towards all. This is the bhava of a saint, a jnani or a god-realized person, and is said to be the highest attitude. In order to develop this attitude, it is necessary to have regular association with saints and persons of such caliber. No matter what sadhana you do, ultimately, you have to come to a saint or a realized person. Those who bear this in mind and commune with the saints are able to attain this attitude easily. The saints bring wisdom to the people. If you want to progress on the spiritual path, the association of saints is necessary.

Saints are the stepping-stones, but they cannot carry you all the way to the goal. To reach the roof, you need the ladder. In spiritual life too, you need a ladder. But if you keep holding the saint's hand and tell yourself that he will take you ahead; it will not be possible to progress. Only if God showers His blessings on you, can you get through. Firm faith in God is the reward of all spiritual efforts. Whatever you practise, whether asana, pranayama, kundalini yoga, raja yoga or rebirthing, the reward has to be faith. But nobody has ever acquired this jewel of faith without the help of saints.

Dasya bhava

If you consider yourself to be a servant of God, all the qualities of the servant should be expressed in your attitude. Then God becomes your centre, the focus of your life's work. What is the psychology of a servant? How does he think? What is his mentality? That mentality must develop in you. If it does not, then it means your relationship with God is not yet defined and genuinely felt. Your relationship with God must bring about the related sentiments. If you think you are a servant of God, then your personality must develop all those related qualities. How does a servant think? How does a mother think? How does a daughter think? Everybody has a particular psychology. It is not enough just to pay lip service and proclaim, "I am the servant of God."

What the servant does is not the choice of the servant; it has to be the choice of the master. That is known as *seva* (selfless service). I am doing whatever I have been instructed to do, and not just anything that comes into my head. You have to accept whatever pain and trouble the master gives without any complaints, because a servant has no choice. His discomfort and pain are of no consequence to his master. "O Lord, you are my master and I am your servant. Accept me as your servant." You have to be willing to accept all the pain and troubles that He gives you as the will of your Master. The servant cannot expect or hope that his master will redress the problems of his wife and children. The master's attitude is, "You are the servant. You either work under these conditions or get out."

Sakhya bhava

God is always with you, the friend who never leaves you. Anyone in life can desert you or disappoint you, but not God. Swami Sivananda used to say, "God is the breath of my breath, the prana of my prana, and the life of my life. God is my closest friend and my greatest support, my only reality." This is the only truth in life, but most people remain unaware of it. They never experience the nearness of God, the friendship of God, due to narrow mindedness and the influence of worldly associations. If you remove the insulation, then the power of God will begin to flow through you. Every saint has expressed the same sentiment: God is my closest friend, nearer than my breath, my very life.

Vatsalya bhava

The easiest bhava to adopt is the attitude of the worthless son: I am of no use to anyone. I am a thief and a crook. I am a dishonest, treacherous, fallen, lowly creature, yet I am yours. This is the most appropriate bhava in the kali yuga. The most honest and best bhava is that of the worthless son. God, I do your pooja, but my mind is not in it. I go to the temple, but only out of fear so that I may not become a widower or a childless person. I worship Lakshmi, so that I may have money to buy a motorbike or a bicycle. God, I worship you for my own sake, for my own benefit only.

Otherwise I have no great love for you. If I can get what I want without going to you, I will not take the trouble to come to you at all. I am this type of fallen creature, but I am your son. You may give me what you think I deserve. You may slap me, hit me with a stick, and throw me into the river or, if you wish, you may put me on your lap and grant me deliverance.

In this relationship, God is a benign mother or father. It is alright if you ask for some favours sometimes, with a pure mind like that of a child who asks his parents for something. Since you live in this world and tend to get into difficult situations, it is not wrong to ask Him for help to overcome the hurdles of life. Eventually, you should overcome the habit of asking favours from Him, because God knows what is in your mind and will fulfil it. You do not have to be scared of Him, regardless of what you have done. God is not a policeman, magistrate or judge. God never punishes anyone; it is your karma which punishes you. This is the law of nature. You do not have to worry about what God will do. Even if you steal in front of God, nothing will happen to you.

Once Mulshanker, who later on became Swami Dayananda, was observing vigil on *Shivaratri* (dark night of Shiva). As he lay awake during the night, he observed a rat nibbling at the image of Lord Shiva. He wondered why the Lord was not scaring the rat away. As a result of this incident, Swami Dayananda started preaching the philosophy of nirakara Brahma, formless God. Once one of my good Aryasamaji friends asked me why the Lord was not scaring the rat away. I told him that it was not the department concerning God. Even if someone shits on God, He is not going to react, for that person is like a son to Him. If your son spits in your face, you will still love him. If your child comes home covered with dirt and straightaway sits in your lap, spoiling your nice Banarsi sari, what will you do? In the *Ramacharitamanas* it says that when Rama came to Dasharatha, covered in dust and dirt, the king smiled and lifted him up into his lap.

Madhurya bhava

The relationship between lover and beloved is the highest culmination of worship. It is the merging or absorption in the Lord. The attitude of sweetness and gentleness is called madhurya bhava or *Radha bhava*. The feeling of a lover for the beloved suits some people, but it is the most difficult to develop. How will you adopt madhurya bhava? Will you wear a sari and dance before God? Many sadhus wear saris, dance and sing; it comes naturally to them. Not everybody can have the same relationship with God. That is not everyone's cup of tea. Madhurya bhava is very difficult for most people. The last pronouncement in *Ramacharitamanas* is the most beautiful and correct pronouncement: "Even as a lustful man loves a woman or a miserly man loves money, may I love God." There is nothing beyond that.

You cannot realize anything unless you are mad after it. If I suffer from Rama psychosis or Krishna neurosis, it is well and good. Tell me, what is the use of suffering from fear psychosis or sexual neurosis? It is better to have some good mania, so that you get something positive from it. Paramahamsa Ramakrishna was known in Bengal as a mad man during his lifetime. Now, thousands worship him as a God, but when he lived, many people such as Keshav Chandra Sen called him a maniac. Ramakrishna used to say, "It's all right, if you call me a fool. I accept it, if you say I am mad." The madness should be like this. In order to realize God, whom you have never seen, your emotions must be directed totally in the right direction.

If you think of yourself as the beloved of God, all the symptoms of a deep erotic relationship must arise in you, so that you feel the pangs of separation intensely and lose sleep over Him. Mirabai has written in many verses about her sleepless nights, pining for God. She said that separation from God causes deep agony, like being a fish out of water. The relationship of madhurya bhava is one of extreme intensity, which leads to an excess of affection and absorption into the form of God. The madhurya bhava of Devaki and

Kaushalya, who had extreme affection, was at this level. But this intensity is very difficult to experience. There has to be absorption in the feelings and consciousness of the loved one. The mind has to be totally absorbed.

Madhurya bhava succeeds only when God showers His grace on the devotee. There are many examples of falling from this path. Sadhus and mahatmas, especially in Braj, the Mathura region, have done the upasana of madhurya bhava and slipped. When they generate the bhava of a woman within them, it is natural for the sexual desire to crop up. Not just anyone can adopt this path. The person whose heart is like that of a child can adopt madhurya bhava. Only those who have no guilt complexes can have the heart of a child, so madhurya bhava is for them. When the love for God becomes deep and intense, you are able to see God everywhere, in everybody, just as a lover sees his beloved everywhere. Experiencing That, you also become That. Wherever you look, you see God. That experience is the purpose of life. All other activities like study, service, fulfillment of desire, rearing children, keeping accounts, have to be done, but all that is maya.

There is no need to leave home in order to experience this, but you should always think about it. What is God? How can I communicate with Him? If I am He, how can I realize it? That thought should be constantly in your mind. If you are part of God, how can you experience it? You have forgotten that you are a part of Him. If you have amnesia due to a brain injury, you will have to be told your name, because you won't remember it. In the same way, you have forgotten God – this is also amnesia. This realization is the goal of life. Other things are not the real purpose of life, because twenty to twenty-five years from now they will all end. This is just a game of the ego in which you are all involved. It is not that the world is cursed, I am not denigrating it. Everybody has to live in the world. The world is like a pool of mud. You can choose whether to live like the lotus or the worm, but at any rate you will have to live in this pool of mud.

10

Types of Upasakas

The practical aspect of bhakti yoga is upasana. Any practice that facilitates the worship of God, remembrance of God and contemplation on God is called upasana. This includes ritualistic worship, recitation of mantra, meditation, the study of the scriptures and service. The word upasana first occurs in the Vedas. The *Rig Veda* says, "*Ya atmada balade yogya vijva upasate presiam yasya devah*", which means 'the entire animate kingdom, including the devas, worship the One, who is the giver of the Self and of life.' The upasana of nirakara Brahman, which is beyond name and form, is described in the Vedas. The Puranas describe the names and forms of sakara Brahman, so that the seekers can perceive the state of Brahman.

While following the path of upasana, the coordination of body, mind and intellect is required. These three aspects of upasana: healthy body, firm mind and clear intellect, are important requisites. In the yajna ceremony, for example, the priest purifies the body of a worshipper. Yajna, ritualistic worship and external offerings are physical activities in upasana. Generally, the upasaka first works on the physical plane, following the directions of his spiritual preceptor. The worship of God with water, flowers and incense, burning of lamps and offering of food is upasana on the physical plane.

The mind and intellect are essential agents in upasana. Thinking is an action of the mind, and the mind is guided by the intellect. There cannot be upasana unless the deity stands before the mind. For the vision of the deity, the mind must be associated with the qualities of the deity. Paramatma is invisible to the external eyes, but can be experienced by the mental eye through worship of the deity. Intellect also plays an important role, because the upasana cannot be practised unless and until a decision is taken. The intellect becomes sharp by the practice of upasana. When the intellect is awakened, the upasaka can differentiate between hallucination and true perception. This point is the real beginning of upasana.

Therefore, physical, mental and intellectual involvement is necessary for progress in upasana. Different types of individuals practise different types of upasanas, according to the level of their mental development. At the *tamasic* (inert) level, upasana is performed through gross, instinctive worship and rituals, bringing pleasure to the senses. The base instincts are systematically transformed by regular worship of the terrifying forms of God, and the fear of their wrath keeps the upasaka in line. Through such forms of worship the inertia and ignorance of tamas is gradually reduced and rajas emerges.

With the emergence of *rajas* (dynamism), the mind begins to open. Qualities such as intelligence, understanding and discrimination develop under the influence of desire, ambition and greed. Rajasic upasana is worship performed with selfish motives. Each person wants to enjoy a healthy, successful and prosperous life, and at the same time, to overcome the threat of enemies and misfortune. Many upasanas are introduced at this level to achieve this double purpose. In the *Rig Veda*, for example, we find hymns for the cure of diseases, like tuberculoses. There are also many beautiful hymns, invoking and supplicating the powers of nature.

At the initial rajasic level, people struggle with nature and its devastating occurrences, such as cyclones, floods, droughts, earthquakes, diseases and death. They worship and pray to the powers of nature to overcome or avert these destructive incidents. The worshipper asks the deities of nature, which represent the elements, planets, rivers, oceans, lakes, mountains, forests or harvest, to control these powers and make them beneficent. Another important upasana at this level is ancestor worship, or *pitri pooja*, performed for the forefathers who dwell on the subtle plane, but protect the living generations of each family.

The qualities of rajas are further honed and thinned by upasanas, such as mantra repetition and worship of personal deities. With the reduction of rajas, sattwa begins to emerge. Rajasic upasana performed for individual liberation awakens sattwa. Yogic techniques are prescribed in this category: (i) external forms of yoga, such as *shatkarma* (six cleansing techniques) and asana, purify and balance the body, (ii) pranayama awakens the energy and controls the mind and senses, (iii) meditation focuses and stills the mind and redirects the outgoing energy towards the Atman, or Self, which is within.

Rajasic upasana may also be performed for the betterment of humanity, whereby the upasaka realizes that his spiritual evolution and that of the community are of equal importance. God pervades the entire universe and is microcosmic as well as macrocosmic. This view brings a change in the form of upasana. The approach of service to humanity gives a social form to the sadhana, and the upasaka becomes sympathetic to the entire world. Action performed without any individual selfish motive is pure devotion to Paramatman. At this point, the upasana of seva becomes sattwic. Here the individual soul merges with the existence of all beings, and the upasaka experiences a lovely relationship with the world.

The tamasic and rajasic qualities of human nature, such as, anger, greed, hatred and jealousy, are slowly annihilated by upasana and replaced by the positive qualities of forgiveness, forbearance, calmness, friendliness, love, compassion, and humility. These are sattwic qualities, which automatically lead towards God. At the sattwic level of upasana, the upasaka is transformed and becomes one with the universe and with God. He remains in the bodiless existence of pure consciousness. This is the state of samadhi, which the mind and intellect cannot reach and words cannot describe. It is the state of an enlightened person, whose life is divine.

Live the divine life

In any form of upasana, whether tamasic, rajasic or sattwic, a concept of God is an essential requisite. When the seeker wants to start an upasana, the question he must first ask is what to worship: nature, a personal deity or God? The deity or form for worship represents God, and the deities are innumerable. One may also adore a stone, which is colored with vermilion, without any particular figure, name or virtue. This is a very pure form of worship, where the stone represents only the transcendental being. However, this stone can give the upasaka whatever he desires, according to his shraddha or faith.

Man is an individual entity; therefore he is the upasaka or worshipper of God. The relationship between man and God is that of worshipper and worshipped in the beginning. Actually man is a psychophysical creature. The mind affects the body and the bodily disorders affect the mind. Therefore, the stability of both is required for upasana, and this steadiness is acquired through faith in God. Man has all the qualities of an animal. The lifestyle and behavior of man are his distinguishing qualities. He can live a life, which leads towards moksha or God-realization, by following the *purusharthas* (worthy human aims) of artha, kama, dharma and moksha and the instructions of shastra, or he can lead an instinctive life.

Thus the concept of upasana in vedic culture presents all the aspects of an individual's relationship with God: tribal, social and global, including nature worship and the worship of ancestors, deities etc. The aim of all these forms of worship is to uplift the human consciousness from earthly associations to the eternal and infinite existence, which is called moksha. Therefore upasana is a path to human perfection, an instrument for *moksha vidya* (experience of liberation). The path of upasana may be categorized by rites and rituals, cults and customs, but there is one continuous stream of spiritual aspiration behind all of these, to live the life divine. The saints and seers have shown us that man is capable of living a divine life on earth, and they have given the path of upasana as the means.

Four stages of life

Upasana is the journey one undertakes to discover and experience the Atman and Paramatman. The upliftment of human consciousness is impossible without upasana. There are different types of aspirants in spiritual life. Some feel that they are chained to the wheel of samsara and wish to get off. They want to be free from the cycle of birth and death and rebirth. A few of those seek the way out of samsara. Of the few, those who actually walk the path are called upasakas. Those who reach the state of ultimate knowledge and become unified with the deity are called siddhas.

In ancient India, life was organized in such a way that the highest human aspiration could be fulfilled. The lifespan was divided into four distinct stages, called *ashramas*. In each stage, different responsibilities were emphasized for the evolution of that age group. Accordingly, the types of upasana prescribed for each stage was also different and each stage of life was conducive for the development of a specific type of upasaka.

1. *Brahmacharya* (up to 25 years) is the period of youth, education and the acquiring of knowledge in order to gain a livelihood. *Sandhya vandana*, (worship at dawn and dusk) sun worship, including *surya namaskara* (prostrations to the sun), *Gayatri mantra* (mantra to enhance learning) and pranayama, are practices prescribed during this stage of life.

2. *Grihastha* (from 25–50 years) is the period of household life, during which the upasanas of a more ritual nature, yajna and yoga are recommended.

110

3. *Vanaprastha* (from 50–75 years) is the period of retirement when the individual devotes his life to study of the shastras and performance of the inner upasanas, which lead to communion with God.

4. *Sannyasa* (from 75 years onward) is the period of renunciation, spiritual experience and liberation of the soul. The upasana here is total merging with God.

By living in accordance with the ashramas, the development of upasana throughout the entire life is spelt out. The upasaka gradually achieves unification with God in the course of life and then guides others in their efforts in the same direction. When upasana is performed in this way, with a purified mind, the upasaka attains the real knowledge of Paramatman. That knowledge creates intimate love for God and then he is called a bhakta. The knowledge of supreme bliss generates ecstasy in him and he sings God's names and glories for the rest of his life. This is the state of para bhakti.

FIVE LEVELS OF UPASAKAS

Generally speaking, there are five levels of upasakas, or devotees, who represent the path of spiritual evolution through upasana. These five types of devotees all worship God and sing His name and praises, but with different motives.

1. Artha upasakas

The artha upasakas worship God to be relieved of their sorrow, sickness and distress. These devotees ask for help or a solution from God when they are in a fix, in misery or beset with problems. At such times, when they become desperate, helpless, agonized and frightened, they remember God and surrender to Him to overcome their crisis. For example, a man may be dragged into a court case. There may be an official enquiry by the government against him. He may have income tax problems. His young son may have fallen sick. There are countless predicaments and problems that may confront a man. When such a man turns to God, because he is caught in an unavoidable calamity, he is called a desperate devotee.

Of course, God knows all this. The reason why this person is unable to overcome his worldly sufferings is that the two qualities of faith and trust are missing in his life. By performing upasana, he can activate these qualities for a short time only, but not constantly. Faith in God will bring him out of crisis situations a few times, but this will not happen every time. People suffer because of their own desires and expectations. When the suffering becomes unbearable and there is no other way out, then they turn to God. They perform upasana, develop intense faith in God, and then the crisis slowly goes away. After that, they resume their life as before and forget about the upasana and God. But when they are in the crisis, that is the crucial time when they should transform their life totally.

2. Artharthi upasakas
Those upasakas who pray to God for any form of wish fulfillment, such as, acquiring a husband or wife, progeny, money or property, are called artharthi bhaktas. These upasakas desire something that they are unable to attain in life and turn to God to ask or beg for it. For example, everyone desires a son. They believe that without a son there will be no future breadwinner in the family or anyone to perform their last rites after death. So everyone wants a son to earn money, to support the father, and to provide for his well-being during the onward journey after death. A son is believed to buy a ticket for the father's posthumous journey by performing his last rites. Some people also worship God to ask for a job, for prosperity in business, to pass exams and so on. Such upasakas are called devotees with desire; they have an axe to grind. These are selfish bhaktas, who seek gratification of their personal desires from God.

Shabari, Draupadi, Dhruva and Prahlad all worshipped God and sang His name. Just see how much strength there is in the name of God! He solved the problems of Prahlad,

112

delivered Dhruva, and saved the honour of Draupadi. They all prayed to God for attaining a purpose, and God fulfilled their wishes. Their bhakti was artharthi, to fulfil a specific end. But Shabari had no vested interest in worshipping Lord Rama. Her bhakti was *nishkama*, desireless; she was simply lost in love.

You should tread the path of upasana for the love of God. There is no end to desires and you will never be able to fulfill them all. One desire leads to another, like the waves of the ocean, which arise incessantly one after another. When a situation occurs in which you experience God helping you, then and there you should transform your life and give it a totally new direction. It has also been said in the *Srimad Bhagavat* that, "If you get God's love, you get everything." The definition of God's love varies. Somebody who does not have a son gets a son. If there are many problems before a marriage, they get solved. An incurable disease is cured. People accept these instances as God's grace.

The form of grace varies from person to person, especially for worldly people who are suffering from the sorrows of everyday life. They do not have the willpower to bear this sorrow. What if that man does not get a son? It is a great anguish for him. He badly wants a son, so he goes on breaking his head on God's image. These things cannot be understood by people because they are swinging on the pendulum of happiness and misery. Each one has his own desires, which are most important to him. Your desires are not important to me, but they are most important to you. You want God to bless you with a son, so you promise to offer one litre of milk in the temple. He blesses you and in exchange you spend just eight rupees, no more than that, on a litre of milk.

You also want release from karmas, but you have so many compulsions, desires and wishes, that you cannot escape them, even if you want to. There are thousands of desires, each of which costs a life in itself. Many of your pleasures have been fulfilled, yet the desires are innumerable. Suppose you have a wish to be free of karma. You have money, you are physically able to sing the glory of the Lord, and your children are settled. You could buy a small house in a village, have a garden, and pray morning and evening to the Lord. Would you ever think of doing such a thing? No, what would happen to your grandchildren? So you are stuck.

3. Jignasu upasakas
Those devotees who are curious about God, who want to inquire about truth, are jignasu upasakas.

Such devotees are curious to know what God is. Their devotion to God is motivated by a search into reality, into the nature of God and the soul. They want to know what rebirth is. The number of such devotees is limited, but there are some like this. They leave their homes and the temptations of material life to inquire into God and spirituality. They have a spiritual goal. I was one such devotee, but not any longer. I have taken my name off the list of such jignasu devotees. But this type of devotion inspired me when I started on the spiritual path.

I was beset with transcendental questions, such as, what is life, what is the nature of the world, where does man come from, where does he go after death, what is the sun, what is the moon, what is creation? This is the jignasu upasaka. He has a questioning mind and seeks knowledge about God by every means of worship available: singing bhajans in His praise, doing kirtan or japa, performing austerities, practising pratyahara, withdrawing from the world of the senses, or practising meditation. Such devotees try out dharana, dhyana and samadhi, prompted by the urge to know God. The number of such devotees is not large. The first two categories contain the highest percentage of humanity; most people belong to them.

4. Jnani upasakas
Those devotees who are saturated with subtle knowledge and discrimination are called jnani upasakas. In jnana

upasana meditation leads to realization of the Self. Here knowledge comes first, then contemplation. The upasaka goes to a guru and hears a particular truth, then contemplates and meditates on it. The thought process continues unabated; you go on thinking point by point ceaselessly. You forget everything around you, like a scientist mulling over problems. That is called *nidhidhyasana,* and when the process is complete, the meaning becomes clear to you. Before coming to this path, the upasaka should have four qualifications: *vairagya* (detachment), *viveka* (discrimination), *satsanga* (spiritual associations) and *mumukshutwa* (desire for liberation).

These four qualifications are necessary; otherwise there will be mistakes in the process of thinking, and thinking is the system of meditation. Systematic thinking through the purified mind, thinking on a particular point according to the instructions of a guru, leads to meditation. Jnana comes only after purification of chitta. Sitting in one asana, you think about your ishtha devata, your personal deity, or Brahman, the cosmic being. You must have an outline for your thinking, which is provided by the guru and in accordance with the logic of the shastras. In jnana upasana the thinking process is absolutely logical; there is no place for illogical thinking. The thinking is systematic and orderly.

Jnana upasana is a difficult, analytical approach, which can be made only by one who has a pure mind, a thorough background of the scriptures, and the company of a guru. This is said in the Upanishads. However, it is a logical process and therefore it is accessible to everyone. You can have any kind of background. The background of the thinking process may vary from culture to culture, from people to people, but one thing is true: the process of knowledge in western philosophy ultimately leads to scepticism. You know the proverb about seven blind persons talking about an elephant. So, in jnana upasana, an experienced teacher should guide the line of thinking carefully.

115

The jnana upasaka realizes the principle of truth on the evidence of the saints, and the revelations and dictums of the great philosophers, who said, *Tat Twam Asi*: "You are That" or *Aham Brahmasi*: "I am the cosmic light", and that becomes the guideline. The saints have said, "Realize your real nature", which means that behind the shadow of the body and the mind, behind the passions and emotions, behind the ever changing experiences, there is an eternal consciousness within us which has homogeneity at its root, and which is just cosmic, without beginning and without end. The experience is an absolute experience, which has no other dimensions of experience.

Ultimately, the attainment of jnana depends upon God's grace and the upasaka's capacity to experience it. To be worthy of God's grace, you must become aware of His grace. God's grace does not descend; it is always there. His grace is within everybody at all times, but we do not realize it. There is a beautiful sloka (2:46) in the *Bhagavad Gita*: "To the brahmana who has known the Self, all the Vedas are as useful as is a reservoir of water, when there is a flood everywhere."

5. Premi upasakas

Some people pray to God because they are in love with Him; they are the *premi upasakas*. These types of devotees are those who love God, like the gopis or Hanuman. Such bhaktas have nothing to ask of God. They have no selfish motive, they seek no benefit from God. They do not want happiness or success in life, solutions to their worldly problems or release from sorrow and suffering. They turn to God out of love for Him. Chaitanya Mahaprabhu and Mirabai were such devotees of pure love. I have cited them as examples, but such devotees are a rarity. In order to experience this state, an intense love of God is required, in which the mind is fixed on God without any diversifying thoughts.

The intense love of God does not depend on destiny or on horoscopes. It does not depend on anyone but Him. He will give you that intense love if He wants. Intense love can only be gained by the grace of God, not from any other practice. No method exists to attain para bhakti. To awaken bhakti, find a genuine guru to surrender to and serve. Be hospitable to people and do japa of God's name. You may go on pilgrimages, visit temples, fast, attend satsang and do pooja. These upasanas will awaken mild bhakti and you will begin to feel good, but this is not para bhakti. Para bhakti is not ordinary love; it is extremely intense love. It is the divine love which great saints have realized. For twenty-four hours of the day, whether eating, drinking, sleeping or awake, they are lost in this love.

In para bhakti, the bhakta merges totally and completely with God. He has no awareness of his own identity. He no longer thinks of himself as a bhakta. His mind is so immersed in God that he feels himself to be God. He becomes one with God. At one point during my sadhana, I received guidance everywhere I went, but I thought it was my inner being who was speaking, my super-soul. Who is my super-soul? There is no super-soul! God is the first and the last. Everything is God, who I have not seen and perhaps will not even see in the future. A mahatma once said, "A doll made of salt went to the sea to measure its depth and ultimately lost itself in the water." This is what happens to us; on knowing God one becomes Him.

Engross your mind in God

In the course of life, you may be afflicted with different kinds of suffering due to pain, disease, death, poverty, loss of friends, ill-repute and so on. In such situations you must find a way to absorb your mind in another subject where it dissolves totally. There have been many great men in this world and almost all of them were afflicted with some disease or problem. Napoleon was epileptic, despite which he became one of the world's greatest military generals. Julius Caesar suffered from epilepsy. Isaac Newton was sick throughout his life. Adi Shankara suffered from severe fistula. Ramakrishna Paramahamsa had cancer, but still he lived for eighty years. Swami Vivekananda had diabetes and suffered frequent bouts of depression; he still shook the whole world and established his name in the annals of great men.

How did they all deal with these sufferings? They identified themselves with God, Brahman or Atman, and not with disease and suffering. Therefore, the wise ask God only for those things that are appropriate for their spiritual evolution, and not for the removal of suffering, disease or pain. When you consider yourself to be sick, then you are sick. But if you do not consider yourself to be sick and think of yourself as an artist, a musician, a scientist, a fighter, a saint, a sevak, then the question of disease does not arise.

I have mentioned a few great people who have established their names in this world, people whom history will remember for at least a thousand years. They suffered from severe diseases but did not allow the disease to become a barrier in their lives. Ramakrishna could have said, "I have cancer," and stopped singing kirtans and bhajans, but he did not do so! Vivekananda could have said, "I have diabetes, so now I must rest and take insulin," but he did not. When you identify with a sickness or disease then you suffer from disease neurosis twenty-four hours of the day.

Disease neurosis means your mind is engrossed in sickness, so you are sick. However, when your mind is engrossed in God's name or in spiritual life, then the disease only follows behind like a tail. How can that matter? You can let the disease follow behind you like a tail. Just as a dog has a tail, your tail is called diabetes. For all upasakas, *Bhagavat naam*, the name of God, is a medicine, whether they are arthi, artharthi, jignasu, jnani, or premi bhaktas. It has been said in the *Ramacharitamanas*:

> *The yogi keeps awake by repeating His name,*
> *So do those who are detached from creation.*
> *They experience that Brahman joyfully,*
> *Who is indescribable, without imperfection,*
> *Having no name or form.*

118

Those who want to know His hidden movements
Perceive them by repeating His name with the tongue.
Spiritual practitioners repeat the name,
Becoming totally absorbed in it,
They become adepts and obtain siddhis.
When people repeat the name,
Even extreme types of adversities and misfortunes
Are uprooted and they become happy.

11

Relevance of Sakara Upasana

Is God immanent or transcendent? This is the question that philosophers and seekers have been asking for thousands of years. When you say immanent, it means sakara, with form. When you say transcendent, it means nirakara, without form. In vedic philosophy, the concept of God is not confined only to immanence or to transcendence; God is considered to be immanent as well as transcendent. God is beyond everything, beyond time, space and matter, but at the same time, God is immanent, present in all beings. So, the question is not whether God is sakara or nirakara, but whether He assumes a form of His own or whether every form is His form.

Is God only transcendent or is He immanent? Isn't His form the universal manifestation, everything that you perceive? So, God is immanent as well as transcendent. God exists in all forms, from the microbe to the towering tree, from the limited mind to the universal mind. God is in the person who needs your help, and in the animal who needs your protection. A complete idea of God has to emerge in such a way that society will be regenerated, and people will enjoy life. Who knows in what form He may appear before you? He may knock at your door as a crippled person instead of appearing in His four-armed form.

It is easy to understand that God has no form. Yet every form that we perceive, conceive, respect or worship is His form. It does not matter if I worship Rama and you worship Christ or Mohammed. God takes finite and infinite forms. If God does not have infinite forms, He is not God. Take the earth as a simple example. One lump of earth can take thousands of forms and names, but basically it is earth. Why shouldn't we understand God in the same manner? Why should I think that only Rama, Krishna, Shiva, Christ or God is sitting somewhere?

When God incarnates in the physical body He is subject to the *gunas* (qualities) of prakriti. Incarnation does not take place without being subject to the gunas of prakriti. God is nameless, formless and attributeless. He has no place, no name and no colour, but when He incarnates, He has to subject Himself to the laws of prakriti, which are birth and death, sorrow and joy. In the same way you are subject to prakriti; the whole world is subject to prakriti. Therefore, even though Sita is Adi Shakti, when she is born into maya, she is also subject to the three gunas of prakriti, as is Rama.

To worship God with a form is difficult. It is easy to accept God as formless or nirakara. It is even easier to talk about the formless God. Nobody can dispute it, because nobody has seen the formless God. If you describe God as formless, having no fixed name or place, nobody can challenge you, because nobody has seen Him. Whatever you say about the formless God, one has to accept. Refutation or challenge can only come in the case of known things, which both you and I have seen. You and I can dispute over the appearance of a squirrel and describe it differently because both of us have seen it. Once three disciples were quarrelling over the exact colour of the chameleon. They could quarrel, because all of them had seen the chameleon change colour.

God with form, sakara, is very difficult to comprehend, to explain, to accept and to ingest, but it is the easiest thing to dispute. Even a small child can criticize the concept of God with form. It is very nice to say that God is abstract, transcendental, formless, nameless and spaceless. You can believe it and say, "Yes, it is right, I think God is like that."

However, when you say that God has the form of Shiva, Vishnu or Brahma, it is hard to believe. Children and those who have innocent hearts and minds can believe it. But intellectuals will say, "What? God is the son of a king? Krishna, running after girls? He was married eight times! Has God got a wife? God's wife!"

Matter of personal experience

My definition of God will depend upon my personal experience, not on what the books say. How can I accept that God is formless? I may not have seen His form, His beautiful countenance, His hands or His feet. I have not seen His eyes, which are said to be like lotus petals, but I have definitely heard His voice, not once, but twice. When I have heard Him, how can I take Him to be nirguna, without attributes? *Desha,* place, *kaala,* time, and *vastu,* substance, are the three parameters of creation. Desha and kala have no boundaries, no end, because creation is the gross manifestation of *Parameshwara* (sublime God). God did not make this creation; He became the creation. You might have read in the Upanishads, that God transformed Himself into creation; this entire universe is a manifestation of God Himself.

So, God is immanent and transcendent; God is a part of this creation and beyond it also. This is the distinctive feature of Indian philosophy and Sanatan Dharma; no other religion accepts this fact. In my early days, I used to have many problems in Rishikesh, because I believed that God was formless and nameless. Some of my *gurubhais* (guru brothers) used to worship Krishna or Rama and do long poojas in the temples. I used to say, "What are you doing? It is all nonsense!" At that time I did not believe that God could have a form, and if anyone told me so, I said they were wrong, although in vedic dharma, worship of form has been given the ultimate importance. Now, my whole concept has changed, because it is my personal experience.

People have written volumes about God without form. I was born in a family that believed in the formless God and began my spiritual quest with that philosophy. I studied *Adwaita Vedanta* (doctrine of non-dualism) and the works of Shankaracharya. I had never given a thought to God with form, nor had I thought over the formless God, because it is not possible to think of a formless God. The God who has no name, form or abode, colour or attribute, simply cannot be a subject of contemplation. Later on, however, I had many experiences, which made me realize there is somebody talking to me and instructing me. He can talk in English and Hindi. After that, I began to meditate on the God with form and results began to show up very soon. I started sakara upasana after coming to Rikhia with an image of Sri Ganesha. One day Ganesha said, "Satyananda, you have just given me names, now watch and see my maya, my miracles."

This is the background of my transition into sakara worship. In Rishikesh, under the instruction of my guru, I took part in rites and rituals as a duty; my heart was not in it. If I was assigned the duty of worshipping Shiva, I did it. If I was asked to chant *Rudrapath* (Rudra mantras), I did it. But, in Rikhia, I began to light an incense stick in front of the images of Ganesha. Burning incense sticks before all the four images I received of him turned out to be a costly affair. But why only burn incense for Ganesha? All the gods enjoy incense sticks. Thus I made it a daily routine to burn incense sticks in front of all the images in my pooja room. As soon as I get up in the morning, the very first thing I do is light the incense sticks, even before washing my hands and mouth. This is my sakara worship.

What is sakara worship?

Sakara upasana means to worship God according to your own faith and belief. There is an immeasurable quantity of water in the ocean, but you can take away only as much as your container will hold. Similarly, you can only grasp God to the extent and depth of your awareness, feelings, soul, personality and the totality of yourself. I could not grasp the formless, nirakara God then, nor can I do it now, nor will I ever have that capacity. My capacity is limited to lighting a lamp and an incense stick in front of Ganesha's image and singing his praises. In the same way, you can worship God, according to the capacity of your intellect and feelings.

First you should adopt a pooja which delights your heart and can move and melt it. The chosen deity that you worship is called ishta devata, because it is what your heart is attracted to, what your heart wishes for. The ishta devata is that personal form of God, who enthrals and captivates your imagination. You can also read the *Ramacharitamanas* devoutly, profoundly and with understanding. Tulsidas has illustrated this very point of sakara upasana throughout the *Ramacharitamanas*. In fact, this is the theme of the *Ramacharitamanas*, the nirakara becomes sakara; the formless God becomes manifest in a recognizable form.

Tulsidas has not neglected the nirakara aspect of God; he talks about both the God with attributes and the unattainable *kaivalyapada*, the path of final liberation. But the important point he makes is that worship or upasana of God means to set your heart on any aspect of God that attracts and satisfies you, that is within the grasp of your limited awareness, that stirs your feelings and sustains your interest. Whatever you worship and meditate upon seeps into your inner being. It casts an indelible imprint on your consciousness, which passes from birth to birth. You may remain a villain, a bad character, a rogue, in the present lifetime, but there is every possibility of reaching and realizing your ideal ishta in some birth, sooner or later.

I love the sakara God, as much as a Bengali loves rasagulla, a South Indian loves idli and dosa, or a Westerner loves chocolate. No one should have a doubt about nirakara coming down into sakara. Let it be very simple. Choose the form of your ishta devata and worship Him or Her, ring the bell, read the holy books, light a candle and an incense stick, praise him or her, and quietly go to bed. Most certainly God will bless you. God is neither formless nor with form. The truth is that he is both formless and with form. Tulsidas says:

No difference exists between the formless God and the God of form.
Thus speak the Vedas and Puranas, the munis and the wise.
The same formless, unseen, unborn and attributeless God
takes the form impressed by the love of the devotee.

Necessity of an ishta devata

How can you ever see a formless entity, and how can you name a nameless entity? How will you find the one who does not live anywhere? I don't want such a God. I want a God who has a name and a form, who has a home and an address. This makes things easy. Great yogis and saints can find Him anywhere, but I want an easy way to locate His address, so I have enshrined Him in Raghunath Kutir. Everyday I take care of that room. I meditate and worship Him daily, and I can say truly that my God lives there. Why should I say that God is everywhere? Maybe He is, I don't deny it, but where will I manage to keep hold of Him? This I learned from *Ramacharitamanas*. You have tried millions of ways to find Him, but where did you find Him? Where will you worship Him? Everybody is lost and confused.

Even if you say that God has no form I still need a form. The point is very simple. I require a form and, therefore, it is my need. I must have a form of God for myself towards which I feel intense attraction. This is the meaning of the term ishta devata. The word *ishta* means 'I like it' and *devata* means 'divine form'. So, ishta devata means that divine form which I like. I like Christ, I like Krishna, and I like Rama. For others, the ishta devata can be the form of Kali, Durga, Devi or Mary. You may choose whatever aspect you like, but the form has to be there. Even the cross is a form of God, not because Christ was crucified on it, but because it represents your inner, psychic body: ajna chakra, ida, pingala and sushumna. So, the cross is a good form to meditate on, if you like it.

The dissipated mind needs an ishta devata. The mind is power, but right now it is in a state of dissipation. The sunlight illuminates everything that it falls on. That same sunlight, if concentrated through a magnifying glass, can burn. Similarly, the dissipated mind has to be channeled, concentrated, brought into focus, and then it becomes powerful. So, any discussion on whether or not God has a form is meaningless. As long as your mind is in a dissipated state, it needs a form, an ishta devata. However, when you have concentrated your mind and entered the state of savikalpa and nirvikalpa samadhi, where the mind is totally one-pointed and all dualities cease to exist, then you can transcend form. You start with the form and, when it is no longer required, you transcend it.

So, don't be confused or get into strife thinking about whether God has a form or is formless. Only consider whether seeing Him with a form or without form will fulfill you. If you are fulfilled by the formless divinity, that is perfectly all right; if you prefer to see His form that is okay. The scriptures have said that God is "*Alakh Niranjan*". The word *alakh* means 'that which can't be seen' and *niranjan* means 'one without stain', 'untainted'. However, you need a form in order to focus your broken and dissipated mind. If you don't want to see God in a human form, then you may seek Him in various other forms. Divinity and divine power has also been revealed in the form of mantra, yantra and mandala, which are psychic forms.

However, if your mind fixes itself on a human form of God, it is very good, because this is an important aspect of upasana. How can you feel God unless you consider Him to be close to you? Your God does not eat, sleep or talk. If you want to love God, you must have a concept. He is a living God and a living God eats. For instance, my Ganeshaji in Ganesha Kutir changes his dress four times a year. In winter, he wears a warm dress. In spring, I take off all his warm clothes, because he'll be feeling hot! You see, I have a special suitcase for Ganesha. Now he is feeling cold! Should

I not be sensitive to that? If I am not sensitive enough when my God feels cold or suffers with cough, cold and fever, then there is no connection between Him and me. This is the concept.

The difference between you and God must go away. There is a great difference between the formless, transcendental God and myself. So I can't reach Him, and if I can't reach Him, He can't reach me either! The unmanifest God is so far away that He can't reach me and I can't reach Him. There has to be a connection, a relationship with God, like your relationship with your family members. If my son can get sick, so can my God. Whether He gets sick or not, at least I can feel that He is sick. If you can believe that God sleeps and eats, and so His food should be prepared, then that is an indication of your sensitivity. Until you become this sensitive, His form does not materialize in you. It is for this reason that vedic dharma talks about seeing God in human form, such as Rama, Krishna, Vishnu, Shiva or Devi. These forms are used for meditation and are also loved and worshipped by the devotee.

God will come in that form in which you think of Him. You may see God in any form. In the *Bhagavad Gita*, Lord Krishna says, "Among Vedas, I am the Sama; among trees, I am the peepul; among rivers, I am the Ganga; among months, I am Marga Sheersha; among heavenly bodies, I am the moon..." You can worship God in whatever form you wish, and that very form will appear before you. As Tulsidas says in *Ramacharitamanas*: 'Everyone visualized in the person of the Lord the reflection of his own emotional disposition.' If you think that all this is fiction, let me tell you, nothing that exists in this world is fiction; everything is reality.

Ishta devata and guru

When upasana is practised only for spiritual attainment there are certain rules to be observed but if it is practised with a particular end in view then the rules are different. For example, each ishta mantra has a corresponding devata and yantra, and you have to proceed accordingly. But if you are practising for spiritual evolution and the development of your inner awareness, then the mantra can be one and the ishta devata another; both do not have to correspond. Your personal ishta mantra should be repeated morning and evening at a fixed time, for one or two malas, but this does not stop you from worshipping Shiva, Hanuman or Ganesha.

In practices for spiritual attainment, emotions come into the picture. Let us say that I have a very strong feeling for Rama; I like his lifestyle, his divinity. However, my mantra is not the Rama mantra; it is the Shiva mantra. Here the mantra does not correspond to the ishta devata. It does not matter since I am not doing it for any particular purpose but for the purification of the inner awareness, to have a vision of the divine. So first, you have to decide whether you wish to practise for spiritual or worldly attainment. But you should know that the ishta devata belongs to the non-physical, esoteric, spiritual and divine dimension.

Etymologically, the word *devata* means that which radiates, illumines, enlightens, sheds light on, or dispels darkness. The devata is the one who lights up the darkness and reveals the hidden essence. There are as many devatas as there are people. Some worship Vishnu, some Shiva, some Ganesha or Hanuman as their ishta devata. The indigenous aboriginals worship Mahadeva. The Bengalis worship Durga and Kali. You may not see your ishta devata or have any logical proof of its existence, but you still worship your chosen deity regularly.

Externally ishta devata and guru are only two different names, but internally they are one. The basic principle is Atma, also known as ishwara tattwa, atmatattwa, parabrahma, parameshwara, anadi, avinashi, abhokta, akarta, the One who is beyond name, form, place, speech and the sense perceptions. To attain that ultimate principle, you may worship the ishta devata or the guru, because they are not separate in essence, they are merely two different forms. The principle is one and the same, whether you attain the ishta or the guru. The point is how to focus the mind, which is forever running after maya, the mind that is so engrossed in worldly objects, the mind that is running after the shadow, the mirage of desires.

This fickle, capricious, covetous mind needs to be focused, to be applied somewhere to make it one-pointed. You need a prop to act as a focal point. The guru is necessary because he can act as a focal point. Without formal admission, you cannot enter a college. Without the rituals of the wedding ceremony, you cannot be called man and wife. Even if you stay together day and night, you will be considered only as boyfriend and girlfriend, not as husband and wife. But the moment you go around the holy fire seven times and perform the marriage ritual, you will be accepted as husband and wife. Similarly, until you accept someone as your guru you cannot be called a sadhaka or upasaka. Unless and until you get a guide, a guru, you cannot be a traveller on the spiritual path.

You have not yet received the imprint of the guru; therefore, you need a guru. The guru shows you the path. He directs and guides you. The mantra that your guru gives you is the master key to all the locks of your life. Our spiritual masters, the supermen, tell us that far ahead on this path of upasana, there comes a stage where only un-divided awareness resides. Neither the ishta nor the guru survives. *Phutaa kumbha jala jala hi samaanaa*, which means that when the ego breaks, when this puny, petty earthen pot of 'I' shatters, the water inside the pitcher and the water outside become one. Therefore, there is no essential differ-ence between you and me, or the guru and the ishta.

Inner vision of God
Rama was born from Kaushalya 9,035 years ago, in Ayodhya. It is that Rama whom I am thinking about all the time. It is much easier to think about God in a human form. There is no use talking about abstract or intellectual things, vedantic philosophy or this or that. Try to seek God in human form.

This is the greatest sadhana in man's life. Intellectualization and contemplation bring nothing. Telling yourself, "I am Brahman", does not make you Brahman. Even if you say, "God is in my heart", it gives no result. You must see God, therefore, the word darshan, meaning 'inner vision', is used.

You can have this vision in a dream, in meditation or in any state. In the state of darshan there is no awareness of you or me; only the *swaroopa*, or form of God remains. What is the form of God? It is like the form of water, which takes the shape of the pitcher, bowl or glass it is poured into. The form of water is that of a cup, a glass, a bowl, a pitcher, a bucket, a river, a lake or an ocean. Water has no form of its own. Tell me, what is the form of gold? If you shape the form of God in a stone, God takes that form. If you weave God's picture in cloth, God takes that form. Whatever material is used, God takes on that form.

The form which you have decided upon is the basis for the manifestation of your consciousness. This particular form can be your deity, your guru, one whom you love and adore. Always try to develop the awareness of this one, unchanging form. When this form comes to you in the form of imagination or an idea, it means that your awareness is not yet clear; there is some kind of disturbance of mind. When you are able to see that image clearly, as if it were a conscious dream, it means your awareness is coming to the point of consolidation or crystallization. If the form continues in the plane of your consciousness like a vivid dream with color, it means your consciousness is completely disassociated and is functioning independently on the borderline of knowledge.

The image is clear when the consciousness is pure. This purity of consciousness is to be understood absolutely in the spiritual and metaphysical sense, rather than in the ethical or moral sense. In spite of the fact that your mind was running here and there in between the practice, the moment you stop the movement and close your eyes, the image should appear. You can take any image, a circle, a triangle, a rose or a human form, but once it is decided upon, the image should not be changed, even if other forms come to replace it.

Eventually you will be able to see the object as clearly as you see an object with your eyes open. This is the experience of expanded consciousness, or the fourth dimension, which is the ultimate aim of yoga. Through yoga that dimension of consciousness is achieved in which you can see your consciousness as clearly and as real as you see the things outside. In the yogic texts this is called spiritual vision. The classical term for that is darshan, to see an object without the medium of the senses, without thinking, feeling or touching.

All these things that come in the form of an image, an idea, a vision, or a conscious dream, are different manifestations of your own awareness. It is your own being, the Atman, the nucleus of your personality. When you have this vision, when you experience this fourth dimension of your personality, and you are having the higher experience that "I am all", you have completed your upasana.

12

Sankalpa in Upasana

You may remember God and worship Him with different motives, but whatever you do constitutes upasana, and whatever you wish for in this world, you will get. Everything happens in its own way. When a desire arises in the mind of God, He also arranges for its fulfilment. If you worship women, wealth, enjoyment and happiness, you will obtain them but they will inevitably bring misery and sorrow in their trail, just as everything brings its own shadow along with it. Everything in this world has a material shadow. Whatever you wish for in this world, you will get: son, wife, prosperity, success, fame, honour and status. But these will also bring sorrow and unhappiness. However, when you worship God with a heart full of love and wish for that which will allow you to establish a relationship with Him, then there is no question of sorrow or unhappiness.

Choosing a sankalpa

The Sanskrit word *sankalpa* is loosely translated as 'determination', 'conviction' or 'resolve'. Sankalpa converts the dynamic mental force of willpower, or *iccha shakti*, into a living entity. Sankalpa is a science. It is not just a simple idea that you would like something, and if you do a little prayer or worship, it will come about. In a sankalpa, the mental energy becomes stronger than matter; and with such a force, you can achieve what is virtually impossible to attain.

So the sankalpa is not a mere wish or idle fancy related to your self-centred personality. The sankalpa is a plea, a message from your soul to help liberate it from its bondage in your human form. The sankalpa is born from a yearning that comes from beyond any physical, mental or emotional need.

You should have only one sankalpa in force at any one time, and to decide upon it, you must go beyond your intellect. The sankalpa is not something that anyone else can select for you; it can only be decided by you. The sankalpa should originate from a moment of inspiration, when you have been able to listen to the deepest desire, emanating from within you. When your sankalpa has been revealed to you from the depths of your being, and you have accepted it with humility and reverence, you should never question it. Always keep a positive attitude towards your sankalpa, and it will become the means to overcome any obstacle upon your spiritual path.

You should repeat your sankalpa with total conviction and with all your faith, sincerity and devotion. The power of sankalpa is a force that can change the course of your destiny. Whenever you sit for prayer or worship, whenever you remember the Lord or repeat His name, you can reinforce your sankalpa by repeating it mentally at that time. Sometimes you may feel a huge gap between yourself and the realization of your sankalpa. At those times repeat it mentally and visualize it, right there in front of you, in living reality. Such should be the faith with which you hold your sankalpa. The force of your mental energy is capable of tremendous intensity, and if you are able to harness that force, anything that you set your mind upon will come true.

Role of sankalpa in formal worship
Sankalpa has an important role in all poojas. At the beginning of the pooja, the sankalpa is declared by the devotee performing the pooja. The sankalpa specifies the kind of pooja that is going to take place and the desired fruits.

According to the *Dharmashastras* (scriptures on correct conduct), the sankalpa is necessary for the performance of all worship, including the daily bath and offerings, for in strict theory a rite yields its complete fruit only when it is performed consciously. The sankalpa pronounced by the worshipper in the daily pooja is fixed by the scriptural text of the pooja and cannot be deliberately altered. The occasional or *naimittika* poojas have their specific formulas, which differ according to the purpose of the pooja. These optional poojas are characterized by the desire for the fulfilment of a particular material desire.

The sankalpa is absolutely necessary for the success of any pooja or ritual. In the sankalpa, the devotee pledges to fulfil his promise of adoration and is thereby assured of his success to attain the fruits of the worship. The sankalpa declares the place, time, aim and method of the ritual act that he is going to perform. Any astrological details are mentioned, according to the current almanac or *panchanga*. The traditional formulas used here differ according to one's region. Finally the particular ritual to be performed is announced together with the desired results. The devotee is thereby bound to fulfil his promise, but he is also assured of its success.

The sankalpa is not completed until the end of the pooja, when the worshipper expresses his prayer that the deity be pleased with his worship. Then the deity, having accepted the offering of the pooja, will be disposed to fulfil his wishes. Without this final part of the sankalpa, the worshipper cannot obtain any result. This exchange is also indicated by the practice of returning part of the offerings brought to the temple by the devotee. After the pooja the food offered to the idol becomes prasad, god's grace, and is eaten with devotion by the worshippers, who thereby earn merit and communicate with the god.

The performance of daily poojas is a duty of the householder, enjoined by the *Dharmashastra*, and the omission is an offence for which atonements are due. The daily poojas are said to be beneficial to the worshipper on a material as well as spiritual level. The performer of Vishnu's pooja believes that he is always surrounded by the goddess of wealth, Lakshmi, and that he is protected from all negative forces. The bhaktas, who include pooja as part of their spiritual practices, believe that the worship of the Lord is karma leading to moksha, and any acts, which are not done as adoration of god, are futile and cause bondage. The bhaktas contend that all actions are offerings to God and should be done without attachment, in the belief that one is not doing anything; rather that God alone is acting.

Taking a vow

In order to become established in any form of worship, whether formal or informal, you must first make a vow. You can make a simple and small vow that every morning you will get up early, have a bath, and chant Gayatri mantra a specific number of times. Then, irrespective of your workload, you must do it daily. Even if the mind is disturbed, you must still do it. If your faith in the vow dwindles, even then you must do it. The important thing is to do it and do it and do it. The vow that you make is an expression of your will, whether a strong decision or a small oath. You must have studied the principle of crystallization in primary science. If you hang a small crystal, after some time, you will see that small crystal particles kept nearby are drawn to it, until in the end such a large crystal is formed that it falls off.

In the beginning make a small decision at primary class level. Getting up at four in the morning is a small vow. There are thousands of vows, big and small. Celibacy is a big vow, sitting in the middle of five fires is a big vow, sannyasa is a big vow. I am talking about small vows here, not big vows. Suppose you have vowed to get up at four a.m. every day. Even if your health is suffering, you have a cough and cold, and you are unable to do anything else, still you must get up at four a.m. You have taken a vow, so you definitely must do it. You did not say, "I will get up at four, take a bath and do so many rounds of japa." You only said, "I will get up at four a.m." and this does not mean lying in bed wrapped with blankets.

In the same way, you can make a vow to fast on Ekadashi, or whatever vow is suitable for you, and then follow it with regularity. This way the willpower becomes strong and the mind becomes disciplined. When your mind is strong, you will have no need to repent. Your bad habits will change without repentance. Everybody repents; gamblers and drunkards also repent, but it has no effect because the mind is weak. To make the mind strong, a man must be able to make a decision and stick to it without wavering. A gardener decides to plant potato, brinjal and cabbage, so that is his sadhana. Raidas was a cobbler; he decided to make shoes and that was his sadhana. Kabir was a weaver; he decided to make cloth, so that was his sadhana.

Whatever you do or want to do, that can become your sadhana, your upasana, provided you offer it to God. The feeling that 'I am the doer' must not be there. Some work as doctors, some as advocates, some as priests, some do business. Whatever work you do, you must have the feeling of dedication. There are many distractions on the spiritual path: children, household chores, job, money, but these are not the aim of life. They are the means, but not the end. Life is the means to achieve God-realization.

Sankalpa has its own laws of karma. Whether the future is bright or otherwise, everyone fantasizes about the future. But life is formed by your karmas, not by your wishes. However, there are some people who can change their life, according to their sankalpa. In order to make this happen, you have to be like an assassin. You must have the determination to carry a decision through. You must not waver, because karma, wealth, learning and death are all decided on the day of conception and man can only change it through determined efforts to keep his resolve.

All great saints and thinkers used to take vows. History shows us that great warriors also used to take vows. This practice exists in all religions: Vedic Dharma, Islam,

Christianity and Buddhism. For example, Jesus made a sankalpa to tell the truth; and he died to keep it. All world religions have this tradition. They call it taking a vow.

A wish and a pledge

But what is a vow? "God, give me this and, therefore, next year I will not eat bread." No, it is not that easy. If you ask God for a great favour and make a great offering in return, you will never face a loss. If your transactions with God are honest and clear, you will never lose. If you do business with God correctly, you will never be a loser. You can take lessons from the lives of saints and hermits. Prayer for the fulfilment of a wish is a very powerful thing, if it is done properly. It has its own laws. Whatever you want to do, you can do by your own wish. If this wish is made properly, then it is like a bombshell. However, when you make a wish, you must also pledge to renounce something. If a lady wishes for a child, she has to pledge something in return, which is equivalent to the child. For example, God made me victorious globally, and I pledged to return that.

Praying for the fulfilment of a wish is not a simple matter. It has a very deep relationship with God. In your mind there is sorrow and suffering; there are also desires and unfulfilled wishes. You wish to fulfil them all, but you must also give something in return, because your destiny is fixed. If you take ten rupees out of your pocket, you must replace it with something. This is the law of karma. Everyone has to follow these laws, whether it be Rama, Krishna, Asha or Satyananda; nobody can erase them. Everyone is bound to suffer throughout his or her destiny. You can alter the *kriyaman karma*, that is, the actions not yet performed; you can even alter *sanchit karma*, the stored actions, but you cannot alter *prarabdha karma*, destined actions, by any ritual or *anushthana* (prescribed practices).

For altering the prarabdha or destined karmas, you have to make an adjustment. A prayer for wish fulfilment made along with a pledge to renounce something is one such type

137

of adjustment. If you want to live luxuriously, then you will have to renounce something. Therefore, such prayers are necessary. Nothing is impossible to attain in the kingdom of God, but God is a complicated element. You cannot handle Him easily. There is only one-way to handle God, make a prayer, and make a promise which even He does not know of. You, and only you, know that promise, not even I need to know.

When you say prayers for the fulfilment of a wish, you must not ask, "Should I wish for this or not?" It is only on the basis of faith that prayers are made, so why ask the question? It is better to keep quiet. You should not speak about your wish to anyone before, during or after making a resolve. It is a sankalpa, a seed, a resolve that arises from the mind. If you sow that seed and dig it up again and again in order to look at it, then the potential for growth is lost. Bury the seed in the soil of your mind and then forget about it totally.

In 1963, after making the wish, regarding my yoga mission, I had pledged that within twenty years my work would be completed, and then I would leave everything and surrender myself to Him. But I totally forgot about this commitment. Then one day I happened to be in Bombay. All at once I had the feeling that as Trayambakeshwar was nearby, I should go there for darshan, because my ishta devata is Lord Mrityunjaya and the *jyotirlingam* (self-illumined symbol) was at Trayambakeshwar. I instructed Swami Satsangi to hire a taxi and we drove there. The moment I bowed down in front of the temple precincts, I immediately remembered my commitment; because it was there that I had made it. I suddenly realized my mistake.

I had asked Him to do things for me, and in return I had pledged that I would leave everything. He had done the work for me, and the moment my forehead touched the ground in front of Him, I immediately remembered everything. I must have remained in that state for a minute or two. As I realized my mistake, I was thinking, not praying:

138

"Now I have to leave Munger; I must leave everything." So, I returned to Bombay by car, and then caught a plane to Munger. I immediately telephoned Swami Niranjan, who was in New York at that time, and told him to leave everything and return to Munger. He returned, took charge and did everything after that.

Even if somebody digs and asks about your sankalpa, don't say anything, because the feelings of love will work in equal proportion to the secrecy you maintain. The more hidden the seed is, the stronger the plant will be. If you dig daily to look at the seed, then it will lose its power. I had totally forgotten that I had made promises to God. I was totally blissful in my fame and success. I didn't even remember that I had promised Him anything. I had forgotten the promise despite receiving so much from Him! There was never a single obstacle in the development of my mission. When I travelled abroad, people came from all over Europe to listen to me. All the hotels of entire towns were booked out. People were so enthusiastic that Swamiji was coming. Even the Pope and his bishops heard me. This was because whoever is blessed by God is a king in himself.

So, nothing is difficult for one who is blessed by God, but He is a complex element. It is not so easy to pull Him by ropes or to pin Him down. You must pledge some act of renunciation, and you don't have to ask anybody about it; you have to decide it for yourself. Don't consult your mother and father. You give something to God and you take something from Him. God knows how to give and how to take as well. So, you will only receive what you are destined to. I was given whatever was in my destiny. But no one can stop you from praying or worshipping Him. So go ahead.

Be a light unto yourself
On the spiritual path there are two important aspects: one is yourself and the other is God. There is no third aspect. That is what I also consider in my life: first, myself, I have to struggle, I have to strive, and then God and His blessings.

So, firstly, God can be reached only by love. There is no other way. The feeling of love that arises in the mind becomes the sankalpa. When you feel love, devotion and affection for someone, then whatever you think about that person becomes your pooja, your worship, your sankalpa. Secondly, God will meet you only if He wishes, not by your wish. You must remember this. God is approachable only through love and devotion. He will reveal Himself only if He wants to, not because you have tried all the methods.

Actually, nothing except bhakti is necessary in order to find God. There is no other method. All the methods written about in the *Bible*, the *Gita* and Upanishads are just said because we have to do something. You have to lay yourself open to God. Do not be a hypocrite. You should know what you are. Your mind is so filthy, your ideas so faulty, your imagination so dirty, and your speech so rough. You talk about God, read about Him, write about Him, think about Him, but how do you pray? During prayer, your body is all that is there; the mind has gone elsewhere. While doing japa, the mind is roaming all over the place like a delinquent. That is the quality of your personality; that is what you are. You belong to the lower level and yet now you want to gain admission to university! You will fail every year.

You have to be a light unto yourself; it is no use knocking at my door. The most innocent person, who does not know the ABC's of spiritual training, can get realization at any time, if he wishes. No qualifications are required. You do not have to be truthful, celibate or sincere. You do not have to be Christian or Hindu, or put on a sacred thread. Darshan of God can be had by anyone, anytime, anywhere. For God's grace, you do not have to qualify yourself. Many great, truthful, honest and pure people have missed the bus, because they look for God by way of compromise. Always remember that God is never far from you. God should be dearer to you than the dearest.

13

Navadha Bhakti

In the *Srimad Bhagavat* and the *Vishnu Purana*, nine forms of worship are given to develop devotion. These nine forms are known as navadha bhakti. You can select any method, which suits you best, and by practicing that attain illumination and union with the Lord.

1. *Shravana* – hearing stories of God's and satsang
2. *Kirtana* – singing of His glories
3. *Smarana* – constant remembrance of His name and presence
4. *Padasevana* – service of His feet
5. *Archana* – ritual worship of God with or without form
6. *Vandana* – prostration and prayer to the Lord
7. *Dasya* – cultivating the attitude of a servant of God
8. *Sakhya* – cultivating the attitude of a friend towards God
9. *Atma nivedana* – complete surrender of the self.

1. Shravana/satsang

Shravana means listening to the stories of God, attending satsang and reading sacred literature. Hearing about the deeds of the Lord and the saints inspires us. Swami Vivekananda, Swami Ramatirtha, Swami Sivananda, Anandamayi Ma and Neem Karoli Baba are saints of this time, and you will find their disciples everywhere. Direct your mind and feeling towards a saint or a guru for some time. By reflecting on their great deeds, by hearing or reading stories

141

about them, by listening to their teachings in satsang, you will become encouraged and motivated.

What is satsang? The first definition of satsang is association with God, which brings a total transformation in your mind and heart. Attending satsang again and again will open your eyes and reveal to you a new dimension of life. God's words and blessings are pouring down everywhere, but you need to open your mind more and feel yourself to always be in tune with Him. To keep in tune with Him it is necessary to expose yourself to satsang from time to time. With the Lord's grace you will get an opportunity for real satsang where you will experience the presence or association with Truth.

Attend the satsang of sadhus and mahatmas to seek knowledge. Seek the company of saints, sages and wise men, as they do not have any obligation to particular sects, and they are universal in nature and philosophy. This type of satsang gives great happiness and peace, allows your devotion to God to become strong, and develops your discrimination. Of course, the company of the wise is very difficult to obtain but if by God's grace you have it, it will transform you.

The second definition of satsang is to keep company with good literature: the Vedas, Upanishads, *Bhagavad Gita*, *Bible*, *Koran*, *Torah* and many other scriptures. Then there is the literature of saints and swamis, such as Sri Aurobindo, Swami Sivananda and others. There are hundreds and thousands of spiritual books. So, if you cannot attend satsang, then at least read good books like *Ramacharitamanas*, *Srimad Bhagavat* and *Guru Granth Sahib*. *Ramacharitamanas* is the most powerful tonic for generating bhakti. You should make it a point to dive deep into such literature.

You do not have to be a good person in order to attend satsang. A ruffian, tyrant or wicked man can improve with the company of the wise. You may be a wretched person, an incarnation of evil; it doesn't matter. Suppose someone had a bad birth previously or his parents did not give him the right training. Through contact with good company, he can

142

improve. Through negative associations, children of very good families can become spoiled. In the same way, through positive associations, the wretched person can become good.

The company that you keep also depends on your environment and lifestyle. You go to school or college, work in an office, read books, watch films, sing songs, attend social gatherings; these are also associations. Anyone and anything that you interact with in your life is a form of association. However, through satsang a positive transformation definitely takes place. The importance of satsang is that even the most unholy, most untouchable being becomes worthy of respect, worship and honour.

Satsang is the origin of bliss. Without satsang, bhakti is not possible, because you can't create the bliss; it can only be imbibed. You have to be in touch with bliss through satsang, so go to satsang from time to time, sing the Lord's name, and study the scriptures pertaining to bhakti, devotion to God. You should study the lives of saints and great souls. This country has produced many great souls, such as Lord Rama and Lord Krishna, and you should read about their lives. This country has given birth to many householders, like King Janaka, Tukaram, Kabir Das, Nanak Dev, Guru Govind Singh and others, who had children and still led very great lives. This country has given birth to many saints, mahatmas and sannyasins. Read about their lives and receive inspiration from them.

In order to experience God's blessings, you have to spare some time for Him. One thing is sure, God's grace comes as His gift; it is dependent on His will and cannot be acquired through your efforts. At the same time, you still have to make some effort. Attending satsang is a kind of effort. If no effort were required, the saints and sages would not have laid so much emphasis on satsang. The effort made in the form of satsang culminates in awareness of the complete presence of God's grace.

It is only when you expose yourself to the company of divine thoughts and divine association through satsang that you may perhaps become aware of the eternal, spontaneous grace of God, which is always within you. So, people who are on the spiritual path should strive continuously and regularly. The way to attain God is through satsang. In satsang, you should listen to discourses by learned, virtuous, enlightened souls. If you live in that atmosphere, it will help you.

2. Kirtan

Kirtan means singing the glories and names of God. This is the simplest, easiest and surest sadhana, involving the least risk and expense. When you rise in the morning, first sit down and sing God's name; *Raghupati Raghava Raja Ram* is one example. However, you need not sing this kirtan; you can make your own choice. Go on singing the Lord's name for thirty to forty minutes. When you repeat God's name, you don't spend time; you gain time. It is a longterm investment. Repeat this process again when you go to bed at night. Even if you return late at night from a discotheque or a nightclub and you are a little tipsy, it doesn't matter – that's a part of life. You can still sing God's name.

Sing the name of God until your mind melts. Just as sugar becomes one with milk, let the mind melt in God. There is no use controlling the mind, because there is no mind, as such. Just sing His name until you get out! This was the path of Chaitanya Mahaprabhu and Mirabai. Narada continuously chanted the name Narayana, twenty-four hours a day. If you sing the name of God with the proper melody, pitch, and beat, you will enjoy it like nothing else. Good food, sweets, tea and coffee, do not generate as much heat as the singing of God's name. If you are wondering how to become a better person, do a little kirtan everyday.

Kirtan is a part of *nada yoga*, the yoga of sound. The word *nada* means 'flow of sound vibrations'. While singing kirtan, if you close your eyes, the rhythm starts and gradually the vibrational frequencies rise. The higher the velocity, the lower the frequency, and the higher the frequency, the lower the velocity. This is the relationship between velocity and frequency. It is a scientific law. Velocity pertains to the mind. The mind is very active. It has speed, so it has velocity. The mind must lose its velocity and attain frequency. When the mind attains frequency, then many minds become one mind. This is possible through kirtan. When the mind becomes one with the nada, the sound and the mantra, there is no difference between the mind and the mantra. Then the place where the kirtan is sung becomes sanctified and purified.

In the kali yuga, most people are not capable of observing austerities; they belong to the culture of sofas and chairs. Therefore, one should participate in kirtan at home with a few others. Let us start with the family in which there are at least four persons. You can choose any convenient time to sit together with your family, either before meals or before sleeping, and sing the name of God for at least ten or fifteen minutes. You should also take your children to kirtan sessions. Kirtans are held in many places. Small groups of sadhus sit together and sing kirtan. You can go to a guru's ashram for kirtan. There is no special day reserved for kirtan; all days are auspicious for singing God's name.

Just as an animal trainer tames a tiger or a snake-charmer tames a serpent, in the same way, the name of God, the chanting of mantra, must be done properly in a large group, with correct, timing. *Tala*, timing, is an attribute of the mind. By following the tala, the mind goes deep without any effort from your side. You may also play a guitar, *mridang* (clay drum) or harmonium, and just keep on singing the Lord's name. Kirtan is the most powerful form of music and devotion. If you can sing for one hour or more, you don't have to do japa, meditation or pooja. Kirtan becomes your means of worship, your upasana. Just sing God's name over and over again; that is *naam samkirtan*. I sing alone here, but singing alone is not naam kirtan. Naam sankirtan is when ten, twenty-five, thirty people sit down and sing God's name. Singing the stories of God is also very important.

The name can be selected from a number of names by which God is called. It can be Allah, Rama, Govinda or Guru. Whatever name you choose, go on singing it. Start slowly and go on building up the crescendo. As the rhythm increases you become more and more immersed. In the beginning the mind stays outside, but slowly it starts going within. Whenever a kirtan is happening and you get wind of it, go and join in. Recorded kirtans are also available. You can record the kirtan on the spot, bring it home and play it to the children and other family members. There is no harm if Shiva kirtan is sung in a Vaishnava house, if Christian hymns are sung in a Hindu house, or if Rama or Krishna kirtan is sung in a Christian house.

You can sing kirtan anywhere, at home, in a social gathering or at any auspicious get together. This is a very good way to inculcate good habits in children. You should start slowly by devoting ten to fifteen minutes daily to kirtan. This new routine will help to make kirtan your second nature. When you get up in the morning, sit down and sing God's name. You can sing it loudly. What is there to hide? There should be no shame in singing the Lord's name. Why should you be ashamed of worshipping the Lord? If people see you worshipping, they will follow your example. You should sing kirtan every day. You eat every day, so why not sing every day?

Kirtan is very effective. If you sing one kirtan slowly and spontaneously for a period of two hours or even longer, gradually increasing the rhythm, you will reach a deep state of awareness. Restlessness and lack of peace are the greatest enemies of man. When the mind becomes quiet, the impossible becomes possible. All the saints say that kirtan is the only sadhana you can do with relaxation and without any difficulty. In this age of tension and preoccupation, you are never free. You have to work to support your family, and you do not have a lot of time. Even if you have time, you are not able to concentrate the mind. Concentration of mind is very difficult in this age. This is the age of *adharma* (absence

146

if dharma), of tension and confusion. Now there is no other way, except singing God's name.

For those who are crooked, who have tensions, sorrow, misfortune or health problems, it is useless to even talk about concentration. Even with complete harmony in the family, good children and a nice wife or husband, your mind is not able to concentrate because, in the kali yuga, concentration of mind is only possible for a few. Arjuna said something similar to Lord Krishna in the *Bhagavad Gita* (6:34): "In Dwaparyuga, O Krishna, certainly the mind is restless, turbulent, strong and obstinate, and I deem it as difficult to control as the blowing wind." However, it is still possible to sing God's name and immerse yourself in this for an hour or so. This is possible now, but I do not know what will happen in the future. In this kali yuga, in this age, kirtan is as good as medicine.

God's name is always sweet. Sugar is sweet whether you put it in halwa or cake. In the same way, God's name is always sweet, whether you sing or chant it – it has the quality of *madhuram*. There is a song: *Adharam Madhuram, Nayanam Madhuram*. He is sweetness personified. When you get out of bed in the morning with your eyes closed, half asleep, half awake, sing God's name. That is how the day should begin, with God's name: *Sri Ram Jai Ram*. This is a good start in the morning, then you can take a bath and read the *Bible*, *Ramayana, Srimad Bhagavat*, the teachings of Ramakrishna Paramahamsa, Bhakti Vedanta or Swami Sivananda.

Singing kirtans connects you with the Lord and is the quickest and easiest way to realize yourself. Even if you sing kirtan for four hours at a stretch, there are no side effects. Every other kind of yoga, if practised incorrectly, has some side effects, but kirtan has none. Rather it can overcome depression, anxiety, high blood pressure and every other problem. When kirtan is sung the mental state changes towards one-pointedness and *shanti*, peace. This is the real kirtan. The tradition of kirtan is very ancient. Chaitanya Mahaprabhu developed and taught this concept. He used to say that the only path to salvation in this kali yuga is singing the Lord's name and nothing else. Since kirtan can be so useful to humanity, we should be properly trained in it.

Kirtan purifies the entire atmosphere wherever it is sung. When ten, twenty or thirty people sing kirtan together, they generate a powerful energy. The house where kirtan is sung becomes purified and bad spirits cannot reside there. People remain in a positive mental state in that home and all the unpleasantness disappears, because the name of God has the ability to destroy negative energy. When the light of the sun appears, the darkness disappears. The name of God is like light, which illumines and purifies wherever it is sung. When four or five children get together at home and sing film songs, nobody stops them. Similarly, they could get together and sing the name of God. You eat sweets and also chillies, which have a different type of taste. The taste of film songs is of fun, while the taste of kirtan is of peace.

You must have noticed that in some houses someone is always sick, despite the house being pleasant and clean. If people are unwell it means that there are evil spirits residing there and banishing those spirits from the house is not an economical task. If you get a pundit to do it for you, he will ask for a lot of money. The method of kirtan costs nothing and it does the job well. The parents and children only need to sit together and sing the Lord's name: *Sri Ram Jaya Ram Jaya Jaya Ram* or *Sri Krishna Govinda Hare Murare*. If they sing it in unison, repeatedly, it is called kirtan. You may also sing the praises of the Lord; that is called *stuti*. And, asking the Lord for something through song is called *prarthana*.

3. Smarana – remembrance of the lord

In the *Bhagavad Gita*, Lord Krishna says: "O Arjuna, I am easily attainable by that yogi who is ever steady, who remembers Me constantly every day and who thinks of none else." When you repeat the name, it will remind us of God. Name is only a reminder so it doesn't matter what name you repeat. Just repeat the name which attracts you most: Sri Rama, Om Namah Shivayah, Hail Mary, Jesus Christ, etc. Suppose you have come from a Christian background and I give you a clock, which chants the name of Rama. You will say, "No, I don't want it, because I am a Christian." This is a foolish idea. Many Indians intermarry with men and women from foreign countries, and many foreigners marry Indian men and women. Yet we don't see any difference in that; we see the difference only in God's name.

Sri Ram, Jaya Ram, Jai Jai Ram is only a reminder. The idea that it invokes in us is that of divinity. Divinity is total, all comprehensive and universal. Divinity has no form. God's name reminds us of purity, divinity and greatness. We can take any name or read any scripture, whether it is the Gita by Prabhupad, the works of Shankaracharya, the Upanishads, the Vedas, the *Bible*, the *Koran*, the *Guru Granth Sahib*, the couplets of Kabir, Mirabai or Raidas. This makes no difference to our religious beliefs. The taste of salt or sugar is the same in Europe, India and China. What I don't understand is how the difference in God's name cropped up in the first place. It must have been the work of mischief mongers.

When you can remember God every morning and evening with as much single mindedness as you remember your sick child, your beautiful wife, your old mother, your sister who has gone to her husband's house, or a vanquished enemy, you will have reached the goal, your boat will have crossed the river. Feel that God's name is your very breath. Think only about God and do everything for God, nothing else. Talk only about God and devotion to Him. Consider how you can become close to God, and the ways by which you can feel Him in your heart. When you are aware of God, just as you are constantly aware of the pain in a wound, it is called *surati*. If this awareness comes, you are lucky and blessed.

You can feel love for God just as you feel pain and pleasure, joy and remorse, sleep and hunger. Once you

149

have begun to feel that love, you will be the happiest person in this world. The only person who is happy in this life is the one who thinks of God, who lives in God, and for whom the subject matter of life is God. For him, there is no cancer, no poverty and no difficulty. For him, there is only light. In front is light, behind is light, to the right is light, to the left is light, and everywhere is light. Remember Him constantly, as you would remember your beloved, even while eating, drinking and sleeping. Your lover may not meet you, but even the memory gives you happiness.

The simple question is how to be aware of Him all the time without any difficulty or struggle. One should be constantly engrossed in thoughts of Him around the clock, just like the gopis, who used to think about Lord Krishna all the time, while eating, drinking, sleeping, talking, walking, sitting or standing. My guru, Swami Sivananda, used to ask me, "Do you remember His name all the time?" I would reply, "Swamiji, I try but mostly I forget, because I am so busy with administration." He would say, "While doing administration work, you still remember to eat, sleep and go to the toilet. You don't forget those things, so how can you forget God, because His name is your very breath. Your whole life has to be dedicated to remembrance of Him."

My guru also said, "Moreover, you are a sannyasin. A sannyasin's only hope is God's name. A sannyasin, who depends on his scholarship, will not survive in spiritual life; he will certainly have a downfall." The best way to achieve the aim of spiritual life is to remember His name. God's name is an effective force for sannyasins, as well as for householders. Your knowledge and book learning are of no avail; they are only acquired to deceive others. You go on talking and giving lectures to others. This is nothing but recreation. You are just jokers, entertaining others. The kingdom of God is accessible only to those who give God first priority, wherever they are and whatever their circumstances.

One can remember God, whether in the form of light or sound or on the banks of Chitrakoot. This is the most important aim in human life; eating, drinking, housekeeping, family, marriage, and profession are not aims. Man should not live only for these. Suppose you have a very serious problem. You eat, you sleep, you go to the toilet, you go to the office or to work, you go to the shop, you meet your friends, but the problem is always lurking somewhere in your mind. In the same way you must think of God continuously. A man who is absolutely attuned to God will also undergo karma and reap the consequences, but they will not affect him. He will see everything as if in a video film because he has become a witness to the part he is enacting.

Remembrance of God gradually moves you towards perfection. So, whenever you find time, sit down and repeat the name of God. It may be for a few minutes or for one, two or three hours. When it is possible, do japa anushthana for nine days, three days, even one day will do. You can also do an anushthana for one full year if you wish. This is the only way you will become free. Life begins with incompleteness. If you want to take your life towards completeness and perfection, then you should begin with the mantra of wholeness. The only mantra of wholeness and perfection is the Lord's name. So life starts with imperfection and this is natural. When you wish to move towards perfection, you don't have to take up a difficult method or path; just repeat God's name. When you die, your last breath should be the awareness of God's name.

4. Padasevana – worship through service

Lord Krishna has said in the *Bhagavad Gita* (9:27), "Whatever you do, whatever you eat, whatever you offer in sacrifice, whatever you give, whatever you practise as austerity, O Arjuna, do it as an offering unto Me." Think that wherever you are sitting is your temple and whatever you are doing is service towards God. This is what your bhavana should be. If you are harvesting your paddy, think that the field is the temple of God. After all, grains are a devata, a form of God; water is a devata, a form of God; earth is a devi, a goddess;

151

wind is a devata called Pawan, the father of Hanuman. God is everywhere. Keep reflecting on God.

My guru, Swami Sivananda, was a very special person, he could see God in everything. He would call all the sweepers and scavengers, feed and clothe them, give them tea, wash their feet, and ask me to do the same. He would also call the lepers, and he started a leper colony in Rishikesh behind Kailash Ashram on the banks of the Ganga. I would go to the colony to narrate *Ramayana*. There were about two hundred and fifty leprosy patients living there. My guru had huts made for them, had their roofs thatched, and did everything for them. They were taught to chant Rama's name. He forbade them to beg in the streets and would even send them bundles of bidis. They were given goats to rear, because lepers are forbidden to raise cows.

There were so many incidents like this in his life, which I saw with my own eyes. He believed that those who think well of others have tender hearts. One who thinks ill of others cannot have a soft heart. One who thinks ill of others has a hard heart, which needs to be pounded. Prakriti breaks hard-core hearts. Your heart should be so soft, so tender, so sensitive, that it should immediately respond to the cries of agony and pain from others. Draupadi's agonized cries for help reached the Lord, because He has a soft, tender heart. Even if we had been around, her cries would not have touched our hard hearts. We would have escaped with the excuse that we were unaware of what was happening to her.

You should be able to feel the pain of other people, to feel the tragedy in another's life. Before you are able to experience Brahman or the Lord, to see the light or experience enlightenment, you must be able to feel the pain and agony of another person. If you can't feel or respond to another's agony mentally, it means you cannot attain peace, you cannot see the light. Such a compassionate and sensitive heart, which feels and responds to another's pain, will attain God effortlessly. The more distant and unaffected you are from the suffering and distress of others, the further God will be from you. God, Shiva, Rama, Devi, all will be beyond your reach.

Serve the Lord through each and everyone, because anyone could be the Lord. Whenever you help others, it should be with the spirit of offering service to the Lord. If a sadhu comes to your house and you are well off, it is your duty to give him food. However, do not give with the spirit of performing a duty, rather give as if offering it to God. If a beggar comes to your house, do not have the attitude of helping a poor man. Instead, feel that you are being given the opportunity to serve the Lord. It is Him! Who knows? Lord Narayana can come in any form.

In Maharashtra, there lived a mahatma called Namdev. Once a dog was eating bread from Namdev's dish, but when it saw him approaching, it ran away. Namdev ran after the dog with the bread calling, "Please take some butter also." He thought, God can come in any form, because God has no form and can take any form. So, you should be careful how you treat others. God can come as an important person of authority or a big businessman. Everyone will notice such a person and treat him with respect. But if God were to come as a weak person, a blind person or a beggar, you would not treat him with respect, and would give him only small change. This is our normal attitude.

You don't have spiritual eyes, inner eyes; you have *avidya*, ignorance, and *ajnana*, lack of wisdom. You want to see reality with the physical eyes, but it is not possible, so do service to others and it will yield positive results. Service to guru is certainly a very important part of spiritual life and should never be underestimated. Spiritual life begins with seva. Swami Sivananda's fundamental philosophy of life was social service and human service. His priorities were "Serve, love, give, purify, meditate, realize." So, meditation was at the end of his list, a long way off. His spiritual life started with service and culminated in meditation. The beginning of spiritual life stems from service to humanity. When God inspires you to do service, you should take it as his blessing.

Saints are born to help others, to serve others, not to seek their own liberation. Does a river drink its own water? Do trees and vines that grow fruits and vegetables, such as mangoes, guavas, apples, papaya, jackfruit, tomatoes or potatoes eat produce? No, they are grown for all of us. This is called *paramartha*, the highest service. That which helps others is paramartha and that which is of no help to others is selfishness. Man's greatest weakness is selfishness. Devas run after enjoyment, demons are cruel and human beings are selfish. So devas have to learn self-restraint, demons have to learn to be kind, and human beings have to learn to serve.

Service to God's forms is worship. God has two forms: transcendental and immanent. The immanent form is everywhere, in everything. If you serve a tree, you are serving God. If you serve the land, you are serving God. If you purify the river, you are serving God. If you purify the atmosphere, you are serving God. If you help the needy, you are serving God. Then we have the transcendental God also in *Hare Rama, Hare Rama.* I do not object to that, but the realization of God must become a total experience, not partial.

In the *Bhagavad Gita* (11:5–7), while showing Arjuna His universal form, the Lord said: "Behold all my forms, hundreds and thousands of different sorts, divine and of various colours and shapes. Behold the Adityas, the Vasus, the Rudras, the two Ashvins and also the Maruts; behold many wonders never seen before, O Arjuna. Now behold in My body, the whole universe centred in one, including the moving and the unmoving, and whatever else you desire to see."

5. Archana – ritual worship

External rituals are symbolic; they align the mind with what is happening outside to what is happening inside. Only when there is an alignment of forces does the ritual become powerful. Wherever worship is introduced in any form, rituals have followed thereafter. Every religion has rituals. Vedic dharma has rituals, Buddhism, Jainism and Islam have rituals and different Christian denominations have rituals. Each sect, religion and creed has criticized the ritualism of others, but has become stuck in its own characteristic form of ritual. This has a history of at least two thousand years.

In the vedic system pooja is the main form of ritual worship. The meaning of pooja is 'to honour'. The term pooja denotes the ritual worship of an idol or an iconic form of a deity, as well as any other objects that you consider sacred or possessing special powers. Any such ritual, whether performed with special ritual procedures by a person trained in ritualism or by someone without such knowledge, or whether conducted in a temple or at home, can be referred to as pooja. Most poojas are performed daily, like the sandhya, or sun worship. Moreover, pooja has been in-corporated into the performance of certain samskaras, such as *shraaddha* (rite for deceased ancestors), and yajnas.

Pooja is performed in all countries by people seeking their cherished desires. The time, place and utensils involved in the pooja are not exterior ornaments; they are elements of the worship. The sequence of the various parts of the pooja is determined by the logic of inner meaning. Some poojas are characterized with traditionally prescribed ritual procedures, e.g. a pooja consisting of the offering of a fixed sequence of services, accompanied by the recitation of mantras.

The types of pooja are often named after the number of offerings, for example, a pooja with five services is named *panchopachara pooja;* pooja with sixteen services is *soda-shopacara pooja.* A pooja of a simple kind may consist of an offering of a selection of traditional items, such as turmeric powder, kumkum, flowers, sandalwood paste etc., requiring neither much knowledge of ritualism nor much time. In an elaborate type of pooja the number of offerings may traditionally vary from one to 108 or more, depending on one's means, time, family tradition and the occasion.

155

In any standard pooja there are certain preparatory rites to be performed before the worship of an idol can begin. These services include rites for the purification of the devotee, for the implements used, and for the actual place of worship. For example, there is the offering of water to be sipped; salutations to the gods to remove obstacles, prayers to particular deities to obtain their protection, and worship of the bell, the conch, the lamp and the *kalasha* (vessel). There is also a particular service for the success of the worship in which the devotee declares the place, the time, the method and the aim or sankalpa of the pooja to be performed.

The sodashopachara pooja is the standard, traditional daily pooja, consisting of a series of sixteen main services, or upacharas. After the preparatory rites, this pooja begins with the invocation of the deity using the first mantra of the *Purusha Sukta*. The services that follow include offerings of a seat; water to wash the feet; water mixed with sandalwood paste and other ingredients; various kinds of baths; garments; ornaments; food; waving of the lamp during the arati; circumambulation; prostration; and the offering of flowers. Each service is consecrated by mantras from the vedic literature. After the pooja, the food offered to the idol becomes imbued with *prasada* (God's grace) and is eaten by the worshippers with devotion.

There are also occasional naimittika poojas, those performed when a special event arises. These times are usually indicated in the *panchangas* (calendars), and are observed regularly according to the family or temple tradition. Some occasional poojas are performed on certain days of every week or every month, others yearly, or once in several years when an *adhika* (additional) month occurs. As such, occasional poojas at our ashrams include: chanting the *Bhagavad Gita* on Ekadashi; and the chanting of *Sundar Kand* every full moon.

Idols worshipped in pooja are said to be of nine kinds of materials: jewels, gold, silver, copper, brass, mental, stone,

156

wood, and clay. An idol prepared from jewels is considered to be the best, while one made of clay is the most inferior. Idols are also described as movable, those which can be lifted up and carried to another place, or immovable, and those which are fixed on a pedestal and cannot be moved once they have been installed. For the pooja in temples, large idols of stone, wood or brass are used. In the daily pooja at home small brass, silver or copper idols are worshipped, and for occasional poojas, pictures or drawings are often used. For other occasional poojas, like the Ganesha or Saraswati poojas, worshippers will use idols traditionally made from clay.

Various objects are worshipped or honoured on certain occasions and different kinds of offerings are used for the pooja, according to their nature. For example, water for washing the feet is offered to an idol, but to offer it to fire would extinguish it. The sun is worshipped with recitation of hymns from the Vedas, fire by offering oblations, Brahmans by offering hospitality, cows by giving fodder, wind by regarding it as prana, and water by offering water mixed with other offerings.

The most common objects of pooja are idols (murti or pratima) but there are many other objects of worship, including:

- *Bhumi pooja* (worship of the earth) which occurs before the construction of a new building.
- Worship of water from the pooja of the river Ganga on the day of *dasahara* (tenth day of Navaratri).
- Fire is well known from sacrificial ceremonies; a pooja of the fire is performed on *Holi* (a day celebrating victory over demonic forces).
- The sun is worshipped by repetition of mantras in the sandhya rite.
- Food is the object of worship at the *govardhana pooja*, in which the idol of Krishna in his child form is placed.
- Golden coins are worshipped as representing the goddess Lakshmi in the *Lakshmi pooja* during *Deepavali* (the festival of lights).

157

- Brahmins are frequently worshipped at the end of occasional poojas.
- The sacredness of the cow is well known. A cow with a calf is worshipped on the twelfth day of the dark fortnight of *Ashwina* (September/October).
- The vessel (*kumbha* or *kalasha*), that is imagined to be the seat of the universe, is of great importance in many poojas. It is used in the *Durga* worship particularly, but in festivals all gods can be invoked into it. The vessel is never kept empty, but is filled with auspicious objects while vedic mantras are recited. The kalasha is a symbol of plenty and welfare. It is believed to fulfil the desires of its owner and produce various treasures.
- The drawing of a lotus with eight petals, a symbol of the cosmos, occurs especially in tantric texts as a mandala in which divinities are invoked.
- The worship of gurus and teachers is very common in India, especially on the day of Guru Poornima.
- Young unmarried girls are worshipped in the *kumari pooja*, and young boys after their *upanayana* (sacred thread ceremony) in the *batuka pooja*.
- In tantric forms of worship, deities are worshipped and meditated upon.
- Stones such as the shaligram are commonly worshipped as deities.
- The lingam is the most common iconic form used in Shiva worship.
- Attributes like books and weapons sometimes become objects of pooja, e.g. the worship of books on the day of Saraswati pooja, and of tools and instruments of trade during the *Vishwakarma pooja* (Vishwakarma being the engine of the gods).
- Mandalas and yantras invoked with mantras are objects of tantric worship.
- Worship is due when pictures of deities are painted on objects like a wall, a sheet of cloth or a board.

- Animals like snakes are worshipped on special days known as *Naga panchami*.
- Plants are worshipped, such as *tulsi* (holy basil), especially on the *tulasi vivaha* days.
- Trees like the *vata* (banyan) are worshipped by those who observe the *vatasavitri vrata*.
- The *paduka* (wooden sandals) of gods, gurus or saintly persons are worshipped.
- Very commonly areca nuts, betel, represent deities, especially Ganapati Ganesha, when worshiped at the beginning of a ceremony or when many deities are placed in a mandala.

Mantras are considered to be the concentrated essence of divinity and are used to sanctify ritual acts and to establish a communion between the worshipper and the divine.

In the traditional pooja with sixteen services, soda-shopachara pooja, the sixteen verses of the *Purusha Sukta* are the most important mantras. Hymns of praise may occur at two stages of the pooja. They may be recited at the time of the *abhishek*, a special kind of bath. Stotras may further be recited immediately after the completion of the pooja. At the time of abhishek, suktas as well as stotras may be repeated for a specific number of times. For example, the *Shiva Mahimna* stotra for Shiva is repeated eleven times, eleven being the number associated with Shiva in the form of Rudra.

Aratis are metrical compositions in *matra* (traditional tones), sung in praise of the deity as burning camphor or ghee lamps are waved in front of the diety. The singing of the arati may be accompanied by hand clapping and the rhythmic sound of cymbals, drums and bells.

5. Vandana – prayer

Prayer is communion with the Lord; only bowing the head is not prayer. Prayer has its own laws; it is not a simple matter. Praying for the fulfilment of a wish is a very powerful thing, if done properly, and requires a deep relationship with God. When you wish to take up an upasana, pray to God, ask Him, 'What should I do?' He Himself will give you the inspiration. Wherever you are, He is there. Pray to Him and He will show you the way. God can show the way to anybody. If He has shown the way to me, He will show the way to you. He has shown the way to Mirabai. He showed the way to Ramakrishna and Vivekananda. He showed the way to Mother Teresa and all those who sought His advice. The Lord shows the way to whoever seeks and labours for it with a true heart.

God's blessings are for everyone. Suppose it is pouring rain, and you put a corked bottle outside to collect the water. Beside the bottle, you also keep an empty plate and glass. The bottle will not fill with water because it is corked, and the plate will contain more water than the glass. Through prayer, you can keep yourself open and be ready to receive His blessings. Remember that every person has a sequence of development, which is pre-determined, just as an eclipse can be predicted thousands of years before it occurs. You can calculate when a solar or lunar eclipse will take place. In the same way, human life is also based on certain laws. Happiness and sorrow, birth and death, knowledge and ignorance – everything in life has been pre-determined. That is why you should not beat your brow over it, rather, pray to God, and enjoy that communion.

So, earn your livelihood and devote yourself to prayer. Pray to Him and you will find the path. Prayer has two forms. In the first form you express the feelings of your heart before the Supreme Being within you. In the second form you sing a prayer from the scriptures, which is pleasing to you. When you pray to God, always feel that He is listening. In raja yoga, it is said that you listen to your own prayers, but that is very subjective. According to bhakti yoga, the listener is not the personal, conditioned self. There is a higher universal Self within you, apart from this little self, and That is listening. That universal Self, or Atman, is identical with God, Paramatman or Brahman. This is how

160

God can listen to all your prayers within you, and at the same time, be the infinite, cosmic consciousness.

The psychology of prayer is very important for everyone to understand. Prayer is one of the most powerful ways to give expression to the suppressed emotions and thought forms of your mind. You can express all those things through prayer, which you cannot tell to anybody. During prayer, the Lord is a symbol, which you imagine or visualize in front of you, and then you offer the totality of the expression of your heart to Him. By this process, the mind becomes purified and relaxed. When the mind is relaxed, then the physical body relaxes. The tensions in different parts of the body, including the heart, are abated.

Therefore, prayer has an immediate relevance to one's everyday life. But when you talk about spiritual enlightenment through prayer, then the prayer has a much deeper significance. When a yogi retires from the affairs of life and enters into silence, he remains within his own self, uniting with or trying to unite with his own being. That is also prayer. You might have read that Christ used to take his disciples into seclusion to pray. Now, what was their prayer? It was not a prayer that we sing in the temples or the church. Christ was actually taking his disciples into retreat to practise communication with the inner self. That was the prayer.

While many people believe that prayer means asking for something, you should understand the other meaning of prayer as not asking for something, but communicating with one's own inner being. Everybody cannot do this form of prayer, because they do not know the way. You can try it, but you may not be able to do it. You may succeed intellectually, but intellectual communication is of no significance. Inner communication is not a process of thinking: Let me just close my eyes and think that I'm with God and I am one with God. That is hypnosis, and that is what most people have been doing. Prayer is not conducted through the medium of the mind, whether you are asking for something or communicating with the inner self.

161

Ultimately, prayer is purely an expression of inner feelings, not sentiments. In bhakti, this feeling is called bhavana, which means the 'expression of your inner being'. The expression of your inner being is called devotion. The expression of the mind, emotion or passion is called sentiment. Therefore, the saints and sages have composed prayers, because communication with the inner self is extremely difficult. Actually, they did not compose the prayers; rather, they were revealed to them in higher states of consciousness.

It is the poets and ordinary men like us who have composed the prayers. In the beginning an aspirant has to take the help of these prayers to conduct his own feelings. However, there comes a moment when words fail and language is of no avail; expressions become mute and there is a total feeling. During moments of extreme suffering or joy, the means of expression fails and you do not know what to say or how to express it. When the dualities of consciousness are about to fuse into one another and you are in absolute communion, then these external prayers will not have any significance or relevance.

So now, let me say that prayer has two forms, one in which you express and one in which you don't. In the first, words and feelings are the forms of prayer. In the second, silence is a form of prayer. When you pray with words and feelings, you should pray in all love, humility and confidence. The prayer mixed with emotion and feeling is at once heard and fulfilled. Do not simply utter Sanskrit slokas with your intellect. Pray to Him like a child. Remember any event of your life, when your prayer was heard and fulfilled. Recollect the state of your mind at that time. Pray with perfect faith that He will listen to your prayer and fulfil it. Never pray for trifling things. Pray to Him for strength to face life. Pray for viveka, vairagya, love and service. Pray for purity of mind. Pray for meditation and celibacy. Pray for Him to come face to face and reveal knowledge to you. Have faith that He is the kind and all merciful Father, and that He will give all you ask for.

Pray for understanding His merciful acts and loving blessings. Pray to Him for quick spiritual evolution. Pray to Him with all your love, faith and emotion.

7. Dasya bhava – servant

Dasya means servant; wherever you are, be a servant of God. Mirabai always used to pray, "Please Lord, keep me as your servant." A servant just has to do his duty. He does not have be anxious or worried, he has no accountability, no responsibility. He just has to carry out his orders without thinking too much. If the Lord gives an order, you do it. Then things become easy, because you don't have to think or struggle. When it is God's will, everything is easy. When it is man's will, then you have to struggle. The Upanishads say, '*Aham Brahmasmi*' – I am God. But if this is true, why are you so unhappy? Why do you cry? Why are you in ignorance? Why are you subject to tamas, rajas and sattwa?

The duty of a servant, *sevak dharma*, is to do whatever the master orders. If he asks you to sweep the filth, you must do it. A servant does not have a choice of his own. I do whatever I do as an errand for Him; it is His work that I do. If I do japa, it is because He has asked me to do it. If I don't do it, it is because He has asked me not to do it. If I meditate, it is because He wants that, not because it is my wish. Of course, I like to meditate and to do japa, but I will not do these spiritual things simply because I want to, for then my ego comes in. There comes a point when the servant has to sacrifice every personal choice. I have made up my mind to do all that He asks of me. In this way I have discovered my relationship with God, and it fits my personality exactly. Now, my life is an expression of service to Him.

It is not possible to be God's servant and a guru; these two cannot coexist. The servant is always a servant. When that servant becomes the guru of someone else, then he cannot remain the servant of his master. The servant cannot be the master and serve the master at the same time. He has to leave one of the two posts. If he has to remain as guru,

163

then he has to resign from service to God. He has to render his resignation. I am not prepared to do that, because I find service to God more beneficial than being a guru.

You will discover that being the servant of God brings spontaneity into your life. Even if you do not want to love God, you will love Him. Even if you don't want to surrender, you will have to do it. Even if you don't want anything from Him, He will give you everything. Service to God brings spontaneous blessings. You don't have to ask God for anything in a church, temple or prayer hall, because you are the servant. Your duty is to serve, not to ask. Even prayer is not the dharma of a servant. The servant has no choice. His only duty and dharma is to carry out the orders of his master. The master gives you an order and you carry it out. Why should the servant pray to the master? There is no need for prayer.

All disciples should live like servants, but they like to live like masters. They do what they want, not what I want, so there is no spontaneity of relationship. I have a spontaneous relationship with Swami Niranjan, and I want to have this relationship with everyone. Similarly, God wants spontaneity in His relationship with us. When He gives you pain, accept it. When you are in pain, you say it is due to a curse or to bad karma, because you feel that only good things are the blessings of God. Pain is a curse as well as a blessing of God.

For sixty or seventy long years, I was always thinking about what God could be like. Was He knowledge or wisdom? Ultimately, I stopped questioning. I have given up the quest and established a relationship with Him. I have given up looking for the One whom I have been searching for and investigating since childhood. I do not enquire anymore. Now I have decided, whoever You are, I am Your servant. Though I have not seen You, my Master, I am Your servant. I will do whatever You tell me. If You tell me to clean the toilets, I will do it. If You give me the status of Brahma, fine. 'I am the chariot; You are the charioteer.' This should be the attitude of everyone.

After years and years of searching and hard work, I have discovered my relationship with God, who He is to me and who am I to Him. This has been the major accomplishment of my life. I found the answer, and this happened because the ego melted. I realized that whatever I am was His benediction. What I did was His will. What I am is because of Him. What I did was because of Him. What I received was because of Him. In the future, whatever happens will be according to His wish. It was only after the dissolution of ego that the path became slightly visible. When this ego was present, I presumed that I was the doer and I had to suffer the consequences accordingly. If you are the doer, you have to be accountable for what you do, for the good as well as the bad. It is not a one-day affair, or a one-day game.

Right from the beginning of my life, as a disciple of Swami Sivananda, then as a *parivrajaka* (wandering sannyasin), as an administrator of Bihar School of Yoga and as a preacher of yoga, I always had the feeling that there was someone guiding, coaxing, helping and inspiring me. That idea was latent somewhere in me. So I have come to the conclusion that I am His servant, which is dasya bhava. All along, somewhere in the depths of my heart, I have always had the feeling that someone is asking me to do this and I am doing it. Someone is inspiring me to speak and I am speaking. That bhavana, that attitude of a servant, was lurking somewhere in the depths of my personality, and now it has become very clear to me.

8. Sakhya – friend

Sakhya upasana is worship of the Lord as one's true friend, and developing the qualities of a true friend within oneself. The true friend moulds himself, according to the likes and wishes of his friend, and acts as per his wishes, rather than his own. True friendship is free from selfishness and personal desires. The true friend always thinks and acts for the welfare and support of his friend, and never begs from him or compromises with him. Similarly, the upasaka, who worships the Lord as sakhya, never begs from Him or compromises Him through thought, speech or action.

The sakhya is always eager to please the Lord and to take up any work of the Lord, leaving aside even the most urgent and pressing work of his own. Assuming an attitude of neglect towards personal work, he totally concerns himself with the friendship and needs of the Lord. He thinks of the Lord as his closest companion, and always looks forward to meeting Him through meditation, prayers, and all forms of service. In this way friendship is sublimated into a spiritual relationship.

God is microcosmic as well as macrocosmic. So, if you wish to worship God as a friend you must demolish the personal boundaries, which limit your associations, and become a friend to all without exception. This path is also known as *mitra sadhana*, which involves understanding, compassion and caring for all. Be a friend to all. You must be able to consider the whole world as your friend and neighbour. Only a person with a very open mind can do this.

9. Atma nivedan – self-surrender

Total self-surrender is known as atma nivedan, yielding completely to God; it is also called *atma samarpan*. Your faith in God should be so deep that you submerge yourself fully in Him. In the *Ramacharitamanas*, it says: "By the systematic practice of navadha bhakti, you can reach a point of total self-surrender." Before self-surrender can take place, the entire personality has to be rearranged. Self-surrender is not just the thought that you want to surrender; it is an inborn quality. For surrender you require innocence, but you have lost this purity. The heart, mind and intellect have become tough and rigid. In order to soften them, satsang is necessary for a sustained period of time; satsang is a very powerful tool.

Surrender is spontaneous. In order to rise, you have to use energy, force and strain. But to fall down, you do not need to use strength; instead you have to let go of yourself and just drop down. The more worried you are about surrender, the less likely are you to attain it. Don't worry about surrender, worry only about satsang, bhakti, and the discovery of your relationship with God. The test of surrender is whether or not you are able to manage it. In surrender, everything is not beautiful, comfortable and pleasing; it is a trying situation when God tries your true nature. Kabir has very aptly remarked: "His is the house of love, not the house of your aunt. Only he can enter here, who takes off his head and carries it in his hands."

Surrender is totally dependent on God's grace. You can go on practising yoga and meditation but nothing will bring you close to him. Ultimately, you will realize that all is dependent on God's grace. How can you surrender to God? First you have to know exactly what God means, and for that you have to ask Him. You have to pray to Him, "God, show me the path and be kind enough to lead me onto it. I have no mental, physical or moral strength, unless You bless me." So even the form in which God's grace is shown to you, the form in which He is revealed to you or inspires you, should be left to the Lord.

Both destiny and self-effort are useless in comparison to God's grace. The seers say to receive that grace requires complete faith in God. Let your faith in God be so deep that you lose yourself in Him in such a way that sorrow is transformed into happiness. Despair goes and hope comes. Sorrow and pain are like day and night; they come and go, continually changing their positions like a rotating wheel. This is a fact. Hence, let there be some changes in your life to allow the experience God's grace, the ultimate divine grace. Everyone must try to obtain it.

Surrender is the experience of conceding your crude ego. This ego is the basis of your individuality. When you go to the religious places, the temple or church, you pray and also speak a few lines of surrender, "I am yours, all is yours, Your will be done." This is verbal surrender. Real surrender takes place when you withdraw your ego, which is standing

167

in-between you and your divinity, in-between you and your guru, or in-between yourself and your Self. In order to learn how to surrender, you must have a guru. First practise the primary lessons in surrender under the guidance of the guru, and then you can practise surrender to your divinity.

When you surrender yourself to your divinity, then life becomes happy and glorious. Happiness or unhappiness, joy or sorrow, whether your wishes are fulfilled or not you will not care, because you have surrendered yourself to the will of the divine and whatever He brings into your life is welcome. Everybody wants life to be nice, everybody wants happiness and good health. Nobody wants a bad life, nobody wants to be unhappy or unwell. But why should you only want to have your own choice? Why should you choose? Let Him choose. There is a higher reality, a greater law, a universal law. This universal law is responsible for all events, for every experience in your life: your body, your birth, your very existence.

Everything is an expression of that universal law and that universal law is a mighty law. It is an intelligent law, an omniscient law that controls each and every aspect of your life. That realization must dawn. You have seen that from

time to time, nations, races and tribes have experienced this. There are people who have surrendered themselves, who are fully devoted to spiritual life, who are related to a guru, and are trying to establish the union with their inner self. It is for those people that the act of surrender at every level is very important.

14

Use of Symbols

According to Patanjali, you must have a symbol of your choice in order to progress in meditation. In upasana it is said that you must select a form for worship, which you can easily love, and which draws your consciousness towards it like a magnet. You can hold your mind on such a symbol without any difficulty. Many people take the sky or light as their symbol, but they find it very difficult to hold the consciousness there, because one needs something which attracts the attention in order to hold the consciousness. Anything can be used as a symbol, but if the symbol is properly chosen, your upasana will succeed earlier.

Everyone has his or her own symbol, and you must find yours. You can select any image: a circle, a triangle, a rose, a fire flame or a human form, but once it is decided upon, the image should not be changed, even if other forms superimpose upon it. The form you decide upon is the basis for the manifestation of your consciousness. It is a powerful archetype that draws out the deep experiences within your unconscious mind but there is no direct relationship between the symbol and your personality. The personality is one thing and the symbol is entirely different. The purpose of the symbol is to awaken the inner spirit, the inner awareness, so that the external mind will be fused and united with it.

During worship or meditation always try to develop the awareness of the one, unchanging symbol. When this form

169

comes to you in the form of imagination or an idea, it means that your awareness is not yet clear; there is some kind of disturbance in the mind. When you are able to see that image as if it is a conscious dream, it means your awareness is coming to the point of consolidation or crystallization. If the form continues in the plane of your consciousness like a vivid dream in colour, it means your consciousness is completely disassociated and is functioning independently on the borderline of knowledge.

Eventually you will be able to see the object as clearly as you see an object with your eyes open. This is the experience of expanded consciousness, or *turya*, the fourth dimension, which is the ultimate aim of upasana. Through worship and meditation that dimension of consciousness is achieved in which you can see your consciousness as clearly and as real as you see the things outside. In the yogic texts this is called spiritual vision or *darshan*, which means to see an object without the medium of the senses, without thinking, without feeling, without touching. When you have this vision, when you experience this fourth dimension of your consciousness, then you have completed your upasana, and you are having the higher experience of 'I am all'.

Shivalingam

The shivalingam is the symbol of supreme consciousness in the causal form. The term lingam represents the causal body, a state of existence that is invisible and unseen, but is there nonetheless. The cosmic or total consciousness cannot be comprehended; it is abstract, invisible and infinite, but it can be experienced. The ultimate reality is incomprehensible to anyone, even a saint or a yogi, much less an ordinary person. If you want to comprehend that ultimate reality there is only one way; you have to become that. It is not possible otherwise. That consciousness which cannot be comprehended by any means or by anyone, should be comprehended by its symbol, the shivalingam.

170

The shivalingam is a black, oval shaped stone that is not carved or man made. It is found exactly in that shape, and ranges in size from a few inches to about fifteen feet in height. It is brought from the banks of the Narmada River, which originates in central India and flows towards the west, ultimately merging in the Arabian Sea. The shivalingam is an ancient symbol of an event that triggered man's consciousness and brought him from the instinctive level to the state of human being.

In this physical body there are twelve centres which are considered to be important points of concentration for the improvement and awakening of your consciousness. Of these twelve points, three are most important. One is *mooladhara chakra* at the base of the spine; the second is *ajna chakra* at the top of the spine, behind the eyebrow centre, and the third is *sahasrara chakra*, the cosmic brain, at the crown of the head. These three points are considered to be the most important manifestations of Shiva.

The form of Shiva in mooladhara chakra is that of a smoky grey, oval shaped lingam, which has no illumination. The second centre of the shivalingam is ajna chakra, where it is black in colour. The third centre is sahasrara chakra, at the top of the brain, which is said to be the crystal or illumined shivalingam. This concept of Shiva has inspired Hindus for thousands and thousands of years to follow the path from gross to subtle, subtle to causal, causal to transcendental. Shiva represents the spiritual evolution in man, not the evolution of matter. The shivalingam, therefore, relates to the highest consciousness within you, which is trying to manifest.

Throughout India, in every Shiva temple, you will find an oval shaped stone, which is black in colour, never white. This stone is worshipped and concentrated upon in order to awaken the twelve centres in your body. Shivalingams may be *chala*, movable, or *achala*, immovable. The chala lingams may be kept in the shrine of one's home for worship or prepared temporarily for worship with materials like clay, dough, rice or sand, and dispensed with after the worship.

171

They may also be worn on the body as *ishtalingam*. The achala lingams are those made of black stone, which are installed in temples.

In India, we also have the crystal shivalingam, which is called *sphatik lingam*. This sphatik, or crystal lingam, is only found in a few places, and then it is not moved, but a temple is built around it. Why is crystal precious? It has been scientifically proven that crystal has many effects on matter and on the brain; it is not just a simple stone. Crystal grasps all the sound vibrations. Any sound vibration passing through the sound matrix will hit the crystal objects, whether a small crystal ball, a crystal mala, crystal beads, or a crystal lingam. When you expose yourself to the sphatik lingam, something begins to happen in your brain and consciousness.

This is exactly what happened millions and millions of years ago. When your ancestors confronted the large rock of crystal, their consciousness began to explode. That great explosion or awakening, which took place in them, happened on account of the psychic images that they began to see within the mind. Many people who take psychedelic drugs see these images. With the eyes open or closed, you can see them, in meditation you can see them, and in dreams you can see them. Those images that you see relate to the movement of an inner consciousness.

In Samkhya philosophy and in Vedanta, the causal body is known as the *linga sharira*, the subtle body, which is there but you can't see it. When you see the sphatik lingam, it explodes the images from the causal body or the unconscious within you, and which were in your ancestors also. With that leap the human evolution started. With that leap, you began to know that you exist. Worship of and meditation on the shivalingam is considered very important, because it can explode the inner source of awareness, where infinite knowledge is hidden and where the possibility of the great evolution of man is stored.

In India, there are thousands of temples, where this oval shaped shivalingam is worshipped, but of all these, twelve

172

are considered as jyotirlingams. The word *jyoti* means 'light' and jyotirlingam means illumined lingam. These are not Narmada lingams; they are crystal lingams. Eleven of these are situated at different places in India and the twelfth is in Nepal. Every jyotirlingam has a special name. The name of the jyotirlingam in Nepal is *Pashupatinath*, which means 'Lord of the beast'. The names of the others are Somnatheshwar, Mallikarjuna, Mahakaleshwar, Omkareshwar, Kedareshwar, Bheemashankar, Vishveshwar, Trymbakeshwar, Baidyanatheshwar, Nageshwar, Gushmeshwar and Rameshwar. Each year, hundreds and thousands of people go on pilgrimages to these places.

There is an important celebration in the month of March, on the fourteenth day of the dark fortnight, called Shivaratri, or the night of Shiva. This is an undeclared holiday in India. Nobody goes to the office. The whole day everybody fasts; they don't even take a drop of water or a drink of tea. They only repeat the mantra *Om Namah Shivaya*. In the evening they go to the temple, where worship of the shivalingam goes on all night. The people sit close to the lingam and many priests and Brahmins go on chanting the thousand names of Shiva, one after another, throughout the night. Above the lingam is a copper vessel with tiny holes in the bottom from which water continuously drips onto the shivalingam. All night long the water drips and drips, and the people meditate.

Shaligram

The shaligram is important to the worshippers of Vishnu, just as the shivalingam is to the worshippers of Shiva. Although pronounced shaligram, the correct Sanskrit word is *shalagrama*, which is one of the names of Lord Vishnu. The origin of this word is traced to a remote village called Shalagrami near the source of the Gandaki River in Nepal. Vishnu is known there as Shalagraman. This village is a pilgrimage centre, and the stones used to prepare the image of Vishnu came to be called shalagrama. This stone is also found at another place called Muktinath, situated at a high altitude in Nepal.

Shaligrams are natural formations, which are spheroid in shape, smooth to the touch, and black, red or mixed in color. Each shaligram has a natural hole at the top, inside of which spirals can be seen, reminiscent of the discus. There are many types and qualities of shaligram bearing such symbols of Vishnu as the conch, lotus, chakra and garland, but the authentic shaligram must also have a small golden ring on the top.

Lord Vishnu is said to reside in the shaligram, which bears his emblems. It is, therefore, a highly venerated symbol of worship which is handed down in the family from generation to generation. It is not an object to be purchased or sold. No blemish is attached to the shaligram. Even if it is broken, defaced, burnt in fire or otherwise disfigured, it does no harm. The worship of shaligram does not call for elaborate pooja, not even mantras or sacred water is required. By the worship of shaligram, all the sins accrued in crores of births are eradicated.

Shaligrams are never installed in temples, but are worshipped in the home privately. Once a shaligam is kept in the home, its worship, although simple, becomes obligatory. Possessing and worshipping shaligram will confer certain permanent benefits. It is not only a spiritual symbol, but also manifests mystical and magnetic powers.

Conch

The *shankha* or conch is also a natural formation derived from the shell of an aquatic animal, and highly revered as a symbol of worship. Since the conch is held in the hands of Lord Vishnu, it has become an object of worship. Whatever is held in God's hands becomes sacred. The conch symbolizes the cosmic space, whose attribute is sound. It is believed that the sound of the conch kills certain bacteria, keeps away poisonous creatures and evil spirits, and averts earthquake and other natural calamities.

In ancient times the shankha was blown during warfare to signal the beginning and end of each daily battle and it was also blown triumphantly to signify victory. Even today, you will hear the resounding note of the conch rending the air when it is blown at the time of sandhya worship (sunrise and sunset), and when it is used to initiate or end any form of worship or chanting performed in the home. The shanka is also blown at various times during the daily poojas performed in temple worship. During the abhisheka worship the conch is used as a vessel for pouring water, as the water in God's abode is considered sacred.

There are many types of conches. The *dakshinamukhi*, south-faced or reverse coiled conch, is important in tantric rituals. Nobody can keep the dakshinamukhi conch except *parama-hamsas* (self-realized sannyasins), without the full ritual worship and matching of the planetary constellations and zodiac signs. The people who have them in their homes might have inherited them from forefathers who were tantric sadhakas.

Swastika

The word *swasti* means 'auspicious', and the swastika is a symbol of auspiciousness, denoting a good or propitious event or existence. It is also worshipped as a symbol of Vishnu, Ganesha, the Sun and light. Generally, each and every religious ceremony starts with the drawing of a swastika. It is also drawn at the holding area where pilgrims gather before being admitted to the place of pilgrimage and on walls of temples. The swastika represents the wheel of the world, which turns eternally around a fixed and unchanging centre, God.

Lotus

The lotus is a spiritual flower and represents purity. Each of the gods and goddesses hold a lotus in their hand. Sri Lakshmi stands on a lotus, and Brahma arises from a lotus. Water does not wet the petals of the lotus flower, although it sits on top of the water. In this way, the lotus symbolizes the spiritual attitude of a devotee, who remains in the world, but

175

is unaffected by it. As the sun rises, the lotus flower gradually opens. Similarly, as the spiritual knowledge increases, the aspirant gradually blooms within. The psychic centres within the human body are also referred to as lotuses, and in this context each of these lotuses refers to a different expression of the kundalini shakti.

Angavati

There are many popular, auspicious diagrams that are seen in the homes during worship. These diagrams are often drawn on houses or shops in a particular white powder called *rangoli*. They are also painted on the walls of temples and engraved on copper plates, which are worshipped daily along with other images of gods. These diagrams include, chakra, swastika, lotus, and various yantras. *Angavati* are said to be symbols of different deities, and their worship pleases that particular deity, who in turn bestows rewards on the worshipper. The symbols are an *anga*, or part of the deity, which cannot be separated. Therefore, worship of these diagrams is called angavati upasana.

Kavacha

Kavacha refers to a sectarian mark, consisting of lines, curves, circles, spots and designs, which are painted on various parts of the body. The use of these marks brings the aspirant under the protection of a particular deity. The kavacha is said to protect the upasaka against negative forces. There is also a practice of wearing a stone, a piece of metal or a piece of paper, charged with mantras. The one Brahman is here invoked by different names in order to protect different parts of the body, so that the aspirant may utter the mantras of his ishta devata.

Mudra

Mudra is the ritual of manual gestures. There are 108 hand mudras used for the various acts performed during worship. The five fingers of the hand represent the five great elements

176

and their contact with each other pleases the respective deity of the elements, who accepts the worship. Mudra gives pleasure to the devatas. Different mudras are used in the worship of Shiva, Vishnu, Ganesha, Devi and Durga. Mudras are psychic, emotional, devotional and aesthetic gestures, which give moksha. Yogic mudras are attitudes of energy flow, intended to link the individual pranic force with the universal or cosmic force. Dancing postures also include mudras. The method of worshipping the gods through dance mudras is an effort of man to attain moksha. Nataraja is a form of Shiva, who is pleased by dance.

Yantra and mandala

Yantra and mandala are two types of visual symbols, used in worship and meditation. The yantra is a geometrical diagram, like a triangle, intersecting triangles, hexagon and circle. Yantras were known to all cultures in the past. They are very powerful, universal forces by which you can identify and communicate with the Divine. Just as you have radioactive fields and electromagnetic fields, so you have yantra fields to which you can connect through worship or meditation.

Space cannot be defined by less than three lines, so the triangle is considered to be the first form to emerge out of creation. Thus the triangle is known as *moola trikona* or the root triangle. The downward-pointing triangle represents the root matrix of creation or prakriti, and the upward-pointing triangle represents purusha or consciousness. The intersection of a downward and upward pointing triangle is often found in a yantra, representing both consciousness and energy.

The circle represents the cycle of timelessness, eternity, where there is no beginning and no end, and it implies the process of birth and death, as an eternal cycle of events. The square is the substratum on which the yantra rests, and denotes the physical or terrestrial world, which ultimately has to be transcended. The whole visual concept of the yantra, although symbolic, forms a pathway from the outer physical experience to the innermost chambers of creation and existence.

Mandalas may be two-dimensional or three-dimensional. A photo or picture is a two-dimensional mandala, for example, the picture of your ishta devata or the photo of your guru. The drawing of a tree, a mountain, a trident, a flower, the full moon or the sun, is a pictorial mandala. The second type of mandala is three-dimensional, like a statue. One who worships or meditates upon a murti or statue is not an idolater. The spiritual consciousness, the Atman, has no name and no form. At the same time, if you want to evolve spiritually, you have to create a symbol of that formlessness.

That formless and nameless consciousness has to be explained in terms of a symbol. That symbol is called a murti and it is three-dimensional. When you concentrate on a particular murti, then it is easier for the mind to transcend itself, because the mind has certain special characteristics. The three-dimensional murti can help the mind to concentrate, transform or restructure itself as quickly as possible. Indian philosophy believes that the ultimate principle is formless, nameless and timeless, but, at the same time, if you have to restructure and transform your mind, you need a base. These symbols have a very deep effect on the mind, and when used for worship or meditation, they provide both a base and a way of going into your Self.

15

Mantra Upasana

Mantra is a major aspect of upasana. Mantra is a word or combination of words, which connect the upasaka with higher dimensions of consciousness. Sound is the primordial form of energy, the original substance and basis of the whole universe. This universe with its solar systems, its invisible fields of energy, is an expansion of sound energy. This sound is known as 'mantra' in yoga, and in the *Bible* it is called 'the word'. Any religion or sect may use mantra, but it is neither religious nor sectarian. It is not Hindu, Christian, Islamic or Jewish. Mantra is a form of sound vibration, and sound has different stages of manifestation.

Every type of sound from the primordial to the manifest state undergoes transformation, changes in frequency, velocity, and so on. Mantra is one of the manifestations of primordial energy. Each letter and syllable of the mantra penetrates deep down into the various levels of your consciousness. Mantra is the science of sound vibration. Sound is an explosive force. Even the gross form of sound can completely destroy a large rock. As sound attains higher frequency, the mind also attains a higher frequency. With the evolution of sound, the mind also evolves.

Therefore, the mantra that you receive from your guru is an important force and element in the process of your spiritual experience. The constant repetition of a mantra has an effect on your consciousness. While repeating the mantra you should

179

try not to concentrate the mind or fight with the mind. You must ignore the mind, because there is no such thing as mind. As you are aware of the mantra and go on repeating it, you will find that everything settles into a capsule of experience. This experience is born of mantra; it is not a quality of mind.

The hallucinations and imaginations that you experience are the qualities of the mind. An experience of kundalini or psychic upliftment is not a product of mind. You will have to ignore the idiosyncrasies of your mind: mind is passions, ambitions, jealousy, fears, insecurities and depressions. Let them be! Do not worry at all about the mind. That disassociation can be attained only by mantra. Through continual practice of the mantra, your awareness gradually becomes disassociated from the mental neurosis and obsessions. This is the meaning of mantra. The word mantra literally means 'by the repetition of which you are freed', you are disassociated, by the contemplation on which you become free. Therefore, mantra should be understood in this light.

When you practise mantra, in the beginning there are certain methods which you have to adopt for some time: practising mantra with the mala, with the breath in various chakras or in the path of sushumna. Sometimes you pronounce it audibly, increasing or decreasing the speed, and sometimes you repeat mentally. There are many ways of practising mantra. The best way is to repeat it audibly, then whispering, then mentally. Finally, practise it with your natural breath, deep breath and deeper breath. These are the four main ways of practising mantra.

The audible repetition of mantra has greater velocity and less frequency. When you practise mantra with your natural breath, it has greater frequency and less velocity. The greater the frequency, the greater the strength, willpower and vision it gives to your consciousness. There are many kinds of mantras, such as universal or personal; some are long, some medium, some short. Important universal mantras include: Aum, Gayatri, Mahamrityunjaya and *Ramacharitamanas*, which is a collection of mantras.

Aum (Om)

Meditation on the mantra Aum is one of the most important vedic and upanishadic upasanas. Aum is the first mantra to appear in the *Rig Veda*. According to the vedic tradition, the mantra Aum is reserved for sannyasins, and the Gayatri mantra is for householders. The mantra Aum is very powerful, and if you practice it as a sadhana, your whole mind will be consumed without difficulty. Therefore, the mantra Aum is designated for sannyasins, who have transcended the obligations of society.

The mantra Aum is a combination of three sounds, four *matras* (units of time taken to pronounce a vowel) and four levels of awareness. The three sounds represented by the mantra Aum are 'A', 'U', and 'M', which represent the three dimensions of consciousness. 'A' represents the waking state, 'U' the dream state, and 'M' the unconscious state. The *Mandukya Upanishad* says that the first stage of consciousness is objective, the second stage subjective, and the third stage unconscious. These three states are known as *jagrat, swapna* and *sushupti*; waking, dreaming and sleeping

While chanting Aum, you pass from one stage of consciousness into another, because the letter 'A' represents the conscious mind, 'U' the subconscious mind and 'M' the unconscious mind. The mind undergoes transformation in the states of waking, dreaming and sleeping. Awareness of the external objects through the medium of the mind and senses is known as the waking state. When the mind is devoid of the association of the senses, but is aware of the objects already perceived, that is known as the dream state. In the dream state you can perceive the objects subjectively, because you have already perceived them in your waking experience. But when the mind is not cognizing subjectively or objectively, it enters the causal state, which is called deep sleep.

These three states of the mind represent your veritable existence. The whole universe is classified into these three planes of existence, so Aum represents the total existence. It is not just a sound, which has been picked up at random, nor is it a holy word that represents any particular religion. The mantra Aum is a formula, an equation. The letter 'A' represents the objective, perceptible world, 'U' the subjective, mental world, and 'M' the unmanifest world.

Aum is the equation of the entire creation: the creation that was, that is, and that shall be forever more; and also what is beyond these three. Creation has to be understood in terms of time. Space and object must exist in time; time, space and object are inter-related factors. One of them cannot exist without the other. These three again are categories of the mind, and mind cannot exist without these three. If there were no time, no space and no object, there would be no mind. And conversely, if there is no mind, there is no time, space or object.

When you think about things, when you feel hatred, love, passion and compassion, that is not mind; these are the manifestation of mind, *chitta vritti*. Manifestation of mind is not the mind. Very few people have been able to see the mind at any level, and those who can, either can go insane or attain *jivanmukti*, liberation. Mind is that powerful substance of consciousness, which is formless and abstract. You can only see its patterns: *raga, dwesha, kama, kroda*, anger, passion, greed, hatred, but these are not the mind. The *Mandukya Upanishad* states that the consciousness manifests on the lower plane, in three stages. Sensory perception is a manifestation of consciousness; dreams are a manifestation of consciousness, and profound sleep is also a manifestation of consciousness. When I say consciousness, I mean the Atman.

So, Aum is a combination of three sounds, 'A', 'U', and 'M'. These three letters or sounds represent the three periods of time, the three stages of individual manifestation, and the three dimensions of intelligence. However, the Upanishads say that these three letters alone do not constitute Aum. There is a fourth sound, but that sound is formless and beyond the three dimensions. This fourth level of experience is referred to as *anahad nada*, or soundless sound. Here there is no sound, there is no vibration. It is an experience beyond time, space and object. It is the experience of consciousness itself, and there is no duality.

The waking, sleeping and dreaming states represent the gross manifest individual consciousness. These three states of the individual self are known as relative existence; they are not absolute or ultimate. They represent the creation or the manifest nature. But there is an unmanifest dimension as well, which is known as turiya, the highest dimension of creation. As such, in the Vedas, Upanishads and other books, Aum represents the *nada,* or the sound principle.

The written symbol of Aum has three curves: ॐ These curves scientifically represent the three factors responsible for the perceptible universe. There is an upper curve, a lower curve, and a curve that is attached to the centre of the two looking like the tail of a monkey. These are the three curves that represent the totality of the cause of creation. These are the three letters and equal three *matras.* The fourth matra, which is transcendental and has nothing to do with the universe, with time, space and object, is apart from these three curves. That is what you call the new moon and the star over it. But it is not a new moon; it is a curve, losing itself.

When you meditate on Aum, you begin to lose the area of mundane awareness. As you go deeper and deeper into meditation, you lose certain levels of your mind. That loss of a level of awareness is represented by what you call the fading moon; it is the fading shape of a curve. The fourth curve has been fading and fading, and looks like a little curve. On the top of that curve is a point, and this point is called bindu. In fact, the whole universe comes from the bindu. Something happens at the level of the bindu, and the whole creation manifests. Here, the bindu means the totality of awareness, focused, concentrated and isolated from every realm of experience.

In meditation you will not think of name and form. You will forget your surroundings; you will forget your past and your future, and you will even forget that you are meditating.

183

When everything is completely removed from the area of awareness, when nothing exists except the meditator, when even the meditator is eliminated, and when the object of meditation is also eliminated, pure awareness remains. There is neither manifest awareness nor unmanifest awareness; there is neither awareness of the meditator nor awareness of the meditation. The point of bindu represents no awareness.

You can meditate on the mantra Aum mentally or you can repeat the sound aloud. You can chant Aum in many ways: with a short *A* – transiting through *Uuu* and long *Mmmmmm*; or with a long *AAAaa* and a short *Mmm*; or by intoning all the three sounds equally. These are the three important ways of producing the Aum sound. When you want to manifest a sound, you have to open your mouth. And when you want to stop the sound, you have to close your mouth. When you open your mouth it is Aaaa. When you close your mouth the sound produced is Mmmmmm. So, from the production of sound to the cessation of sound, there is a third process called *Uuuu* in-between. If you produce the sound *A* and want to close it – *M*, the sound *U* comes in-between only partially, for a short time.

Gayatri mantra

The Gayatri mantra is an important aspect of Surya upasana. Gayatri is referred to as the Mother of the Vedas and this mantra occurs in the *Rig Veda*, the oldest written literature in the library of mankind. So human beings have been chanting the Gayatri mantra for a long time. There is no restriction for this mantra, because its effects are benign. Children are initiated into the Gayatri mantra at the age of eight and the practices of pranayama in a ritual called *upanayana samskara*. This ceremony is obligatory for all Hindu children, and is performed at the critical juncture when the child is about to leave infancy behind and enter into childhood.

Gayatri mantra represents the cosmic prana and is practiced in two different ways. One form of Gayatri is used for mantra yoga; the other is utilized for pranayama, because the syllables of the Gayatri mantra correspond to the correct length of the breath. The Gayatri mantra contains 24 syllables, which are repeated in mantra yoga as follows:

Om Bhur Bhuvah Svah Tat Savitur Varenyam
Bhargo Devasya Dheemahi Dheeyo Yo Nah Prachodayat.

For incorporation during pranayama, the repetition of the mantra is a little different:

Om Bhur, Om Bhuvah, Om Svah, Om Mahah, Om Janah,
Om Tapah, Om Satyam, Om Tat Savitur Varenyam Bhargo
Devasya Dheemahi Dheeyo Yo Nah Prachodayat.
Om Apo Jyotirasya Mritah Brahmah Bhur Bhuvah Svah Om.

Those who practice pranayama should remember this mantra and adjust the breath, according to the mental repetition. The inhalation, retention and exhalation must be adjusted on the basis of the Gayatri mantra. For elementary pranayama, the repetition of one Gayatri mantra represents the duration of one inhalation. During breath retention, you should repeat the mantra twice. While exhaling, you should repeat the mantra twice. For higher pranayama the ratio is 1:6:4.

Gayatri is not just a formula or a combination of words. All throughout the Vedas and Upanishads, time and again, it is said, "Aum is nada; Gayatri is prana". Gayatri is created from Aum, and Gayatri manifests in two stages. In the first stage of Gayatri there is only a mention of three states of individual self. The three states of individual self are known as relative existence. These three states of individual self are not absolute and not ultimate. They represent the creation or the manifest universe, but there is an unmanifest universe as well. This unmanifest universe is known as turiya, or the highest dimension of creation. As such, in the Vedas as well as in the Upanishads and other books, Aum represents the nada of the sound principle. In the order of creation, this sound is further developed. The developed state of Aum mantra is known as Gayatri.

185

Gayatri mantra represents what we call the cosmic, total or original prana. *Bhur, Bhuvah, Svah* represent the waking, dreaming and sleeping, states of the individual self. But in the later stage of Gayatri, not three but seven states are mentioned. These are the seven planes of individual consciousness, starting from the gross and culminating with the subtlest. The practice of this mantra invokes the seven stages of individual consciousness in this life, and in the after life. This means that the individual self can go on ascending from the lowest possible rung of manifestation to the highest possible rung, which is the seventh or absolute state: *Bhur, Bhuvah, Svah, Mahah, Janah, Tapah, Satyam.*

Mahamrityunjaya mantra

Mahamrityunjaya is the great healing mantra that gives protection from all negative forces and can change one's destiny. The Sanskrit word *maha* means 'great', *mritu* means 'death', *jaya* means 'victory' and mantra is a word of great power. The Mahamrityunjaya mantra consists of 34 sound syllables, as follows:

> *Om Tryambakam Yajaamahe*
> *Sugandhim Pushtivardhanam;*
> *Urvaarukamiva Bandhanaat*
> *Mrityormuksheeya Maamritaat.*

"We worship the three-eyed one (Lord Shiva) who is fragrant (in a state of supreme bliss), and who sustains all living beings. May he liberate us from (the eternal cycle of birth and) death. May he lead us to immortality, just as the cucumber is released from its bondage (the vine to which it is attached)."

The Mahamrityunjaya mantra is a potent combination of sounds that, if repeated with faith, dedication and perseverance over a period of time, leads to victory over the fear of death, and eventually to victory over death itself or moksha, realization of the immortal aspect of the Self. It is therefore known as a *moksha mantra*. It is stimulating and heating,

186

bestows longevity and cures illness. It wards off illness, evil forces, accidents and death, by creating a protective psychic shield around the practitioner. It is said to destroy sorrow and poverty, and to fulfil all of one's desires. Anyone who wishes to remove obstacles in life and overcome difficult situations should repeat this mantra regularly. If chanted a minimum of eleven times, the last thing before sleeping at night, it will ensure a better sleep and positive dreams.

The devata of the Mahamrityunjaya mantra is Rudra, who represents Lord Shiva in his fierce and destructive aspect. This mantra was revealed to the Rishi Vashishtha, while he was in a state of deep meditation. It is to be found in *Shree Rudra Prashna* (Rudra's Question), in the fifth chapter of the *Taittiriya Upanishad*, which belongs to the *Yajur Veda*. It is mentioned in many places in the *Rig, Yajur* and *Sama Vedas*. The mantra itself is actually comprised from mantras, which are found in the three Vedas: The *Rig Veda* (7th mandal, 59th chapter, 12th mantra), the *Yajur Veda* (3rd chapter, 60th mantra), and the *Atharva Veda* (14th mandal, 1st chapter, 17th mantra).

The Mahamrityunjaya mantra is also to be found in the Ayurvedic scriptures. In the *Prakriti Khanda* of the *Brahma Vaivarta Purana*, it has been said that Lord Krishna gave the knowledge of Mrityunjaya to the wife of Sage Angira. In the *Sati Khand* of the *Shiva Purana*, Shukracharya has called it *Mrita Sanjeevani Vidya* (the knowledge which leads to eternal life). Shukracharya expounded it to Sage Dadhichi.

The Mahamrityunjaya mantra can be chanted individually or in small groups. The chanting can be conducted by the family and friends at home, or in any other place where you wish to create a positive, protective and high-energy field. The mantra is also chanted during auspicious occasions, such as initiation ceremonies and havans. It is best to use your japa mala, but any other mala of your choice can also be used. The mantra is chanted 108 times in a constant, fixed rhythm. One person should lead the chanting by repeating the mantra once or twice to set the speed and swara, and then the others may join in. The person guiding the chanting should make sure the speed is kept constant.

Ramayana

Ramacharitamanas is beautiful description of the *Ramayana*, the life of Lord Rama. You don't have to spend long hours chanting or reading this text, but do it regularly. You shouldn't do it for two hours one day and then forget about it the next. Just read or chant a stanza or two, for five or ten minutes a day. Even if it takes one whole year to complete the text, what does it matter? Someone might ask, "Where is that person, who can be called good?" You will find the answer in this holy book. Make it a rule to read the *Ramayana* regularly, just as you make time for taking a bath, eating, sleeping or going to the bathroom.

In the same fashion, you should make time for chanting God's name and for self-study. You do not have to labour too much for this. You don't have to take on a big burden in your life. Many people take an overdose of God's name as though this will bring great benefit. No, you need not do that because for that you would have to change your lifestyle completely. Only saints can manage such an overdose. If you also require an overdose of eight to ten hours of worship, then change your lifestyle, your eating, drinking and sleeping habits.

Ramacharitamanas is chanted in the ashram every morning at four o'clock. Sometimes there are only one or two people chanting, and at other times the number increases to eight or ten or more. If you perform this reading in your home there is no need to gather a crowd. If the head of the house returns from work and goes to sleep after eating dinner, those who were at home all day should do the reading. Then God will dwell in your home. Shouldn't God dwell in your house? So, to invite God and to find a place for Him in your home, you should do the chanting of *Ramacharitamanas* regularly. To have God's power in your house, how much time do you need? Even ten or twenty minutes will do – read two stanzas only.

Everyone wants happiness, health and wealth. Those people who don't understand Hindi at all can still chant *Ramacharitamanas* every morning. What need is there to understand the *Ramayana*? Do you need to understand rasgulla? Do you need to understand samosa? There is simply no need to understand the *Ramayana* because it has not been written by a poet. A divine soul was invoked within the person who wrote the *Ramayana*. When any great power says something through you, when any great power writes through you, it is called mantra. When any great power makes you speak, it is called a blessing; otherwise we are all the same human beings.

On some days it may happen that only one person in the home chants *Ramayana*. On other days the chanting may happen with the full participation of family members. But don't stop the chanting, even for a single day, whether you understand the *Ramayana* or not, whether you like it or not, whether the mind is diverted, distracted or confused. You sleep just as you used to sleep, you eat just as you used to eat, so how can you miss doing the *Ramayana*? Everything goes on as usual through pain, distraction and depression. Do you miss any of your work? No, so why miss the *Ramayana*?

You say you don't get time, so take only ten or twenty minutes. Just read one verse. In every house, one person can be given this duty. Just as it is the duty of the wife to cook the food, the duty of the man to earn and the duty of the grandmother to sort the rice, similarly, the duty of reading one or two verses of the *Ramayana* should be given to one person. You will see that happiness, wealth, health and good samskaras will be maintained in every home through this practice.

Anusthana

Anusthana is a traditional form of upasana in which a particular mantra is chanted intensively. There are many kinds of anushthana, but the two most important are sadhana anusthana and purascharana anusthana. *Sadhana anusthana*

189

is done on all ten days of Navaratri. During this time, simple, bland food is taken and no work is done. *Purascharana* is a long anusthana in which the mantra is repeated as many hundreds of thousands of times as the number of mantras or letters it contains. For example, if the mantra is of five syllables (discounting the *Om*) such as *Om Namah Shivaya*, it must be repeated 500,000 times, which means a total of 5000 malas.

Purascharana of *panchakshara*, or a five-syllable mantra should be performed once in a year. This practice can be successfully completed in ten days, during the period of *Navaratri*. If you repeat fifty malas every hour for ten hours every day, it will take ten days. You will need to attune your mind with the breath, and synchronize the breath with the mantra. Practise this with calmness and quietness of mind. It is very difficult and requires a great deal of practice to repeat the mantra fifty thousand times per day. If you can sit for such long hours, you can try it.

The fixed number of repetitions can be completed in a short period of time or over a long period at your convenience. If you do not want to undertake the full number of times, you can do half or a quarter. The anusthana is initiated on an auspicious day, for example, the day of an eclipse, when the number of mantras and the duration of time is fixed, and a sankalpa or vow is made to complete them. After many years of practice, the sound waves awaken the causal body. We call this *mantra siddhi*, the perfection of the power of mantra.

When japa anushthana is performed for spiritual purposes, it constitutes a part of upasana. When it is performed for the fulfilment of a selfish motive or attainment of siddhis (psychic powers), then it is a part of tantra shastra. In the first case the upasaka can select his own mantra and the type of anushthana, or he might receive the mantra in a dream or in meditation. It is advisable, however, to seek the help of a guru. The guru is aware of the psychic personality, of certain defects and inclinations of the upasaka to react too intensely or with unbalanced emotion.

The mantra of Durga, the devi or symbol of the higher aspects of the unconscious, is a powerful mantra which releases great forces when repeated. It would definitely have an adverse effect on the upasaka with uncontrolled emotions and unbalanced mental faculties if these powerful forces are aroused before he is able to control his emotions and mind. The effect of the ram mantra is very soothing and calming on the mind. The shiva mantra will usually develop a sense of detachment, of ecstasy and absolute indifference. An aspirant with these attributes is called a *masta*, which means 'one who is carefree' or even 'absolutely blissful.'

In order to achieve the desired effect with a particular mantra, regardless of its intended purpose, it is of utmost importance that the correct pronunciation is taught by an expert, not only grammatically but also phonetically. It is stated that the advice of a guru must be sought at any rate and in any case. A mantra which can be selected from a book is only for achieving its ends, whereas the beeja or seed mantra, which is recited together with the mantra, is only effective when a guru charges it while giving it to the disciple.

In order for a mantra to be effective, it must produce the intended sound waves through correct pronunciation. This will produce the corresponding colours and in turn will create the intended geometrical forms and figures. This procedure should be intensified and accompanied by proper thought waves. Besides the correct pronunciation, the proper intonation, pitch, mental concentration and application of the creative mind or imagination, is most essential.

In 1992, I performed the *ashtottarshatlaksh* (one hundred and eight lakhs) mantra purashcharana. I did not meet anybody that whole year. It took me three hundred days, from morning until evening, to complete ten million, eight hundred thousand rounds of japa. It was a great success. After completing the purashcharana, my body and mind were both healthy, and I heard the inner command, 'Love your neighbours as I have loved you. Provide for your neighbours

191

as I have provided for you.' This was a very beautiful commandment. Christianity also preaches, 'Love thy neighbour.'

Regular anushthana mantra sadhana helps one perfect a mantra and realize its power. There is so much power in mantra but today, people have forgotten about this tremendous power and how it can be utilized. If you ask for God's blessings through the practice of anushthana, many things can be achieved: offspring, property, employment, salvation, obeying religious duties or dharma. The conflict between men and women or between friends, and the suffering of many people can be relieved; it can all be removed through the perfection of mantra. In ancient times even wars were fought through mantra.

There are various regulations for different types of japa; there are no common rules for perfecting a mantra. The rules vary according to the mantra and the objective behind the japa. Some mantras are used for the attainment of specific desires and others are general. Mantras may be tamasic, rajasic or sattwic, for the fulfilment of tamasic, rajasic or sattwic desires. The rules differ from person to person, after considering his endurance. One general rule will not apply for everybody, so it is essential to follow the advice of your teacher or instructor.

During anushthana, one important requirement is to take light meals. There are also particular observances to be followed as to how to sit, how to sleep, how many times you should eat, etc. A lot of energy is required for this sadhana, so all the physical activities must be kept to a minimum. Although an anushthana of thousands of malas may seem an impossible upasana to complete, it should be done at least for one day, one twenty-four hour period in your lifetime. This is only possible when you can sit with your back straight and your mind constant for many hours at a stretch. Otherwise, you will be yawning, feeling lazy, sleepy or tired.

You may enjoy life; you may acquire, accomplish and accumulate a lot in life. You may see different places, have a lot of experiences, but the ultimate destiny of man is to realize that which is beyond name, form and senses; that which you cannot perceive with your eyes or conceive with your mind is beyond name and form. You can only see or realize that when the external lights are extinguished and the inner light burns. In that inner light alone, you can perceive that which is beyond. It can be called any name you wish, but it is something else. I live here in seclusion for this purpose, because I do not think that life has any other meaning.

16

Tree Pooja

Pooja is performed not only in the temple or shrine room; it is often done outside also for trees and other natural phenomena. Pooja is expressing your sentiments and identifying with the object of worship. When you perform tree pooja, you come in contact with nature. This *sambandh*, contact or communication, has to happen for spiritual development. Communication is being able to interact with the environment with inner sensitivity. If you see someone suffering on the side of the road, you may feel to go and help. If you see a withered plant in need of water, you may feel to give it water.

Even a simple act like giving water is a form of communication. You are conveying your sympathy and compassion, and that is what is received. In this case words have no meaning. When you are able to develop empathy with a plant, a tree or any other object of creation, you are connecting your energy with it. The energy inherent in that tree comes alive, which is the principle of ecology. Tree pooja is a simple daily ritual, taking only five minutes around sunset. It involves meeting your plant every day, whether it is a large tree in the garden or a small pot plant on the kitchen windowsill, and performing the following ritual.

Every day at sunset, light a small candle or an oil lamp in front of the tree, place a flower there, light a stick of incense and pour a small bowl of water at the base of the tree. Along with these offerings, a prayer of thanks and gratitude can be said to the tree. Then for ten seconds close your eyes. Become that tree. If the tree is unhealthy, feel the sickness of the tree and also say a prayer for its wellbeing, "May you become strong and healthy. May you nurture life." After some time the tree will become healthier and stronger. If you continue with this practice with full faith, trust and compassion, you will understand that the tree is responding to your pooja. Of course, the process has to be developed; it cannot happen in a day or a week. You have to fine-tune the frequency of your brain to receive the waves being transmitted by the tree.

The *jyoti* or flame offered to the tree represents the Atman and its awakening, not only in you, but also in the tree. The incense purifies the environment and cleans negativity from your mind, the flower is given as recognition of the beauty of the divine, and the water symbolizes the nurturing of spiritual life. You cannot see the roots of the tree, and similarly, you cannot see the spirit, the essence of your own existence. When you offer water to the roots of a tree, it symbolizes an offering to your own spiritual thirst and the nourishment of your own inner world.

This is the beginning of your connection with nature, not just admiring the tree, but feeling a connection with it. A great deal of satisfaction, fulfilment, happiness and inspiration comes through this connection. That is the spirit of ecology. Some nature movements say to hug a tree. So, in tree pooja, you adopt a tree, worship a tree, become one with the tree, and feel for the tree. Although tree pooja looks simple it has a deep meaning because it is worshipping Mother Earth, the source of all nourishment and life.

Tree pooja is a way of honouring and remembering that transition in evolution where matter is no longer inert, but contains a spark of life and consciousness. Trees are worshipped as a symbol of life, because they provide oxygen, fruits, seeds, wood and shade. Trees purify the air, water and soil, and provide shelter and homes to thousands of other species. Trees are worshipped because they represent all the

195

divine qualities of the mother, endlessly giving, nurturing and sustaining all life forms. Without trees, there would be no oxygen to breathe and all beings would die. From ancient times, many cultures have worshipped plants and trees, and regarded all flora and fauna as sacred. This reveals the sensitivity, foresight and refinement of such cultures.

The atmosphere has two aspects: physical and spiritual. The physical ecosystem depends on the spiritual ecosystem. If the spiritual ecosystem of any place gets spoiled, the physical ecosystem cannot function correctly. This is why it is so important to plant and also to care for trees, especially those having an *adhyatmic* or spiritual vibration. In this way we can help to keep both the spiritual and environmental ecosystems pure.

God pervades each and every atom of creation. God lives not only in human beings, not only in the poor and the sick, but also in the trees. I get up at five a.m., take a bucket and water the trees: tulsi first, then the peepal tree and then all the other trees in my garden. I have fixed an order of priority. While watering them, I go on chanting my mantra simultaneously, and I feel that I am being blessed by each tree. This simple practice does me immense good. What better exercise can an old man like me have than watering plants?

Why do I do this? Because trees are devatas, gods. Tulsi is a goddess; Rudraksha is a god. Rudraksha is Shiva's favourite. Mahatmas were enlightened and attained wisdom under trees. Lord Buddha was enlightened under the banyan tree and became a jnani. Dattatreya, who was the embodiment of the trinity, Brahma, Vishnu and Mahesh, was enlightened under the gular tree. He attained jnana and samadhi under a tree.

Tulsi

Tulsi is a gentle female energy, a sweet little goddess, and should be treated like the queen that she is, the queen of medicinal plants. She is also a plant of power, a powerful lady, a friend, a physician and an ally. When you have tulsi around, you are protected, and she will bring beauty, health,

196

elegance and grace into your life. Wherever there is Tulsi Mayi there is *pavitrata*, purity, for she is the great purifier, both of the body and of the environment. If you plant nine or eleven tulsi trees in your garden, the air will be pure and bacteria-free within a wide radius.

Tulsi is one of those plants that possess divine qualities to invoke the descent of devatas, illumined beings, and increase the spiritual vibrations. The tulsi plant is extremely sensitive and aware, and quickly able to register the vibrations around her. She loves to listen to all Sanskrit chanting, to hear the name of God in the form of kirtan, and she is especially fond of ragas sung to the accompaniment of the tampura.

Another name for tulsi is *Hari Priya*, the beloved of Lord Narayana. Her leaves are always offered along with the food offering, given as prasad after worship of Krishna, Rama or other deities. She is a symbol of Goddess Lakshmi, the consort of Lord Vishnu. The tulsi leaf is the only type of prasad that can be used more than once in worship. After being washed, it can be offered again. Traditionally, in temples, the priests keep water and tulsi leaves in a copper pot and offer three small spoonfuls as prasad to devotees, who drink part of it and sprinkle the remainder on their heads.

In India, as early as 3000 BC, sacred plants were becoming a source of medicine. Plants were regarded as the home of divine spirits with powers beneficial to mankind. By the time Ayurveda became an established science, these beneficial plants had long been acknowledged in the vast medicinal pharmacopoeia contained in plants. The Ayurvedic physicians analyzed tulsi for its healing properties. Although this dispelled much of the superstition connected with tulsi and other plants, it did not diminish the reverence in which tulsi plants are held. Tulsi is known as the mother of Ayurveda.

Tulsi vivaha

The Sanskrit word *vivaha* means 'marriage'. The marriage of tulsi and shaligram is celebrated in the Paramahamsa Alakh Bara every year on *Ekadashi,* the eleventh day after *amavasya* (the no-moon night) in the month of *Kartika* (October/ November) with full ceremony, just like a human marriage. This is also the day of *Deva Utthana*. *Deva* means 'god' and *utthana* means 'to rise up' or 'awake', so it is the day when the gods, or certain dormant energies, awaken.

In this marriage the tulsi plant is symbolic of the energy of goddess tulsi, while the shaligram is symbolic of the energy of Lord Vishnu. Sindoor, mangala sutra, bangles, sweets and marigold malas are offered. A yellow cloth, symbol of Vishnu, and a red cloth, symbol of tulsi, are tied together and offered. Arati is performed and tulsi and shaligram are enclosed in a special bamboo structure or *mandap* covered with a brightly coloured cloth, while they have their honeymoon, which lasts for a few days.

Tulsi pooja

In the *Devi Bhagavat* it is written that, "One who worships tulsi with the mantra *Om Shreem Hreem Kleem Aim Vrindaa-vanyai Swaahaa*, attains all siddhis." The goddess tulsi, who dwells in the tulsi plant, will appear and grant this boon as she is a benevolent force, presiding over all the *lokas* or planes of existence. Those who wish to be righteous and live a happy and prosperous family life worship tulsi. Virgins pray to her for good husbands. Either in the front, back or central *angan* (courtyard) of most Indian homes there is a *tulsi-chawra*, or altar, bearing a tulsi plant. Pooja of tulsi is part of the daily morning ritual of most Hindus, whether they understand the scientific purpose behind this worship or not. The common belief is that where tulsi resides, auspicious vibrations, peace and prosperity always dwell.

Tulsi is especially worshipped during the lunar months of *Vaisakh* (April/May), *Shravan* (July/August), *Kartika* (October/ November) and *Magh* (December/January). After bathing, the worshipper offers water, flowers, kumkum, sandal paste, *nevaidya* (food) and incense to tulsi, who is then circumambulated. In the evening her arati is performed, along with pooja of the household deities. Arati is performed by waving incense and a deepak before her in a clockwise direction. Vaishnavites in particular worship tulsi with full reverence and due observance of scriptural injunctions. Traditionally, before she is worshipped, she is nurtured for a period of three months. Side by side with tulsi, it is customary to have a pot of kusha grass or sugar cane, which are symbols of Lord Vishnu, like the shaligram.

Tulsi is the ishta devi of this akhara, and her worship is performed twice daily at sunrise and sunset. I was able to do *panchagni sadhana* only because of the blessings of tulsi. I prayed to her for one thing only: "Keep me fit!" That's all, nothing more. I stand before Tulsi Devi, facing West and blow the conch three times, turning full circle to include all the directions. Then, I perform *anga nyasa* so as to purify my body. Finally, facing East, I touch the split shaligram to my forehead before ministering to my fire, the *Maha Kaal Chitta Dhuni*, the celestial fire, which has burnt continuously since my arrival in Rikhia in September 1989.

In the ritualistic worship of tulsi, childlike faith is most important. The secret of all rituals is the faith of a child. For an intellectual tulsi is just a plant, but for me, tulsi is not a plant; she is a Devi. In the *akhara* (traditional training place for sannyasins), I dedicate everything to tulsi before giving it as prasad because in this locality everything belongs to her. Whenever I give a golden bracelet, nose ring or hair ornament, I am in fact offering them to her, as she is the owner of the akhara property. All the ornaments are dedicated and offered to her first and foremost, and then presented to the new brides of our neighbourhood. Tulsi is the presiding deity of the spiritual and vedic darshan. She is the head of all departments of pharmaceutical flora.

The first feature of this akhara is the worship of tulsi. We preach only tulsi pooja and daily chanting of *Ramacharitamanas* for forty minutes. Worship of tulsi for health is a must. Health is the first need of every human being, whether a beggar or a millionaire, a sannyasin or a householder. This is the teaching of the scriptures: *dharma, artha, kama, mokshnam, arogyam moolam uttarnam*. The Vedas tell us that for the practice of dharma (righteous conduct), artha (earning wealth), kama (fulfilment of desires) or moksha (spiritual pursuit), the first requirement is health. One way of attaining sound health is to worship tulsi, the queen of all medicinal herbs. You do not even have to eat the leaf, just pray.

The priceless value of tulsi

Once, Satyabhama, one of Krishna's wives, weighed him against her legendary wealth. She asked him, "My Lord, I value you so deeply that I wish to take your weight in gold." Krishna agreed, and a large set of scales was brought. With an amused smile dancing on his lips and a mischievous twinkle in his eye, Krishna sat on one side of the scales, and Satya Bhama began to place her gold on the other side. However, no matter how much gold she placed on the scales, they would not move at all! She placed all she had on the scale, but to no effect.

Satyabhama became distressed, because she had completely run out of gold and no more would even fit on the scales. Then Rukmini, Krishna's first wife, who understood the *lila* or play of Krishna, took a single tulsi leaf and placed it on top of the pile of gold with her full devotion. Immediately, the scales began to move and Krishna's weight was measured. The priceless tulsi leaf represents devotion, and this story shows that even a small leaf offered with devotion means more to the Lord than the wealth of the whole world. This is the greatness of tulsi.

> *Yanmoole sarva tirthaani yannagre sarva devataa*
> *Yanmadhye sarva vedaascha Tulasi taam namaamyaham.*

"I bow down to the Tulsi, at whose base (the roots) are all the holy places, at whose top reside all the deities (divinity), and in whose middle are all the Vedas."

Bilva

The bilva or bel is Lord Shiva's tree and it grows in almost all parts of India, irrespective of the nature of the soil. Shiva is always worshipped with its leaves, and it is said that this tree is much loved by him. It is found in the courtyard of all Shiva temples throughout India. The bilva is also found in Devi temples, where it is worshipped. At midnight, on the evening before Durga and Kali poojas, a tantric ritual called *beel varan* is performed with the appropriate mantras. A particular energy is taken from the tree and placed in a vessel. This energy is then transferred to the statue of Durga or Kali to charge or empower it for the coming pooja. The process is called *prana pratishtha*, the establishing of the life force in the statue. When the pooja is over, the energy is released in a process called *visarjan*.

In the *Atharva Veda*, bilva is described as so sacred that its wood may not be burned for fuel. It is still worshipped today as a totemic deity by the Santhal, the indigenous tribes in India. The dark trifoliate leaves symbolize the three eyes of Lord Shiva, and contain a small percentage of Shiva's alchemical substance – mercury. These leaves have a very pleasant aroma, are used in the worship of both Shiva and Devi, and form an essential ingredient in tantric rituals. It is said that offerings of water sprinkled on these leaves at any shrine will always remain fresh. *Sri Bilva Shtakam* (v. 5) states, "Donating a thousand elephants, and horses, and giving offerings to crores of *kanyas* (young virgins) is equivalent to offering one bilva leaf to Lord Shiva."

According to the *Shiva Purana* (7 AD) the bilva tree is the manifest form of Lord Shiva himself, while all the great *tirthas* and other pilgrimage places are said to reside at its base. One who worships the shivalingam, while sitting under the Bilva, attains the state of Shiva. Washing the head by this tree is said to be the equivalent of bathing in all the sacred rivers. One who performs bilva pooja with flowers and incense achieves Shiva loka, and has happiness and prosperity bestowed upon him. The lighting of the deepak or lamp before this tree bestows knowledge, and enables the devotee to merge in Lord Shiva. The *Shiva Purana* also claims that if the devotee removes the new leaves from one of the branches of that tree and worships the tree with them, they will be freed from vice, while one who feeds a devotee under the bilva will grow in virtue.

The hunter and the bilva tree

The *Shiva Purana* also relates the following myth. Once there was a cruel hearted hunter by the name of Gurudruh, who lived in the lonely forest. On the auspicious day of Maha Shivaratri he had to go out hunting, because his family had nothing to eat. Maha Shivaratri, the great night of Shiva, is the most sacred time for fasts, prayers and offerings, when even the most involuntary acts are made holy, if pleasing to Lord Shiva. By sunset Gurudruh had not been successful in the hunt. Coming to a lake, he climbed a tree and waited for some unsuspecting animal to come and drink. He did not notice that the tree he had climbed was the bilva tree. Neither did he notice the shivalingam beneath it, nor the water pot hanging in the branch just above.

After some time a gentle deer came to quench her thirst and Gurudruh prepared to shoot. As he drew his bow, he accidentally knocked the water pot, hanging in the tree, and some water fell down on the shivalingam beneath, along with a few bilva leaves. Thus, unknowingly and unwittingly, Gurudruh had worshipped Shiva in the first quarter of the night. As a result his heart was a little purified by this act performed on such an auspicious night. Meanwhile the deer, startled by the movement in the tree, looked up and saw the hunter about to release his arrow. "Please do not kill me just yet," pleaded the deer. "I must first take care of my children, and then I will return to be food for your family." The hunter, whose heart had been softened a little by the accidental worship, on noticing the beauty of the deer, let her go on condition that she would return on the morrow to give her body as food for his family.

Later that same night, the sister of the deer came looking for her. Once more the hunter took aim, and once more, without his being aware, the water and the bilva leaves fell down upon the shivalingam. Again, unknowingly, the hunter had worshipped Shiva in the second quarter of the night. The effect of this was that Gurudruh's heart was further purified. His pranas softened a little more, and he allowed this animal to also go and tend to its young, providing it returned the next day to provide him and his family with food.

In the third quarter of the night, the mate of the first deer came in search of her, and again the strange worship took place as the hunter took aim for the third time. But the hunter's heart was beginning to melt due to the worship, and he let the deer's mate go also for the same reason and under the same conditions. Later, when the three deer met together, they discussed who should go and offer himself to the hunter. Even the children offered to give their lives. Finally the whole family decided to surrender to the hunter together, for none of them could bear to live without the others. Thus they set off towards the lake with heavy hearts.

When they arrived at the bilva tree, Gurudruh was very pleased and relieved to see them, and he immediately prepared for the kill. He took aim for the fourth time, but in the same accidental manner as before, worship in the fourth quarter of the night took place unknown to him. This final action of Gurudruh brought about a complete change of heart and, as he was about to release the first arrow, his heart overflowed with pity for the innocent deer. Tears filled his eyes at the thought of all the animals he had killed in the past, and slowly he lowered his bow. Greatly moved by the selfless action of these animals, he felt ashamed, and allowed the whole family of deer to leave unharmed. Such is the purity and spiritual power of the bilva tree that, even without his knowledge or conscious effort, the cruel-hearted hunter had been transformed into a man of compassion and understanding, and was delivered from his past bad karma by the grace of Shiva and the bilva tree.

Rudraksha

The word rudraksha is composed of two words: *rudra*, the fierce aspect of Shiva, and *aksha* 'eye'. So, rudraksha is the eye of Shiva. Rudraksha is a large tree, about the same size as the banyan tree, with a smallish spear-shaped leaf. It grows in mountainous regions like Nepal, where the best rudrakshas are to be found. The fruit of this tree has a hard seed, the formation of which resembles the human brain. These seeds are dried and worn as malas, especially by the followers of Lord Shiva, who are known as *Shaivites*.

The rudraksha has a soft core through which a hole is pierced for threading it. In the best quality beads, the central hole is already there; one does not have to make it. Rudrakshas that do not have this natural hole are of an inferior quality. A good quality bead will sink when put in water, but a false one will float on top of the water. When stringing a rudraksha mala, all the faces should be aligned, and silk thread, gold or silver should be used.

The smaller rudraksha beads are commonly used for japa. The rudraksha mala can be used or worn, even if the aspirant drinks alcohol or eats meat, unlike the sensitive tulsi, which requires the practitioner to have a more sattwic diet and lifestyle. According to the tantra shastras, the specified number of beads to be worn is as follows: around the neck, twenty-seven or thirty-two; around the forehead, forty; around the ears, six; around the wrists, twelve; and on the upper arms, sixteen.

In the *Akshamalik Upanishad* it is written that out of all the malas made of pearls, silver, crystal, shankha (conch), gold, tulsi and sandal, rudraksha is the best. The *Devi Bhagavat* states that the large bead is best for those who worship Shakti. The *Shiva Purana* states that Lakshmi stays where the rudraksha is, and that it has miraculous powers.

The shastras speak of four colours of bead. The white or brahman bead is considered to be of the finest quality. The red or kshatriya bead comes next in regard to value. The yellow bead or vaishya is third in rank, while the black *(shyam)* or shudra bead is the least valuable. According to the shastras, the different colours should be worn, according to one's *jati* or caste.

Faces of rudraksha

When dried, the rudraksha bead is about the size of a marble, although there are smaller varieties also. The value of this bead is determined by its size and also, more especially, by the number of 'faces' or *mukhis* it has, because some of them carry an extremely powerful energy. It is the energy contained in it, or its potency for spiritual practice, that gives its value. The number of faces, from one to twenty-one, is also symbolic of various philosophical concepts.

The one mukhi rudraksha is very rare and represents Shiva himself, the 'One Reality' or pure consciousness. It is highly prized by sadhakas and temples alike. The one who wears this one mukhi rudraksha gets remission from even the gravest sin of killing a Brahmin. The possessor of this rudraksha becomes elevated in status and lacks for nothing.

The two mukhi rudraksha represents Shiva and Shakti (Ardhanarishwara). The one who wears this rudraksha is absolved from all sins, whether intentional or unintentional. This rudraksha controls sexual desire, develops mental peace and concentration, and awakens the kundalini.

The three mukhi rudraksha represents Agni, the Lord of fire and purification. It removes the sin of killing a woman. It makes the wearer dynamic, gives strength and freedom from disease.

The four mukhi rudraksha symbolizes Brahma. It washes away the sin of killing a man. It sharpens the mind and increases the ability to absorb and memorize.

The five mukhi rudraksha represents Kalagni, the fire of death. One who wears this rudraksha gets remission from sins incurred by eating food that ought not to be eaten and enjoying a woman who ought not to be enjoyed. This rudraksha protects the heart and should be worn by persons with heart condition. It facilitates peace of mind and allows the wearer to overcome obstacles in life.

The six mukhi rudraksha represents Kartikeya, the six headed god, who is Shiva's eldest son. All sins are removed by wearing this bead on the right wrist. It develops siddhi or success in any work. It removes materialistic desires and cures diseases, like hysteria, fainting, blood pressure and women's problems.

The seven mukhi rudraksha represents the god Adi Sesha, and has the power to absolve the wearer from the sins of theft. It counteracts negative planetary positions, and averts violent or premature death.

The eight mukhi rudraksha represents Vinayaka, the elephant god. It has the power to remove corruption and deceit. It develops mental peace and concentration when worn. It is beneficial for business and acquisition of wealth. It also cures paralytic strokes.

The nine mukhi rudraksha represents Bhairava and is worn on the left hand. It empowers the wearer and makes him mighty, like a god. It embodies the nine powers of God and leads to salvation. It especially suits the devotees of Durga. It rids the wearer of the sins incurred by aborting a child in the womb one thousand times and killing Brahmins one hundred times. It cures all heart diseases.

The ten mukhi rudraksha is rare and represents Yama. It protects the wearer from the ill effects of psychic power, evil spirits and snakebite. It has great medicinal power. The eleven mukhi rudraksha represents the eleven forms of Rudra. It is worn on the head and bestows the benefits of performing the *Ashwa Medha Yajna*. Worn by women, it improves the ability to bear children and increases the longevity of their husbands. It controls the spread of contagious diseases.

The twelve mukhi rudraksha is the abode of the twelve Adityas. It is worn on the ear to invoke Surya, the Sun god. It guards the wearer against any injury incurred from the horns and teeth of animals, from various diseases and from anxiety. The wearer assumes a god-like aura and is respected by all. It also represents Vishnu and is worn by those who aspire to be *brahmacharis* (followers of Brahmin, masters of the senses). The wearer radiates with brightness and is able to resist the lure of the senses.

The thirteen mukhi rudraksha represents Kamadeva, the god of love. The very fortunate wear this rudraksha, as it has the ability to fulfil every wish and earns the wearer respect and stability.

The fourteen mukhi rudraksha represents Nilkantha or Tripurari, and transforms the wearer into Paramshiva. It is the eye of Shiva and awakens the third eye of wisdom. It also protects the wearer against all diseases.

The fifteen mukhi rudraksha represents Pashupati, and gives spiritual awakening. Its supernatural power guards the wearer against theft.

The sixteen mukhi rudraksha is known as Gauri-Shankar and bestows the blessings of Parvati and Shiva. It is mostly worn by sannyasins.

The seventeen mukhi rudraksha represents Vishwakarma. One who wears a mala of this rudraksha will achieve wealth and spiritual power.

The eighteen mukhi rudraksha represents the Earth and is worn by women and children. It protects women against premature delivery and children against disease.

The nineteen mukhi rudraksha represents Narayana. It fulfills all material desires and sharpens business acumen.

The twenty mukhi rudraksha represents Brahma. It enhances knowledge, bestows mental peace and improves visual power.

The twenty-one mukhi rudraksha is the rarest and represents Kuber. It bestows wealth and all the good things of life, and removes adversity.

Nothing is impossible for the wearer of rudraksha, even liberation, and simply looking at or touching a rudraksha is beneficial. Rudraksha beads are kept for pooja or worship to earn the grace of Lord Shiva, who brings illumination and auspiciousness. Each mukhi or face has its own personal mantra by which its inherent power can be invoked and the wearer blessed by its ruling deity. However, even without the chanting of these mantras, the cosmic vibrations envelop the wearer.

Rudraksha and Ayurveda

Rudraksha is hot in nature, and has magnetic and electric power. It is widely used in the preparation of Ayurvedic medicine. Wearing the mala helps to regulate the blood pressure. The five-faced rudraksha mala monitors blood pressure and cardiac ailments. It must be worn next to the skin to have the required effect. Also, to control blood pressure, put two five-faced rudraksha beads in a glass of water, just after sunset. Drink the water first thing in the morning before any other intake.

The rudraksha mala is also excellent for tranquillizing the mind and removing nervous disorders. It destroys worries and induces positive thoughts and a peaceful mind. For nervousness and coldness due to shock, hold a large five-faced rudraksha tightly in your right palm for ten minutes. You will regain your confidence, and the body will start warming up. In addition, rudraksha are said to be good for those who suffer from diabetes. The therapeutic and spiritual effect of the rudraksha is due to the fact that whenever the bead touches the skin, human magnetism and electricity is produced.

Rudraksha and the chakras

The rudraksha bead is also related to the chakras or energy vortexes in the human spine. The one-faced rudraksha is related to vishuddhi and Lord Shiva. Another name for Shiva is *Akasha-adi-pati*, the Lord of space. The *tattwa* or element ruling vishuddhi chakra is space. The two-faced rudraksha is related to anahata chakra, the air element, *vayu*, and *Ardhanareshwara*, the half-male, half-female form of Shiva. The three-faced rudraksha is associated with manipura chakra and the God Agni, This bead is ideal for those who suffer from inferiority complexes, subjective fear, guilt and depression.

Swadhisthana is represented by the four-faced rudraksha, which is the symbol of Brahma and creation. The wearer gains the power of creativity when blessed. The element of this chakra is water, *apas*. The five-faced rudraksha bead is

208

related to the five-faced form of Rudra, and is connected with mooladhara, which is governed by the element earth or *prithvi*. This bead is good for everyone and anyone can wear it. The wearer of the five-faced mala gains health and peace.

The wrath of Rudra

Devotees of Shiva believe the rudraksha bead to be the hot tear of rage which fell from Rudra's eye as he beheld the effrontery of mankind in the face of the Creator. The name Rudra is from the Sanskrit root *rud*, which means 'to weep'. According to legend, the Destroyer had been meditating for many, many years for the wellfare of all creatures. When he came out of his samadhi, he wept when he looked down from his abode on Mount Kailash and witnessed man's ambitious, unnatural and arrogant technology. His tears rolled down from Kailash to the earthly plane and took the form of the Rudraksha tree.

In its arrogance, mankind had lost its link with God and built a towering metropolis or 'Triple City' to symbolize its own greatness. This magnificent creation, however, disturbed the balance between the earth, the atmosphere and the sky, and so Lord Shiva, in his destructive aspect of Rudra, was forced to right the balance. In the *Mahabharata* it is written, "The Lord of the universe (Shiva) drew his bow and unleashed his arrows at the Triple City (*Tripura*), burning its demons, and hurling them into the western ocean, for the welfare of creation. Then the three-eyed God restrained the fire born of his own anger, saying to it, "Enough! Do not reduce the world to ashes."

Peepal

In Sanskrit the peepal is called 'ashvattha', while in English it is known as the 'sacred fig'. The peepal is a huge tree, whose roots travel extensively and branches spread expansively, giving a wide area of shade. It grows throughout India, particularly in temples and their vicinity. Lord Vishnu is said to dwell in this tree, and it is believed that planting, watering and worshipping it brings prosperity to the planter and the surrounding environment.

The wind playing in its heart-shaped, tapering leaves has been likened by Indian poets to India's oldest musical instrument, the *venu* or flute, and indeed it has a magic all of its own. The peepal is deeply associated with both the origin and the symbiosis of life. It is therefore also referred to as 'the tree of life'. Indians believe that the wood from the peepal was used to light the original sacred fire with which the gods granted knowledge to humanity. In the remains of the Indus valley civilization, seals were found depicting the peepal encircled by worshippers, who were aware of its sacred power.

In the *Bhagavad Gita* (10:26) where Krishna tells Arjuna the different symbols of perfection in the material world, he says, "Among all the trees I am the peepal", which shows us the greatness and divinity of this tree. Krishna also refers to the peepal, or ashvattha, as a symbol of kundalini, the roots of which are in the human brain and the branches the pranic pathways and nerves in the body (15:1): '*Urdhvamoola-madhahshaakham ashvattham praahuravyayam. Chhandaamsi yasya parnaani, yastam veda sa vedavit.*'

Countless Indian legends tell of sages meditating under the peepal, and it is therefore thought to induce illumination in those who seek its shade for purposes of sadhana.

An invocation from the *Rig Veda* also refers to this in the following verse, "He, (Vishnu the preserver) the powerful and the holy, holds straight this tree in unsupported space. Its rays, whose roots are high above, stream downward. Deep may they sink within us and be hidden."

The sacred fig is also the Buddhist symbol for consciousness. Under this tree, Lord Buddha, 'the compassionate one', experienced *nirvana* or enlightenment, and to this day it is worshipped by Buddhists, who call it the *bodhi* tree, or the 'tree of enlightenment'. Buddha is very often depicted by his devotees as having a body in the shape of a peepal leaf.

The peepal in Ayurveda

The peepal was known by Ayurvedic physicians to contain mercury. They used the tree's medicinal properties to maintain health of the vital functions: circulation, vision, lungs and kidneys. According to Swami Sivananda, "The seed is a laxative, refrigerant and astringent. It is useful in constipation, in spermatorrhoea, hoarseness of the voice and thirst. The tender leaves increase semen and are useful in fevers. It is a good appetizer and increases the digestive fire. The juice obtained by incising the tree is useful in fissures of the feet." Swami Sivananda gives the following prescription for fever, sexual debility and impotency: "Boil two tablespoons of the tender leaves in eight ounces of milk, add two tablespoons of sugar and drink." For skin diseases, and for keeping the body cool, he recommends the following infusion: "Soak one teaspoon of powdered bark in twenty ounces of water for half an hour and then strain." So we can see that the peepal tree has practical as well as spiritual applications.

17

Serving and Giving

You don't have to go to a temple or church to worship God or to please Him. You can worship God by serving the poor, the destitute, the disabled, the sick, the hungry, the naked and the helpless. You can give your love to the orphans who are loved by no one. If you want to perform the highest worship of God, become the servant of the downtrodden, do whatever you can with your mind, knowledge, influence and might to help the poorest of the poor, the lowest of the low. God loves those who love Him in this form. You don't have to become a swami, sannyasin or yogi. You don't have to practise asana, pranayama or meditation.

Give your attention to those people who are completely neglected by society, who nobody bothers about. If you cast a helpful eye towards such people, God will turn his grace towards you. This is not only what Satyananda preaches; all the holy books, the *Bible, Koran, Ramayana* and Vedas, tell us this. Christ, Mohammed, Sri Krishna, Mahatma Gandhi and all the great teachers have said the same thing. God is called *deenabandhu*, friend to the unfortunate, helpless and lowly. Have you ever read about an *amirbandhu* God, who is friend to the rich and fortunate? If you believe that God is a friend to the poor, then you should play the role of benefactor to the poor. In this way, you and God will then become very close to each other.

You must have read or heard about Mother Teresa. What an inspiration she has been to us all. She was so blessed by God,

212

she enjoyed such grace from God, that she could serve the most neglected, condemned and despised members of society till her last breath. She picked up those people whom nobody even dared to look at. She would pray: "Lord, make us worthy to serve our fellow men throughout the world, who live and die in poverty and hunger. Through our hands give them this day their daily bread, and through our understanding give them love, peace and joy. Amen." This is the sum and substance of spiritual life. It is atma bhava, the best teaching of Vedanta.

Atma bhava means complete sympathy for others. It means to feel the pain and distress of others, as if it were your own; to feel the poverty, sickness and calamities of others, as your own. This is the highest philosophy of Vedanta, and Mother Teresa could put it into practice. Are you ready to spend money on the poor? A single doctor's bill is nothing less than three hundred rupees. Can you spend that much on the poor from your own pocket? You are ready to spend everything on yourself, but you are not prepared to spend one paise on a poor man! And still you talk about God! But God will not be pleased if you simply fill your own pocket. You have to respect and care for all of his creation, his maya.

The poor people of the world are a challenge to your spiritual life, whether in Asia, Africa or anywhere else in the world. There are people suffering mentally, physically and economically. What percentage of your income are you spending on them? A single bottle of liquor costs a minimum of one hundred rupees and it evaporates within no time. Similarly, people complain that cigarettes have become very expensive, and yet they smoke their money away. Miss these things for just one day and divert that expenditure to the poor and needy. Humans confine their feelings within the family bonds. You have a strong feeling that 'this is mine' and 'that is yours', but you should note that your sadhana, your pooja, your worship can never be successful, as long as your neighbour is in distress.

Ten percent of your income must be spent on God's creation, on His maya. This is the purpose of spiritual life.

Otherwise, do not talk about God. Ten percent of thirty days is three days, so whatever you spend on your own enjoyment and luxuries for three days in one month should go to the poor. Some people enjoy non-vegetarian food, some enjoy eggs, some go to see movies and some enjoy themselves in other ways. They spend four or five hundred rupees easily on their enjoyment and pleasure in a day. Three days' expenses would amount to fifteen hundred rupees or so. Abstain from these pleasures just for three days and divert this money for the education of a poor girl.

How can you serve the poorest of mankind? Who will tell you all this? You have to find out how to serve God in this way. If you want to attain nirvikalpa samadhi, savikalpa samadhi, bhava samadhi or samadhi of any type, damned or blessed, if you want to have a vision of divinity, then ultimately you will have to find a way to serve the poor. Your body, blood, soul, youth, wealth, intelligence, everything should be geared to serving and raising mankind to a proper position. There are innumerable poor widows in our villages who have no future and no life of their own. They are condemned to a meaningless existence, with neither *bhoga* (enjoyment) nor yoga before them. They are made to feel useless.

This is the state of society that I am pointing out to you. Have you ever given a thought to reforming society, to making it better by serving the poor and needy? It is right to do pooja or to read the *Ramayana, Bible or Koran*. It is right to visit a church, mosque or temple. It is right to seek satsang, the holy company of sadhus and sannyasins, but the most important worship of God is to see Him and serve Him in this world of His creation.

> *Jale Vishnu thale Vishnu*
> *Vishnu parvatamastake*
> *Jvaalaamaalaakule Vishnu*
> *Sarvam Vishnumayam jagat.*

214

Vishnu is in the oceans,
In the land, in the mountain peaks,
In the garland of flames,
In every nook and corner of the world.

This means that Vishnu is omnipresent. He pervades the whole earth. God, you are immanent in everything. You are present in all forms of manifestation. You are there in the mango trees, in the water and in the soil. Water is present everywhere in the form of all created beings. Air, fire and space are also everywhere. God is present everywhere. This is a fact, it is not a theory; you must translate this into practice and let it become a reality in your life.

In *Nasadiya Sukta* the rishis wonder whether or not God exists at all; they raise the questions: If He is, then where is He? After creating the universe and the pageant of this world, has He become extinct? Why are we wasting our time in this idle pursuit of finding God? If He is, He is here and now among human beings. Look for Him where He is most needed, not in the temples where people are pouring wealth on His idol.

The temples of Shiva, Vishnu and Baidyanath are full of wealth, and all the temple trusts have full coffers. The temple of God is very rich, but the God living among the poor and the downtrodden in the guise of a lame or blind man is needy. Go and look for Him in destitution, hunger and starvation. Go to those houses where there are no hearths to cook even one square meal per day – because God also lives there. Yes, God lives in the church and the temple, but have you ever thought that God also lives in a poor man who is suffering? Have you ever realized that when you see a poor man and deny his need, you are denying God within him?

The philosophy of atma bhava is very simple, but can you practice it? I consider the entire Rikhia Panchayat to be my ashram. Every house here is my house. The pains and pleasures of every member of every house are my own. Their poverty is my poverty and their happiness is my happiness.

215

That is not a social philosophy; it is vedantic philosophy. You have to see yourself in everyone, and you have to see everyone within your own self. If you write to God, C/O Everywhere, I will deliver your letter to Him.

Worship and devotion to God are performed in a variety of ways. We teach asana, pranayama and kundalini yoga to the affluent who have a lot of leisure. We teach them many things, but does it mean that God lives amongst the rich and does not live amongst the poor, the hungry, the sick and the distressed? Have you ever thought about this? Have you ever felt that God lives in the poor? Enlarge the scope of your sadhana from mere asana, pranayama, japa and meditation to the service of those who are in need. If you are a mason or carpenter, you could help them to build a house. If you are a brick maker or know something about agriculture, horticulture or animal husbandry, you could help them in those ways.

What I am propagating is the Care for the Unfortunate culture. This should become a part of your sadhana. Imparting know-how to those who lack that knowledge is also dharma. Dharma and *sat karma* (right action) are the foundations of worship and spiritual life. If you care for the unfortunate, God will definitely bless you with peace and tranquility. Nobody thinks of going to the house of a poor man and lighting a lamp. Nobody thinks of visiting the 'have-nots'.

When a child is born in your own family you immediately think of a crib, and there are elaborate preparations in anticipation. But when there is a newborn in someone else's family all you do is give good wishes and greetings. If you only give good wishes and greetings to someone who is born today into a very poor family that will not help him. Go to his house and give the child a warm sweater, give him a crib, and give some tonic and some money for the mother. This is a practical sadhana I am giving you.

When you see somebody suffering and you think that he or she deserves it, you should see this as an impurity of your mind. Such impurities disturb the peace of mind in deeper states of meditation. If you bring in compassion, you begin to cultivate the samskaras that will help you clear all the obstacles of procrastination, so that your mind becomes purified and peaceful, allowing you to raise your consciousness into finer states.

Giving prasad

When a saint, a sadhu, a sannyasin or a higher soul gives something to someone it is called prasad. The word prasad means that which is offered to God. Prasad is from the hands of the Almighty Lord. Therefore I offer everything: rickshaws, bicycles, tools, even cows and bulls, in my worship of God. These items become offerings, just like flowers or sweets, and then I distribute them as prasad. There is no stamp of donation on them; they are the Lord's prasad. Of course, there are different types of prasad but the giving of any prasad, either to the 'haves' or the 'have-nots' should be viewed as a form of worship. It is not business or commerce or charity or gift giving; it is a form of worship.

When a *rajarishi* performs sadhana and then distributes prasad, he should give that which reflects his higher qualities. A rajarishi is somebody who has lived like a *raja*, a king, and also like a *rishi*, a seer. A rishi has inner knowledge, he sees the inner light and hears the inner voice. A person who is a rajarishi has these qualities. So what will he give as prasad? Will he give an ordinary sweet? No, he will give cows to the farmers, bicycles to schoolchildren, houses to poor people. And, this is the prasad that I give from the akhara.

At the *Sat Chandi Maha Yajna*, when the worship of the Mother begins, we offer prasad to all the people who have come. We may give a bicycle, but that is not a donation. I do not give donations either. I only give prasad. I am strictly against donations, charity or alms. Begging for alms is the duty of a sannyasin, not that of a *grihastha*, or householder. A sannyasin has to beg; he cannot donate. A grihastha does not beg; he offers things in charity. I am not God, but there must be a medium of expression for God's grace.

217

The important point is that here in the Akhara I do not give gifts. Whatever sari, shawl, T-shirt or other items you receive, remember that they are not gifts. Every year at the Sat Chandi Maha Yajna, the cosmic Mother is invoked and worshipped through rituals and chanting of mantras. This is an aspect of the yajna that is conducted by the pandits, but it is not the only necessary aspect of the Sat Chandi Yajna. The prasad yajna is equally important and it is known as *Daan Yajna*, donating something with devotion. The Mother is being worshipped not only through the mantra recitation of *Durga Saptashati*, but also in the form of worship, when everyone receives prasad, with the warm blessings of Mother's protection.

God is my benefactor

My panchagni upasana, begins from *Makar Samkranti* (winter soltice) 14th January and continues until to *Karka Samkranti* (summer soltice) 16th July, when the sun crosses two important points in the heavens. Then after the full moon of *Kartik Poornima*, in the best month of the year, *Margasheersha* (November/December), when my anushthanas are over, I offer prasad to the Lord. That prasad is neither fruits nor sweets, bilva leaves nor tulsi leaves. I make offerings of two hundred rickshaws and thelas for the strong young men and auto-rickshaws for the educated men; ten thousand items of clothing for women, children and men; and five hundred good luck kits for the newly wed village girls.

This distribution of prasad has been going on for many years without any institution as my benefactor. God is my benefactor and if He wants me to give, He will give me something and then I will give it to you. If He does not give me anything, then I will not give anything to you, because it means He does not want me to. I simply put the prasad before Him, and in this way we start giving. And, I tell you quiet frankly, that when I sit in front of Raghunathji to do my pooja, I would feel ashamed to offer Him a mere *batasha*, or sweet. After all, my Lord is not a fakir. He is an illustrious emperor, a *Samrat Chakravarti*, and how can you offer a sesame seed to an elephant?

218

Lord Rama may not be a god for you, but you will at least accept that he is the king and emperor of Ayodhya. He is a regal person to whom a paltry prasad like batasha or a betel nut simply cannot be offered! So I said, "No, let me make out a list of the royal offerings to be made to the regal hero, like twenty rickshaws, ten ladies' cycles, sixteen spades, forty saris, twenty dhotis, ten pairs of jeans..." In this way, I go on in my mind, making an offering to the Lord.

At first, I was a bit nervous and worried as to how and where I could get these offerings, especially since I am now totally disconnected from Munger economically, financially and constitutionally. I am an Alakh Niranjan man. I am not a grandfather, enjoying rights over the earnings of the grand-children until the end of my life. I do not care for samadhi myself. I only want to be able to remove the pain and misery of the helpless. It needs God's special power to remove the woes of suffering humanity, to wipe away the tears of crying people. It is a spiritual power, not an ordinary power, which enables one to alleviate human sorrow. If you really want to help people, you need a special power from God. Nevertheless, one day I made a list with great hesitation, and the same evening a telephone call came offering a cow and many other items for prasad. So, by evening everything was arranged.

Prasad means happiness, delight and joy. *Vishad* means unhappiness, dejection and despair. What we receive in the temples is prasad, because we are very glad to receive it. We are glad, because we desire gifts from the gods and goddesses. Similarly, the rickshaw and thela pullers are very happy to receive prasad from Sri Rama. The prasad I distribute is not from Swami Satyananda; it is prasad from Sri Rama. Our swamis visit all the villages in the Rikhia Panchayat to survey and assess the requirements of each and every family and then we prepare the prasad for them, the clothes and sweaters etc. For the children we select toys, slates, pencils, rubbers, sharpeners and Amar Chitrakatha comics. We do not merely offer sweets, flowers and incense as prasad, because we prefer to offer something that will be useful to the family members in the long run. Almost all the rickshaws in Deoghar bear the inscription 'Presented by Sivananda Math', a symbol that indicates prasad from Lord Rama.

No money comes into the villages, not that I am complaining. I keep asking God thus, "God why have you forgotten these innocent, pious, clean-hearted, poor villagers? They are foremost in discharging their religious duties, foremost in manual labour and you have forgotten them." Seventy percent of India is totally ignored and I make this statement on the golden jubilee celebration of your freedom and independence. These village people live only by the name of God; only He sustains them. They enjoy neither amenities nor privileges from their nation. Their own nation has not given them even drinking water. Their nation has not given them any facilities whatsoever. Whatever funds their nation spends are directed towards big cities like Delhi, Bombay, Bangalore and Kanpur. But remember, it is not social service that I am doing for them, it is prasad distribution; it is my worship of God, my upasana. In kali yuga there are only two paths for achieving one's ultimate goal: one is God's name, *naam*, and the other is giving daan or prasad.

18

Yajna as Worship

The concept of yajna is more than fire ceremony; it is the circulation of peace, prosperity, health and well-being. As all these are circulated, we are affected at an individual, social and global level. Yajna is the creation of a mandala, the cosmic image or symbol, at one point in time, at one location in space, which realigns and re-circulates all the cosmic, magnetic energy fields in the universe. Yajna is generally identified as a fire ritual, but there are many other components. The word yajna is made up of three root words: *ya* meaning 'creation' or 'production'; *ja* meaning 'distribution' or 'propagation', and *na* meaning 'assimilation', 'absorption' or 'use'. Thus yajna means a process of producing, distributing and then assimilating.

Yajnas are classified in different groups. Some yajnas are performed for the betterment of human beings, to provide material gains and benefits. Some are done to eradicate difficulties and problems in life, and to propitiate the cosmic and divine nature. Some are performed to purify and recharge the atmosphere and all the elements of earth, water, fire, air and space. Some yajnas are designed to influence the elements, so as to create rain in desert areas, or to heal and charge the elements with nutrients to increase their healing properties. Some yajnas are for the fulfilment of desires, such as the propagation of progeny in certain families and tribes.

In the different scriptures, various other forms of yajnas have been described. Some yajnas may be performed by brahmins, others by householders, and some by kings, emperors or rulers to bring peace and prosperity to their kingdoms. According to history and mythology, a special yajna was conducted in order to bring Rama and his brothers into this world. Similarly, we find evidence in the *Mahabharata* where Draupadi, the wife of the Pandavas, along with her brother, Drishtadyumna, were born together out of a yajna. When performed correctly, the yajna becomes a very powerful instrument for bringing about change. Therefore, yajna should be performed wisely.

In modern language, yajna indicates the process by which the prosperity and wealth of creation is circulated, whether it be material, non-material or even spiritual. The basis of yajna is daan. The word daan means 'offering', which is made for the welfare of all, without any expectations or strings attached to it. This implies the offering of all things that are pious and auspicious, which nurture and sustain life and creation. Daan does not mean giving away our unused, used or useless possessions, which would be disposed of at any rate. It means the giving of pure substances and items, which are fit to be utilized and consumed by the Divine, whose abode is within the hearts of all. During the yajna different items are offered to the Divine and then distributed as prasad, as gifts, to everyone, rich or poor, Indian nationals, or people from overseas.

The purpose of yajna is to connect with the higher, compassionate and benevolent energy, to connect with the spirit or cosmic Self. That's how dissemination of the knowledge took place in previous eras. As people were advancing, they were also disseminating and that has given us the collection of the Upanishads, Vedas, *Shrutis* (scriptures revealed or heard in meditation) and *Smritis* (traditional or memorial law). Yajna is a recreation of the vedic ideas in which you progress and take others with you. This tradition also applies in the material field, so that if one is prosperous, that prosperity should also help others, not only oneself. That has been the ideal of vedic socialism. There are stories that whatever the farmers of old cultivated and produced would be distributed freely to everybody at the end of the season. When kings and emperors returned from wars, they would distribute their plunder freely to ensure that everyone in society had an equal share. In the same manner, all kind of distribution takes place during the yajna.

You live in a world, which is bound by action. In this context, the offerings made during a yajna are considered to be the most superior form of action. These offerings are called sacrifice, because they have no selfish or self-oriented motivation. The oblations are offered as sacrifice during the yajna through the divine intermediary of fire, known as Agni Devata. These offerings are then expanded through the agency of fire into the spatial and causal dimensions, thereby reaching the Divine, who receives and enjoys their subtle essence. By making such offerings during the process of yajna, peace and happiness are generated within the individual, the environment and the society.

Happiness is further amplified, because in receiving these oblations, the Divine also becomes happy with you and with the world in which you live. In this way, a positive life cycle is engendered. You nourish the gods with oblations and upon receiving them the gods further nourish you. In this way you are freed from disease, poverty, starvation, and all the vicissitudes of life. Your life is blessed with divine grace and you feel yourself to be a part of the Divine, which is the realization of heaven on earth. So, although the giving may seem to be a small act, remember that it has that element of self-sacrifice in it. Such actions bring you closer to the Divine, which is within and all around you at every moment.

Rajasooya Yajna

The only people, who are authorized to perform the *Rajasooya Yajna*, are emperors, kings and yogis. Traditionally, rulers performed this yajna after they had conquered a kingdom or an empire. Emperors and kings performed this grand yajna to distribute their material wealth; yogis do it to distribute their spiritual wealth. In the known history, very few people have performed Rajasooya Yajna. In remote antiquity, Sri Rama had performed this yajna after he had won the battle against Ravana, and that established him as a just emperor. Later on Yudhisthira, the chief of the Pandavas, performed this yajna after the conquest of all the kingdoms, following the establishment of Indraprastha.

In this age, about 1200 years ago, an emperor of India, Harshvardan, performed the Rajasooya Yajna and gave out his entire treasury. Still there were people, who had not received daan, so he gave them the clothes off his body. Still there was someone left, to whom he gave the last clothes that he was wearing and remained naked. The sister of the emperor, Rajeshwari, tore off a piece from her sari and gave it to him to cover himself. When the emperor walked out of the palace, covered only by the piece of sari, a man said, "I have not yet received anything." The emperor gave him that piece of sari, which his sister had given to him for covering his nakedness.

There are different ways of performing Rajasooya Yajna. I am performing it not as a conqueror of land, wealth or people, but because I was able to establish an empire of yoga, which is the need of today in our civilization. Yoga works at spiritual, mental and physical levels to improve the quality of life, and that is also the concept of prosperity in today's society. We have plenty of wealth, but what we lack is the quality of life. We have gained riches and lost peace of mind. I am performing the Rajasooya Yajna to re-establish peace of mind, contentment, happiness, joy and well being.

The purpose of performing this yajna is spiritual, and the result is also spiritual. The performer is as important as the act of performing a Rajasooya Yajna. The yajna is the vehicle, the means, by which the energy of the performer spreads throughout the world. If a saint or an enlightened being performs the yajna, that person is giving something of himself during the yajna as well: his attainments, his peace, his knowledge, his inspiration, his motivation are also being distributed along with the yajna.

For each type or class of person performing this yajna, different time guidelines are given. Emperors have to perform it for three years, but if a spiritually enlightened being performs it, then it must be conducted for twelve years. It is not the sort of thing you can do on a whim. The Rajasooya Yajna that I am conducting will culminate at the end of twelve years. This is the time allotted for the yajna performed by a saint. Each yajna will have a different routine and emphasis, so as to invoke the qualities that we lack in life. Symbolically, these qualities will be given in a form or shape, such as an object or item. For instance, the first year cloth was distributed, because this is the necessity of life. The first gift was of cloth and the final gift is of gold. I have declared that when the yajna culminates after twelve years, at the end of the sankalpa, even knowledge will be gifted through transmission, *shaktipath*. And if possible, even self-realization will be distributed. Yes, it is an item.

Sat Chandi Yajna

The medium of the Rajasooya Yajna is the *Sat Chandi Yajna*, in which the Mother Goddess, Chandi is invoked and worshipped. Chandi represents the energy of transformation, which is psychological, spiritual and social. That is the basis of the Rajasooya Yajna. Chandi is a very peculiar concept in the tantras, as well. She is the goddess of transformation, change, and the power of Chandi is invoked to bring about an inner transformation in life. You need to invoke Lakshmi for external transformation, to manage the inflation and recession. Chandi is to be invoked for inner transformation.

Sat Chandi is not an ordinary yajna; it is one of the most sacred yajnas of tantra. The techniques of the Sat Chandi come from the highest esoteric tantric rituals. Tantra is a very powerful science, and tantric yajnas invoke tremendous energy, shakti. I am not referring to the tantra that you know

225

about through books, which has been defined as the yoga of sex and free living, but the traditional tantra that is performed to purify and free yourself from weakness and negativity. Tantra is a process of invoking and experiencing the divine force within. This divine force does not come naturally or spontaneously, although it is inherent in everyone; you have to prepare the receiver of the mind.

You are surrounded by radio waves but you are unable to see them. In order to materialize and to hear those waves, you need to have the right instrument, whether it is a radio or a transistor. You also need the ability to tune that instrument, because when the receiver is tuned, you can hear any station you wish. The same applies to the cosmic energy; it surrounds you, internally and externally, above and below, and it is the force responsible for creation, sustenance, transformation and change. The Sat Chandi Yajna prepares you to receive the highest forces of the Divine through the recitation of mantras, performance of rituals and giving of prasad.

The word *sat* or *shat* means 100; and Chandi is the name of the Mother Goddess, the cosmic creator. From the tantric tradition and viewpoint, Chandi is the goddess responsible for the change and transformation that you experience in your life. At the same time Chandi is also a mantra. So, *Sat Chandi* means recitation of the Chandi mantra 100 times. Chandi is the aggressive aspect of the Mother, who comes into existence when all human and divine efforts have failed. Her glories are described in the 700 verses of *Durgasaptashati*, which form the mantra. Mythologically there is a long story behind this tradition, which is full of deep insights into spiritual life. The 100 repetitions of the Chandi mantra, contained in the 700 verses of *Durgasaptashati*, is the process, which is used to invoke the cosmic power.

Mantras are words of power, which create a specific vibration in the environment. Mantras purify the environment. The concept of mantra exists in many mystic traditions, which in the past have used mantras to aid the function of

226

the elements, to control the elements, to harness them for the betterment of society, the planet and creation. Nowadays, the mantras that we recognize are those that give control over the natural processes with the strength to manipulate events. Therefore, mantras may seem like magical spells, witchcraft and wizardry, but in reality they have a different function to perform; they focus the cosmic power. You can feel the strength and power that is created when the mantras are being chanted and everyone is participating. The vibrations become a cosmic power, which pervades the entire region, including your own body and self.

The mantra of the Sat Chandi Yajna is a different experience altogether that induces an altered state of consciousness at the conscious, subconscious and unconscious levels. The power of the mantra is harnessed for spiritual upliftment, and at the same time, used to create a different environment of peace, prosperity and beatitude. Different things can happen at many levels. In yajna, the energy that is invoked by the chanting of the mantras and the creation of yantras and mandalas focuses the cosmic power. It is an incredible experience; thousands come to be in the presence of the yajna, to hear the mantras, to spend ten minutes there, and then go away.

Sat Chandi Yajna is performed to invoke the blessings and auspiciousness of the Cosmic Mother. We are worshipping the Mother, the *Adi Shakti*, the original or primal mother, who was not born from a womb. We are worshipping that eternal Mother, who has no particular form, but every form is Her form. We should not say that She is formless, although it is true that She has no particular form; but it is Her glory we see in the sun and moon, and in all forms of life. The Cosmic Mother, the cosmic energy being worshipped here, is inherent in each and every object of creation. There is no form in this world that is devoid of this cosmic presence. Once we become aware of this cosmic presence within and around us, we will begin to love that divine nature, which some people call God.

Loving God is a personal expression, it is not a matter of religion. Religions are systems that can evoke that feeling, but love of God, feeling for God, and experiencing God are not religion. Loving God is a natural form of expression in which we are aware of, connected to and filled with the presence of that cosmic force. So, here we are worshipping the Mother, the cosmic energy, whom yogis know as kundalini shakti, Vaishnavas as Lakshmi, Shaivas as Gauri and Amba, Christians as Mary. The Mother is the giver who nourishes life and at the same time, She has the power to bless everyone.

During the worship performed in the yajna, no image or idol is used. The invocation is done for *shoonya*, the unmanifest, attributeless existence. There is no idol of any God or demi-god. We have only invoked the formless into a formless space. We have only invited a nirguna, formless, placeless, eternal, infinite Atma, having no name. We have given Her a name and a sex, because we are used to it. Otherwise, She is neither male nor female. We have invoked Her and placed Her somewhere within that space; we don't know where that space is. We have invited the attributeless Shakti into shoonya. Only a cloth is put around something to represent Her. God can be created anywhere on earth, in water, in fire, in air or in ether.

Kanya kumari pooja

Kanya worship is an important part of Shakti Tantra and of the Sat Chandi Yajna. This is a new philosophy of life, where a little girl can be acknowledged and worshipped as a replica of the Divine Mother. This concept of the kanya is unparalleled in man's philosophy. Kanya means 'virgin'. In India, girls officially become kanyas, or virgins, at the age of nine. The concept is fully explained in the scriptures of Shakta Tantra. The discovery that a young virgin was capable of symbolizing and representing the Cosmic Mother was made by a rishi. Could you ever think of your little daughter as the replica of the Mother? No. This idea did not come to the average person, but to the rishis, the great seers.

The replica of greed is money; the replica of passion is a woman. The replica of fear is a tiger, and the replica of the goddess, the Cosmic Mother, is the kanya. The kanyas are very pure, simple and innocent. Up to the age of puberty, they don't know the jugglery of sensual life. Once puberty approaches, the hormones transform the body, emotions and mind. However, there are girls who remain virgins mentally and spiritually, even after puberty. They are virginal by nature, and it is these girls who come for sannyasa. A girl may be a virgin in the sense that she has not menstruated or had sexual interaction, but that alone is not virginity. Not every nine-year old girl can be worshipped as a kanya kumari. Virginity is a natural quality that belongs to one's genetic structure. This is the meaning of virginity in vedic astrology.

The concept of kanya kumari, or virgin, is also found in Christianity. Although Mary was a mother, she was still believed to be a virgin, because she reflected particular qualities that belong to a virgin. One who has the basic quality and divine grace of a virgin can give blessings. During the Kumari Pooja, on the final day of the Sat Chandi Yajna, one hundred and eight girls are looked upon as the form of the Mother and worshipped as Devi. We dress them, feed them and wash their feet, superimposing the concept of Devi on them, and receive their blessings. The kanyas are the Divine Mother's most beautiful form. They represent purity of soul. The soul of man is virgin; its pristine beauty and glory cannot be contaminated. But you cannot see that virgin soul, so you have to form a concept of it.

The kanyas of Rikhia, who host the Sat Chandi Maha Yajnas, represent that virgin reality. They represent your virgin soul, your pure spirit, your inner being, which you are unable to see. This concept is unparalleled. In Devi tantra, the kanya or virgin is considered to be the true embodiment of the Cosmic Mother. We are not her husband or her father.

We are her children and She is our Mother. We should remember this and feel it. In the tantric festival of Sat Chandi, the conductor of every ritual is a kanya. This is the most ancient concept of Shakta Tantra, where a young girl is regarded as the embodiment of divine energy, and there are replicas of the goddess everywhere.

Glossary

Abhisheka – a special kind of bath; an elaborate sacred rite, including chanting of sacred mantras dedicated to a deity during ceremonial bathing of it with fresh water, milk, ghee, honey and banana, often by the continuous pouring of the fluid on the idol from above with the help of a spoon or a conch

Achala – immovable

Achamana – water offered in worship for sipping for mental purification

Acharya – spiritual guide or teacher

Adharma – contrary to dharma or the natural order; disharmony; wrong actions; not fulfilling one's natural role in life

Adhyatmic – spiritual vibration

Adi Sesha – eternal support of the world in the form of a serpent

Adi Shakti – primal force behind creation

Adityas – resplendent suns; twelve in number

Advaita Vedanta – the philosophy which supports the view that the supreme being (Brahman) is the only eternal, unchanging reality; non-dualistic philosophy of Shankaracharya

Agama – scriptures denoting the esoteric traditional worship of Devi tantric texts

Agarbhati – incense

Agni – element of fire; god of fire and purification; witness of worship in fire ceremonies; symbol of the light of the Sun on Earth

Agnihotra rite – small fire ritual, performed daily at dawn and dusk

Aham Brahma Asmi – literally 'I am Brahman'; one of the four Mahavakyas or greatest spiritual sayings of Advaita Vedanta

Ahamkara – ego; awareness of existence of 'I'

Ahimsa – absence of violence from within; non violence on every level to all living beings

231

Aim Hreem Kleem – three beeja mantras repeated regularly while chanting the invocation to Devi; mantras representing Maha Saraswati, Maha Lakshmi and Maha Kali respectively

Aitareya-Brahmana – portion of the Vedas, describing the use of mantras in various yajnas, attributed to Rishi Aitareya

Ajamila – a great sinner who crossed over the ocean of worldly existence through kirtan

Ajapa japa – continuous, spontaneous repetition of mantra; meditation practice in which mantra is coordinated with breath

Ajna chakra – psychic and pranic centre situated at the top of the spinal cord; seat of intuition; centre where guru's commands are received

Ajnana – lack of wisdom

Akhara – traditionally a place for training in arms, particularly for sannyasins; place where sannyasins perform higher austerities in isolation

Akshata – unbroken and uncooked rice used in worship as a sign of auspiciousness, well being and prosperity

Alakh – which cannot be seen; flame; inner illumination

Alakh bara – 'invisible boundary', a place of seclusion which preserves sannyasa traditions; the place where paramahamsa sannyasins live

Alakh niranjan – 'that which can't be seen'; uninvolved, untainted or stainless

Allah – name of God in Muslim religion

Allah-o-Akbar – 'God is great', in the Urdu language

Alwars – group of 12 Vaishnava saints from South India

Amara – immortal

Amavasya – fifteenth day of the dark fortnight when there is absolutely no moon in the sky

Amrita – nectar flowing from sahasrara charka; immortality

Amrita bhava – the sense of absolute fulfilment

Anahad nada – sound which cannot be grasped or heard externally; that sound which is beyond sound; the basis of all sound; unstruck sound; unheard sound

Ananda – everlasting, pure bliss

Ananda Lahari – 'waves of bliss'; a devotional poem of 41 stanzas by Sri Shankaracharya in praise of the mother goddess Tripurasundari

Anandamaya kosha – sheath or body of bliss

Anandamayi Ma – Indian female saint

Angan – courtyard

Angavati – sacred diagrams used in worship

Annamaya kosha – sheath or body of matter

Antar atma – inner spirit or soul

Anugraha – grace; transmission of energy; blessings

Anushthana – resolve to perform mantra upasana for a particular period of time in one place, with absolute discipline; performed

Apara vidya – empirical science, knowledge of the material, worldly aspects

Aparadha bhava– devotion with a sense of guilt

Aradhana – to be fully immersed in worship of the deity with intense reverence

Arati – service or rite of worship involving waving of lights with reverence before a deity

Archana – ritual worship of God with or without form or attributes, usually through Vedic or Tantric methods

Ardhanareshwara – the half-male, half-female form of Shiva

Areca nut – betel nut (often mixed with other ingredients when) offered to a deity in worship to scent the mouth; used in worship to represent devi

Arghya – water offering made in a vessel during worship into which several ingredients like sandalwood paste, unbroken rice grains, etc. have been mixed

Arjuna – Lord Krishna's disciple in the *Bhagavad Gita*; one of the three son's of Kunti, third of the five Pandava brothers and a mighty warrior with expert knowledge of weapons

Arta – devotee who worships to alleviate distress, illness etc.

Artha – accomplishment; attainment in all spheres of life; material need, prosperity; one of the four purusharthas

Artharthi – devotee who worships seeking wealth, possessions, children etc.

Arya samaj – a reformist group founded by Swami Dayananda Saraswati, interested in re-establishing Vedic customs and upliftment of women

Asakti – attachment

Asana – offering a seat for the object of worship; steady and comfortable meditative pose

Asanavidhi – rite or service performed by a devotee for taking his seat to conduct his pooja

Ashram – place of spiritual retreat and inner growth through internal and external labour

Ashrama – stage or period of life, of which there are four according to the ancient Vedic tradition: brahmacharya (student), grihastha (householder), vanaprastha (retirement) and sannyasa

Ashtottarshatlaksh purashcharana – ten million, eight hundred thousand rounds of japa mantra

Ashwa Medha Yajna – a ritual in which a horse is released and the ground it covers measures the sovereignty of the monarch

Atma bhava – attitude of perceiving the Self in all; feeling and experiencing yourself in others

Atma jnana – knowledge of the Self

Atma nivedana – ninth form of bhakti when even the last vestige of individual identity is dissolved in cosmic awareness; complete surrender of the self

Atma samarpan – total self-surrender

Atma(n) – individual soul; spirit; self; self beyond mind and body

Aum – or 'Om', universal mantra considered to be the origin of all other mantras; cosmic vibration of the universe; name representing the concept of God

Aum Namah – 'Aum is the name of God'

Avadhoota – one who is free from all worldly attachments or mental illusions, who is beyond duality; one who has transcended normal consciousness; sixth order of sannyasa tradition

Avahana – the tantric science of invocation; welcoming service or rite invoking the deity into the image of worship

Avatara – incarnated soul of divinity, God

Avidya – ignorance, illusion; also described here as poverty

Ayodhya – capital of Lord Rama's kingdom; also considered to be the creator's eternally shining city

Ayurveda – Vedic system of medical diagnosis and treatment

Baidyanath Dham – a temple of extraordinary power, and the temple precincts of the jyotirlingam at Deoghar, Bihar, dedicated to Lord Shiva

Bala Mukunda – the beautiful child Krishna

Bali – a powerful demon blessed by the trickery of Lord Vishnu during his incarnation as a dwarf

Batuka pooja – ceremonial worship of young boys

Beeja – seed, root

Beeja akshara – seed or original sound syllables

Bel tree – see bilva

Bel varan – a tantric ritual to the bilva or bel tree

Benares – also known as Varanasi or Kashi; place of pilgrimage in India; known as Lord Shiva's city

Bhagalpur – city in Bihar, India

Bhagavad Gita – Lord Krishna's teachings to his disciple Arjuna, delivered at the commencement of the battle of Kurukshetra during the great war recorded in the *Mahabharata*

Bhagavat naam – literally, 'the name of God'

Bhajan – devotional song about various forms of God; singing God's name

Bhakta – devotee of God

Bhakti – literally, 'divine love'; pure intense inner devotion or love; channelling of the intellect, emotions and self towards a higher purpose

Bhakti marga – path of devotion or bhakti

Bharata – India; literally, 'land engulfed in light'; also the name of one of Lord Rama's brothers

Bhasma – sacred ash worn by Lord Shiva

Bhava – attitude, feeling

Bhavana – feeling, emotion; ability to perceive subtle vibrations

Bhishma – great warrior of *Mahabharata* fame

Bhoga – experience of, and craving for pleasure and enjoyment; sensory indulgence and gratification

Bhumi – earth

Bhrumadhya – eyebrow centre; related to ajna chakra in the psychic body

Bhumi pooja – worship of the earth

Bhupura – the square and outer protective force of a yantra

Bhutas – evil spirits, also known as pretas and rakshasas

Bible – the holy scripture of the Christians

Bighas – measure of land; 5/8 ths of an acre

Bilva – the 'stone fruit' tree; a sacred tree whose leaves are in triplets and are specially offered in worship of Lord Siva; the leaves and are considered to be Shiva's prasad; also known as the bel tree

Bol Bam – literally, 'Speak the name of Lord Shiva'; mantra used by pilgrims to Baidyanath

Book of The Dead – Ancient Egyptian scripture of spiritual teachings regarding death, written in hieroglyphics (picture symbols)

Brahma – first of the Hindu trinity, represents creation; God as Creator

Brahma bhava – highest state of realization: the Supreme Spirit and individual spirit are one; worshipper experiences all as God

Brahma vakya – word, speech of God

Brahma vidya – knowledge of God

Brahma yajna – daily personal worship of God; sacrifice made to God

Brahmacharya – living in constant awareness of Brahman; self-restraint; abstinence

235

Brahmacharya ashrama – first stage of life to twenty-five years of age, devoted to learning and study

Brahman – Absolute Reality the one Supreme Reality; ever-expanding, limitless consciousness

Brahmana bhojana – feeding a Brahmin upon completion of pooja

Brahmarishi – realized sage

Brahmastra – an ancient weapon with immense destructive power described here as faith (shraddha), the ultimate weapon of spirituality

Brahmin – literally, 'one who is one with Brahma'; member of the priestly caste; one of the four varnas or divisions of the caste system in India; one who is spiritually inclined

Buddha – 'illumined one'; an enlightened sage who lived in India about 2,500 years ago, whose followers created Buddhism

Chaitanya Mahaprabhu – saint of India, who glorified Lord Krishna with his chanting of kirtan

Chakra – psychic energy centre relating to the evolution of man

Chakravarti – emperor, sovereign of the world; ruler of the charka or country

Chala – movable

Chandana – sandalwood paste

Chandi – the form of Durga who killed the demon Chand; the goddess responsible for change

Chawra – altar

Chetana – consciousness

Chhandogya Upanishad – part of the *Sama Veda*.

Chitrakoot – one of the places where Rama stayed with Sita and Lakshman during his fourteen year banishment from Ayodhya

Conch – large shell that is blown in battle, during ritual worship and on auspicious occasions

Daan – gift, philanthropy; to give away

Daan Yajna – giving something with devotion or as sacrifice

Dakshina – service or rite in pooja in which a gift of money offered to the deity on two betel leaves and sprinkled with water; gift offered to a guru; situated on the right or southern side

Dakshinamukhi shankha – south-faced or reverse coiled conch, important in Tantric ritual

Dal – pulse; lentils

Dama – mental restraint

Darbha (durva) grass – wheat grass, auspicious offering in pooja

Darshan – real vision; to glimpse; to see; to have an inner vision and blessing of the divine power; blessing received just by seeing an enlightened or divine being or God; to see an object without the medium of the senses, without thinking or feeling

Darshan Shastra – scriptures on philosophy

Dasahara – 10th and final day of the nine day worship of the cosmic Mother during Navaratri

Dasaratha – an emperor of India who ruled as king of Ayodhya and was the father of Lord Rama

Dasya bhakti – devotion expressed by cultivating the inner attitude of a servant with God as the Master

Dattatreya – sage of ancient India; one of the forms of Vishnu, combining the nature of all three gods, Brahma, Vishnu and Maheshvara

Daya – mercy

Deenabandhu – friend to the unfortunate

Deepa pooja – worship of the lamp

Deepa(k) – small lamp fed with ghee, waved as an offering in front of the deity, idol

Deepavali (Diwali) – festival of light celebrating Lord Rama's return from exile after vanquishing Ravana; symbolizes the victory of good over evil

Deoghar – literally, 'God's house'; cremation ground of the consort of Shiva in her form as Sati; district in which Swami Satyananda presently resides

Desha – place

Deva – literally, 'illumined one'; higher force or power; a self-luminous being in a male form

Deva Utthana – the day when the gods, or certain dormant energies awaken

Devaki – wife of King Vasudev, mother of Lord Krishna

Devata – god, deity; illumined form; form of divinity; divine being with a particular function

Devata vandana – prayer, salutation to the gods

Devi – a self-luminous being in a female form; divine force, manifestation of Shakti; goddess; Divine Mother

Dharma – natural law; natural role one has to play in life; righteous action; duty, conduct; one of the four purusharthas

Dharmashastras – scriptures explaining how mankind should conduct life in accordance with dharma

Dhoop – incense

Dhuni – sadhana fireplace

237

Dhyana – meditation; a rite in pooja performed as mental purification before worship begins, contemplation on hymns describing the appearance of the deity so as to assist the worshipper to visualize them; absorption in the object of worship or meditation

Dhyana Bhava – expression of constant meditation upon a form of God in the heart

Dosa – a South Indian food, like a very large and extremely thin savoury pancake

Draupadi – great devotee and worshipper of Lord Krishna; daughter of king Drupada of Panchala; wife of the five Pandava brothers

Drishta – that which is seen

Durga – the divinity manifesting as a goddess symbolizing the potent and powerful feminine force; personification of Shakti in her fearsome aspect; Mother; one of the manifestations of the consort of Shiva

Durgasaptashati – tantric text traditionally chanted in worship of the cosmic Mother

Dwaraka – capital city of Lord Krishna situated in the Bay of Kutch

Dwesha – repulsion, dislike

Ekadashi – eleventh days of the bright and dark fortnight in a lunar month

Ekagrata – one-pointedness

Ganapati – another name for Ganesha

Gandha – perfume

Ganesha – elephant-headed, one tusked deity, son of Lord Shiva and Parvati; scribe of the Mahabharata; symbol of auspiciousness, wealth, knowledge, attainment and remover of obstacles

Ganga – sacred Ganges River

Ganga Stotram – hymn in worship of the devi, deity of the river Ganges

Garuda – divine form of an eagle; vehicle of Vishnu

Gayatri mantra – Shakti mantra of twenty-four syllables

Ghanta pooja – worship of the bell

Ghanti-vanti wala bhakti – the bell-ringing-type-of-devotion

Gopis – milkmaids; the transcendental devotees of Krishna

Gouranga – a Vaishnava saint

Grihastha – householder

Grihastha ashrama – second stage of life; householder, married life from about twenty-five to fifty years of age

Gular tree – sacred tree under which Dattatreya received enlightenment

Guna – qualities inherent in all nature; quality or attribute of the mind; three in number: tamas, rajas and sattwa

Guru – dispeller of darkness; spiritually enlightened soul, who can dispel ignorance and illusion from the mind of a disciple

Guru Granth Sahib – holy book of the Sikhs

Guru Nanak – an enlightened sage who formed the Sikh religion

Guru Poornima – full moon day in July when all gurus are worshipped, when guru's grace descends to uplift the disciples

Guru tattwa – inherent element of guru in an individual

Gurubhais – disciples of the same guru

Gurudwara – place of the guru

Haj – the sacred pilgrimage of the Muslims to Mecca

Halwa – a sweet made from roasted flour, ghee and sugar

Hanuman – son of Pavan, god of the wind, and Anjana, a female monkey; devotee of Lord Rama who aided Rama in the rescue of Sita; considered to be the embodiment of devotion, strength and heroism

Hari – one of the names of Vishnu or Lord Narayana

Hari Priya – another name for tulsi, the beloved of Lord Narayana

Hatha Yoga – system of yoga consisting of practices for physical and mental purification to balance energies and awaken kundalini

Havan – fire used in ceremonial worship

Himalayas – the great chain of rugged snow capped mountains running through north India, Pakisthan, Nepal and Tibet; abode of the gods

Holi – festival of colours, celebrating the victory of the gods over the demons

Iccha shakti – dynamic mental force of willpower

Idli – a South Indian food, a steamed, light rice cake

Indra – chief of the gods; a divinity of the atmosphere controlling the elements; god of warfare, bestower of victory and ruler of the senses

Indra loka – abode of the gods

Ishta – literally, 'I like it'

Ishta devata – one's personal deity or symbol of the Supreme; the divine form of God to which you are attracted; the divine form realized within oneself

Ishta mantra – mantra of the chosen personal deity

Ishwara – literally, 'one who rules'; God, the indestructible or un-decaying divine principle; higher state of existence and consciousness

Ishwara pranidhana – surrender to God

Jainism – ancient sect famous for its adherence to non-violence; the most recent Master of the tradition is Mahavir

Japa – repetition of a mantra or a name of God

Jerusalem – holy city; pilgrimage place of the Christians

Jesus Christ – an avatara, the anointed Messiah and enlightened sage whose disciples founded Christianity

Jignasu – devotee who worships for knowledge of God; aspirant, spiritual seeker; preliminary stage of sannyasa

Jiva – individual soul of man which passes through 8,400,000 yonis to obtain the human form

Jivanmukta – a soul who is liberated while living

Jivatma – individual soul

Jnana – true knowledge; wisdom

Jnani bhakta – devotee who worships solely for divine knowledge, experience; wise person

Jyoti – flame

Jyotirlingam – illumined lingam; oval shaped stone worshipped as a symbol of illumined consciousness of Lord Shiva

Kaala – time

Kaba – most sacred place of Muslim worship and pilgrimage in Mecca

Kabir – religious reformer and saint; a great protagonist of Hindu-Muslim amity, influenced by Sufism

Kaivalya – liberation from the wheel of births and deaths

Kaivalyapada – the path of final liberation; fourth and final chapter of Patanjali's *Yoga Sutras*

Kalagni – the fire of death

Kalasha (kumbha) – the vessel used symbolically as the seat of the universe; a symbol of plenty and welfare

Kalasha pooja – worship of the vessel

Kali – aspect of maha shakti, the destroyer of time and annihilator of the ego; a goddess symbolizing the destructive female aspect of divinity

Kali yuga – age of kali: fourth and present age of the world, which began in 3102 BC, with a duration of 432,000 years. During this cycle mankind is at the height of technology, decadence and corruption of spiritual values

Kama – emotional need or fulfilment; one of the four purusharthas

Kamakhya – siddhapeetha in Assam

Kamsa – a demon King of Mathura destroyed by Lord Krishna

Kamya karma – action performed to fulfil a particular desire

Kanya (kumari) – a young virgin female; daughter; a girl between nine years and puberty

Karma – action in the manifest and unmanifest dimension; law of cause and effect of three kinds

Karma yoga – perfected action; yoga of action; action performed with meditative awareness; yoga of dynamic meditation; yogic path of selfless service

Karmakand – precise rituals connected with Vedic sacrifices and other religious ceremonial and sacrificial activities; that portion of the Upanishads detailing the instructions on the proper behaviour and the daily ritual worship for householders

Kartik Shukla Ekadashi – eleventh day of the bright fortnight during the lunar month of Kartik (October/November)

Kartikeya – a son of Lord Shiva, worshipped in South India

Karuna – compassion

Katha – story offered at time of worship

Kathmandu – capital city of Nepal

Kaushalya – wife of King Dasaratha, mother of Lord Rama

Kheer – dessert made from rice boiled in milk and aromatic spices

Khichari – 'mixture of ingredients'; dish made from rice, pulse and ghee

Kirtan – form of worship by the singing of God's name and glories; devotional songs or chanting of mantras with musical accompaniment

Kolkata – capital city of West Bengal, India

Koran – the holy book of the Muslims

Krishna – avatar, manifestation of God in human form; eighth incarnation of Lord Vishnu (the cosmic sustainer); darkness; guru of Arjuna; His teachings are recorded in the Bhagavad Gita; beloved of the gopis of Vrindavan; historical ruler of India

Kriya – action; motion; a yogic practice involving higher techniques

Kriya yoga – a path of kundalini yoga which combines asana, pranayama and visualizations to awaken the dormant spiritual force

Kriyaman karma – in the great law of cause and effect they are the actions not yet performed

Kroda – anger

Kshatriya – member of the warrior class; one of the four varnas or divisions of the caste system in India

Kubera – the divine treasurer

Kumari – unmarried girl; virgin

Kumari pooja – ritual worship of young, virgin girls

Kumkum – vermilion red powder used in symbolic worship to make a dot at the eyebrow centre, as prasad of the goddess; a marking along the parting of the hair which signifies a married woman

Kundalini – the divine energy that transforms human consciousness; evolutionary force; vital force or latent energy residing in mooladhara chakra, often referred to as the serpent power

241

Kundalini yoga – path of yoga which awakens the dormant spiritual force

Kunti – the first wife of King Pandu, a woman who called down the deities Surya, Yama, Vayu and Indra through the power of mantra thus creating her sons Karna, Yudhisthir, Bheema and Arjuna

Laila – character in an Irani love story; beloved of Manju

Lakh – one hundred thousand units

Lakshman – brother, devotee and worshipper of Rama; a hero of the *Ramayana*

Lakshmi – the wife of Lord Vishnu worshipped as the goddess of wealth, beauty and good fortune

Lakshmi pooja – Golden coins are worshipped as representing the goddess Lakshmi

Lalita – the red goddess associated with Sri Yantra

Laya – dissolution, merging

Likhit japa – writing of mantra; form of upasana

Lila – divine play, pastime; cosmic game of consciousness and energy; activity of prakriti and its three gunas

Linga sharira – the causal body or the subtle body

Lingam – smooth oval shaped, black stone used in worship of Shiva

Lokas – planes of existence; dimensions of consciousness

Lotus – a flower which symbolizes the spiritual progress of a devotee unaffected by objects of the sense organs; symbol of the chakras; diagram worshipped as a symbol of Lakshmi

Madhu – honey or sweetness

Madhuparka – prasad mixture offered in worship, made of honey, ghee, milk and curd

Madhurya – sweetness

Madhurya bhava – most intense and sweetest love between lover and beloved, husband and wife

Maha – great

Maha Kaal Chita Dhuni – the fire which has burnt continuously since Swami Satyananda's arrival in Rikhia, September 1989

Maha Kumbha Mela – a great gathering of saints and sages on both the invisible and visible planes held every twelve years when the sun is in kumbha rashi

Maha Mrityunjaya – mantra used for combating disease or death, or for attainment of spiritual immortality; Shiva mantra

Mahabharata – Epic of ancient India involving the great war between the Pandava and Kaurava princes, which chronicles the lives and spiritual development of humans, devas, demons, animals and others

Mahanirajana deepa – service or rite in pooja in which a great lamp is waved in front of the deity

Mahatma – great soul

Mahavakyas – the four highest spiritual sayings: 1) Aham Brahma Asmi, I am Brahman; 2) Tat Tvam Asi, Thou are That; 3) Ayam Atma Brahma, Self is Brahman; 4) Prajnanam Brahma, Knowledge is Brahma

Mahavir – most recent master of the Jains

Maithuna – state of being when bhavana, individual personality, unites with the personality of God

Maithunam utpadayati – the concept of unification of purusha and prakriti

Majnu – character in an Irani love story; beloved of Laila

Makar Sankranti – when the sun begins its journey into the northern hemisphere for six months: 13th to 15th of January; Indian winter solstice

Mala – garland, necklace, rosary made from tulsi, sandalwood, rudraksha or crystal, etc. used as an aid in japa and meditation

Mamta – the feeling of attachment; feeling it is mine

Manasasnana – mental bath, a service or rite of pooja

Manasic pooja – mental worship

Mandala – diagram used in worship to represent divine knowledge or presence, symbolizing the deeper aspects of man's psyche; the abode of a god

Mangalasutra – traditional mala or necklace of black pearl beads which the husband gives to the wife during the marriage ceremony

Manjira – a type of cymbal used in kirtan

Mantra – subtle sound or combinations of sound vibrations revealed to sages in deep meditation, used for liberating consciousness from the limitations of mundane awareness and chanted in mantra upasana

Mantra pushpanjali – service or rite in pooja in which handfuls of flowers, consecrated by mantras, are offered to the deity, image, idol

Mantra siddhi – perfection of mantra

Manusmriti – highly respected code of conduct given by the ancient law giver Manu for the spiritual evolution of all beings

Marga – path

Maruts – divine forms worshipped as gods of the wind

Masta – one who is carefree or absolutely blissful

Mathura – birth place of Lord Krishna

Matra – unit of time

Matrika – literally 'little mother'; the creative force of the letters of the Sanskrit alphabet

Maya – to measure out; creative power; power of illusion; counterpart of Brahman; partial understanding; wrong notions about self-identity

Menakas – divine forms of Shakti

Mirabai – female saint born in the early 16th century in Rajasthan, India; worshipper and great devotee of Lord Krishna

Mitra sadhana – spiritual practice of being a friend to all, without exception; understanding, compassion and caring for all

Moha – deluded attachment

Mohammed – the saint who formed the Muslim religion

Moksha – liberation from the cycles of birth, death and rebirth; inner freedom; one of the four purusharthas

Moksha sadhaka – one who lives life only to attain liberation

Moksha vidya – knowledge, experience of liberation

Moola trikona – the root triangle

Mridanga – large drum made of clay, used as a musical accompaniment in kirtan

Mrityunjaya – conqueror of death; epithet of Shiva

Mudra – in Indian dance: specific physical positions combined with special bhavas or attitudes; in yoga: psycho-neural gesture which alters and redistributes pranic energy within the mind and body

Mukti – salvation, emancipation

Muktinath – place of pilgrimage in the Himalayas, Nepal

Mullah – Muslim priest

Mumbai – capital city of Maharastra State, India

Mumukshuttra – keen longing for liberation from mundane existence

Murti – statue, symbol, image used in worship

Naam samkirtan – group chanting of God's name

Naam smarana – remembrance of God's name; a form of upasana, worship

Nada – psychic or eternal sound

Naga snake

Naga panchami – the day for worship of snakes

Naimittika karma – action performed with a purpose on a special event

Naimittika pooja – occasional poojas performed so as to attain a specific desire

Naivedya – the ritual in worship of offering food or a meal to the deity, which becomes an oblation to the life force of the deity

Nama roopa – all names and forms (of God)

Namaskara – prostration; service or rite in pooja in which prostrations are made in front of the idol; simple greeting by joining both hands; a symbol of reverence

Namaz – Muslim style of worship or prayer which combines specific postures with chantings in Arabic

Namdev – a mahatma from the State of Maharashtra, India

Namo Narayan – 'Salutations to you who are a form of lord Narayana'; used as salutation amongst sannyasins

Nandi – the snow white sacred bull, attendant and favourite vehicle of Lord Shiva

Narada – devarishi, sage, lawgiver and political philosopher mentioned in the *Rigveda, Ramayana* and *Mahabharata*

Narasimha – incarnation of Lord Vishnu in the form of half-man, half-lion

Narayan(a) – a name of god Vishnu, the sustainer of the universe

Narayana bhava – seeing God in all; service of devotees to all beings

Navadha bhakti – nine stages of bhakti, upasana

Navaratri – nine nights; bi-annual festival focusing on the worship of the goddess Durga and Sri Rama

Nayanar – Shaiva saint from South India

Nayanmars – the group of 64 Shaiva saints from South India

Neem Karoli Baba – a famous present day Indian saint of the bhakti marg

Neti-neti – doctrine of 'Not this, not this'; a famous exclamation of the Upanishads related to the impossibility of reducing divinity to any explanation or definition

Nididhyasana – deep state of meditation

Nirakara – formless, without form; unmanifest

Niranjan – immaculate; stainless

Nirguna – a form free of all gunas; without qualities

Nirguna Upasana – worship without form, without attributes

Nirvikalpa – free from distinction, admitting no alternative; a state of samadhi

Nirvikalpa samadhi – state in which the mind ceases to function and only pure consciousness remains; super conscious state

Nishkama – selfless, desireless

Nishkama Upasana – worship without request for worldly desires; worship only to realize the ultimate knowledge

Nishkamya bhava – feeling of freedom from attachment to the fruits of labour

Nishshreyas – devotee desiring only unification with God

Nishtha – devoutness

Nitya karma – daily unavoidable, necessary and obligatory actions including bathing, eating, defecating, sleeping

Nivritti – renunciation of the external world; without vrittis or mental modification; spiritual life

Niyama – personal observances defined by Patanjali as cleanliness, contentment, austerity, self-study and surrender to God

Nritya – dance

Om – or 'Aum', universal mantra; the origin of all other mantras; cosmic vibration of the universe; word representing God

Om Namah Shivaya – Shiva mantra

Om Tat Sat – God is Truth

Pada – path, way, foot

Padaseva/Padasevana – service of God's feet; formal worship to guru, to a mental image of God, to images of God in temples or at home; serving in holy shrines etc.

Paduka – wooden sandals (of gods, gurus or saintly persons)

Padya – water for washing the feet

Pancha tattwas – the five elements of prakriti: earth, water, fire, air, ether

Panchagni sadhana – sadhana of the five fires; meditation in the middle of four fires at each point of the compass, the fifth fire being the summer sun overhead; sadhana involving mastery of the five internal fires: ego, attachment, desire, anger and greed

Panchami – fifth day of each fortnight of the lunar month

Panchamrit – banana, ghee, honey, milk and curd mixture traditionally offered to the deity worshipped in pooja

Panchanga – Hindu almanacs or calendars which give daily astrological details

Panchopachara pooja – ritual worship with five services, (pancha meaning five)

Panchayat – district

Pandit – priest; learned scholar; wise; one trained in performing priestly functions; established in the perception of reality

Para bhakta – supreme bhakta; one who constantly worships God as the one essence in all forms

Para pooja – considered the highest worship in which the devotee experiences and worships nothing but God at all times

Para vidya – transcendental science; the science of God

Paramahamsa – literally 'supreme swan'; sannyasins devoted totally to sadhana, thus approaching the final goal of liberation

Paramartha – the highest service

Paramatma(n) – the supreme or sublime Self; atma of the entire universe, of the individual as well as the cosmos

Parimaladravya – aromatic, perfumed substances offered in pooja to satisfy the deity and to protect the place of worship

Parivrajaka – wandering mendicant

Paropkar – working for the welfare of others

Parsi – people originally from Iran who follow the Zoroastrian religion

Parvati – consort of Lord Shiva in the aspect of daughter of the mountains; his first disciple; mahashakti

Pashupatinath – pilgrimage center in Nepal, where one of the twelve jyotirlingams is located

Patanjali – rishi who codified the stages of meditation in the system of raja yoga; author of the *Yoga Sutras*

Path – any set of mantras to be chanted

Pativrata dharma – rules of a chaste wife

Peepal tree (ashvattha) – a scared tree cultivated throughout India, particularly in temples and their vicinity; Lord Vishnu is said to dwell in this tree; symbol of kundalini; planting, watering and worshipping it brings prosperity to the planter and the surrounding environment; known in English as the 'sacred fig' tree

Peetha – abode; place; seat; synonym for math

Phala – fruit; auspicious offering of fruit given to honour the deity; result of an action

Pinda daan – offerings to ancestors

Pitri – ancestors

Pitriloka – heavenly abode of ancestors, forefathers

Pitri pooja – worship performed for ancestors, forefathers

Pooja – ritual worship; method to bring devotee into the proximity of God; honour, respect; rites

Pooja bhava – external worship

Pooja vidhi – the ways, rules and secrets of ritual worship described in the ancient scriptures

Poojasthana – places of pooja

Poornahuti – the final rite in a fire ceremony or yajna where fruits etc. are offered to the flames and a wish is made

Poornima – full moon day or night

Pradakshina – service or rite in worship where circumambulation is made to offer respect to the deity, image, idol; devotee may also turn himself on the spot, always keeping it to one's right

Prahlada – great devotee of Lord Vishnu

Prakriti – active principle of the manifest world; the aspect of material manifestation in the Samkhya philosophy; cosmic energy

Prana – vital life force; vital energy

Pranapratishtha (or avahana Invocation) – invocation at commencement of pooja by which the deity is made to be present in the idol; ceremony which invokes the life force into the image of worship

Pranayama – yogic technique of breathing, breath control and retention which expands the range of vital or pranic energy

Pranopasana – sacrifice of prana through regulated inhalation, retention and exhalation

Prarabdha karma – destined action; unalterable or fixed karma; the portion of karma that determines one's present life; actions which cannot be altered

Prarthana – worship through prayer

Prasad – food, sweets or other items that have first been offered to the Supreme at the time of worship; consecrated item; grace; happiness, delight and joy

Pratika – symbol used in worship or meditation

Pratishta – installation of a deity of worship

Pratyahara – management of the senses

Prayaschitta (prarathana) – prayer of the devotee the deity's blessing; prayer to forgive deficiencies and offences made knowingly or unknowingly during the worship

Prema bhava – feeling of love; regard

Prema bhakti – devotion by redirecting love towards God

Preyas – worldly desires of the devotee

Prokshana – sprinkling water as purification of the place of worship

Psalm – spiritual poems or verses in worship or glory of God

Puranas – ancient texts concerning the earliest history and mythology of the tantric and vedic traditions

Purascharana – form of mantra upasana, which involves repetition of a mantra hundreds of thousands of times within a specified period of time, and while following definite rules for the practice

Purusha – pure consciousness, name of consciousness in Sankhya philosophy; man

Purusha Sukta – ancient mantras in worship of the supreme consciousness found in the *Rig Veda*

Purusharthas – personal effort; four areas of human endeavour to be fulfilled; artha, karma, dharma and moksha

Pushpa – flower

Radha – foremost transcendental lover and devotee of Lord Krishna; a milkmaid

Raga – attractions; likes

Raghunath – family name of Lord Rama

Raghunath Kutir – residence of Lord Rama in the Akhara in Rikhiapeeth

Raja – king

Raja yoga – 'royal yoga'; codified by Patanjali Maharishi in his *Yoga Sutras*; a system of yoga which awakens the psychic awareness and faculties through meditation culminating in samadhi

Rajarajeshwari – form of devi known as queen of queens; empress

Rajarishi – rishi amongst kshatriyas, the warrior and kingly class

Rajas – one of the three gunas representing the dynamic, active state of mind and nature

Rajasooya Yajna – sacrifice performed by a king entitled to assume the title of emperor

Rakshasa – demon; negative or self defeating force such as jealousy, arrogance, selfishness

Ram Naam Aradhana – worship of Rama; one month program in worship of Rama, held at Rikhiapeeth in 1996

Rama – hero of the *Ramayana*; heroic and virtuous king of the Solar Dynasty; seventh incarnation of Vishnu, the embodiment of dharma

Ramacharitamanas – the life story of Lord Rama as a devotional, poetic composition written by Tulsidas, in Avadhi, a local dialect

Ramakrishna Paramahamsa – a devotee of Kali and renowned mystic and of the last century

Ramayana – an inspired book in verses describing the life of the avatara Lord Rama; the historical version is written by Valmiki in Sanskrit, and the devotion version authored by Tulsidas, as mentioned above

Rameshwaram – pilgrimage center in South India, where Rama stayed while building the bridge to Lanka

Rangoli – juice; designs made in white powder at places of worship

Rasa – blissful essence of love

Rasagulla – an Indian sweet

Rati – intense love or attachment

Rati bhava – intense, passionate feeling

Ravana – a demon king of Lanka who abducted Lord Rama's wife Sita, so that he ensured war with Rama, thus expressing devotion through emnity

Rig Veda – most ancient of the four Vedas comprised of mantras

Rikhia – village in the District of Deoghar, in the State of Jharkhanda, India where Swami Satyananda currently resides

Rishi – a vedic seer; realized sage; one who meditates on the Self

Rishikesh – pilgrimage center in Northern India on the banks of the Ganges River

Ruchi – liking or having a taste for something

Rudra – form of Shiva

Sadhaka – spiritual aspirant; one who practices sadhana

Sadhana – spiritual practice done regularly for attainment of inner experience and self-realization

Sadhana bhakti – devotion to sadhana

Sadhu – a spiritual mendicant; one who regularly performs spiritual practices for enlightenment over a long period of time, with faith and devotion; one who is compassionate to all; a good person

Saguna Upasana – worship with form, with attributes

Sahaja – easy, spontaneous

Sahasrara Chakra – abode of super consciousness; 'thousand petalled lotus'; highest chakra or psychic centre which symbolizes the threshold between the psychic and spiritual realms, located at the crown of the head

Sakama Upasana – worship for worldly gain, e.g. wealth, sons, victory, wellbeing

Sakara – with form

Sakara Ishwara – God with form

Sakha – friend

Sakhya bhava – cultivating the attitude of a friend

Sakshatkara – to perceive that which is not visible to the eyes; direct experience of the absolute

Sama – sensory restraint; tranquility; equipoise, harmonized

Sama Veda – Veda primarily of devotion, worship and contemplation

Samadhana – balance of mind

Samadhi – union with the Divine; culimation of upasana or meditation; state of unity

Samarpan – balanced dedication; surrender

Sambandh – contact or communication; relationship

Samkhya – one of the six darshana or systems of Indian philosophy; based on the division of existence into purusha, prakriti and a number of elements

Sampradaya – tradition

Samsara – illusory world; unending cycle of birth and death

Samskara – education; social rituals that create positive psychic impressions; mental impression; past mental impressions which set up impulses and trains of thought; unconscious memory

Sanatana Dharma – system of eternal values

Sanchit karma – stored, accumulated action; subconscious impressions of past lives

Sandhya – daily personal rite or worship; dawn and dusk

Sandhya karma/Sandhya vandana – prayer and prostration conducted in the morning and/or evening

Sandilya – rishi who authored the *Bhagavat Purana*

Sankalpa – most important service or rite of worship; resolve; will power, determination or conviction

Sankalpapurti – service or rite at the completion of pooja where the devotee reconfirms his sankalpa; wish that the deity be pleased with the pooja and surrender of the merit gained to God

Sankirtan – singing of God's name; form of upasana, worship

Sannyasa – renunciation; dedication; from *sam* meaning 'equable' and *nyasa* meaning 'trust'

Sannyasa ashrama – fourth stage of life, traditionally from age of seventy-five years onwards; total renunciation

Sannyasin – renunciate; one who has detached himself from worldly affairs and strives to attain self realization, moksha; trustee

Sanskrit – ancient language of the Indian/European continent composed of 54 letters

Santhali – an ancient tribe found in Bihar; tribesmen of the region of Santhal, in which Rikhia is located

Saraswati – wife of Brahma manifesting as the goddess of spiritual knowledge, wisdom and the arts; another name for sushumna nadi; an underground river in legend

Sasur – father-in-law

Sat Chandi Maha Yajna – a powerful esoteric tantric yajna to instigate transformation thus enabling the experience of divine life

Satchidananda – three divine attributes: truth, consciousness, bliss

Satguru – true guru who has attained self-realization; the inner guru

Sati – manifestation of the consort of Lord Shiva; also Indian custom in which the wife burnt herself on the funeral pyre of her husband

Satsanga – gathering of spiritually minded people in which the ideals and principles of truth are discussed; being in the company of saints or wise men; 'association with truth', from the roots *sat* (truth) and *sanga* (company)

Sattwa – a balanced state of light and knowledge, one of the three gunas; pure; state of luminosity and harmony

Sattwic – pure

Satya – truth, reality

Satyavan – husband of Savitri in the epic of the *Ramayana*

Saubhagyadravya – substances offered in worship, signifying good fortune: tumeric powder, kumkum, collyrium, glass bangles, a mirror, etc.

Saundarya Lahari – 'wave of beauty'; a devotional hymn to Devi written by Adi Shankaracharya

Savitri – wife of Satyavan in the epic of the *Ramayana*

Seva – selfless service at the feet of God or guru

Sevak – servant; one who lives with a paramahamsa in order to take care of necessary interactions with the realm of duality; devotee with the attitude of a servant

Sevak dharma – the duty of a servant

Shabari – a tribal woman who had intense love for Lord Rama

Shaiva – worshipper of Lord Shiva

Shaivism – tradition where Shiva is worshipped as the supreme deity

Shaivites – worshippers of Shiva

Shakta – worshipper of Devi, the female aspect of God as the ultimate form

Shakti – inner creative energy; vital energy force; power, Mother, manifest power of consciousness, female principle; couterpart of Shiva

Shaktipeetha – place, abode where Shakti is worshipped; spiritual place dedicated to or indwelt by Shakti

Shaligram – spherical fossilized shell mostly found in the region of the Gandaki River in Nepal, it is worshipped as a symbol of Lord Vishnu

Shankara – the auspicious form of Shiva

Shankaracharya – enlightened sage who revitalized the Shaivite tradition, expounded and spread the Adwaita Vedanta philosophy throughout India, and founded the Dasnami order of sannyasa; the spiritual heads of the modern sannaysa traditions from the linage

Shankha – see conch

Shankha mudra – gesture with the hands which imitate the shape of a conch

Shankha pooja – worship of the conch

Shastra – scriptures; authentic text; an authoritative treatise on any subject, particularly science and religion

Shatkarmas – six cleansing practices of Hatha Yoga: nauli, dhauti, kunjal, laghoo shankaprakshalana, trataka

Shatsampat – sixfold spiritual wealth – tranquility, restraint, renunciation, endurance, faith and balance of mind

Shiva – 'auspicious one'; supreme Consciousness; Lord of the yogis; male principle; the aspect of the Hindu trinity (Brahma, Vishnu and Mahesh or Shiva) representing the destructive or transformative aspect

Shivalingam – symbol of consciousness; a black oval shaped stone used in worship as a symbol of Lord Shiva

Shivamahimna stotra – hymn in worship of Shiva

Shivaratri – darkest night of the year when Lord Shiva's marriage to Shakti is celebrated; often referred to as Maha Shivaratri; usually observed on Phalguna (February/March) and sometimes on Magha in the Hindu lunar calendar

Shodashopachara pooja – traditional form of worship with sixteen types of offerings

Shoonya – unmanifest, attributeless existence; void, vacuum, nothingness

Shraaddha – commemorative rites for deceased ancestors

Shraddha – faith, sustained through experience and intuition; reverence

Shravana – form of upasana, worship by listening to the stories of God which tell of His divine name and form

Shreya – spiritual blessing, spiritual abundance, transcendental gain

Shruti – the Vedas; scriptures revealed to or heard by saints in meditation

Siddha – adept or perfected person; one who is able to control the elements and nature; side effect of sadhana

Siddhateerthas – holy places which have retained the vibrations of the austerities of great siddhas; awakened shrine

Siddhi – perfection, psychic power, accomplishment acquired as a result of yogic practice or divine dispensation or birth; power resulting in control over the physical elements

Sikh – a sect originally formed by Guru Govind Singh in order to protect the dharma

Sita – an incarnation of Shakti as the wife of Lord Rama, kundalini shakti, mother goddess, daughter of earth

Sloka – verse

Smarana – for of upasana, worship through constant remembrance of God's name and presence: mantra japa, meditation of God's virtues and names, etc.

Smriti – memory; Vedic texts transmitted by memory, such as Dharma Shastras; traditional or memorial law

Snana – water offered in worship for bathing of the deity, idol, image

Snanottarasvalpa pooja – short pooja after the bath of the deity, idol, image etc.

Sneha bhava – affectionate feeling, like that between brother and sister

Soham – mantra of the breath; used in the practice of ajapa japa

Sphatik – crystal

Sri – Mother Goddess; consort of Lord Vishnu; epithet of respect; auspicious

Sri Chakra – also known as Sri Yantra; the most respected yantra, symbol of the goddess

Sri Vidya Upasana – main tantric worship in the form of external meditation on yantra and internal meditation on the form of the divine mother

Sri Yantra – the most respected yantra which relates consciousness to the source

Srimad Bhagavat – sacred text recounting the life of Lord Krishna

Sthandila – the offering place for the Vedic sacrifices to which the initial worship is given

Stotra – Sanskrit hymn

Stuti – singing the praises of God

Sudarshan Chakra – the weapon of Lord Krishna; sudarshan literally means 'correct vision'

Sukadeva – a maharishi

Suktas – short vedic hymns of praise to different deities

Saundarya Lahari – 'wave of beauty' the entire 105 stanzas of a poem by Sri Shankaracharya in worship of the mother goddess Tripurasundari; it includes the hymn called Ananda Lahari

Surabhi – the heavenly cow, representing auspiciousness and plenty

Surdas – blind Indian poet saint of the bhakti movement

Sushumna – the major energy flow relating to the spinal cord in the body and to transcendental awareness; activated when ida and pingala are balanced

Sutra – thread of thought outlining the ancient spiritual texts

Svetaketu – son of Aruni

Swabhava – innate nature, personality and limitations

Swadhaya – self-study and study of devotional books; self knowledge, self awareness

Swagata – welcoming the Lord or deity

Swami Ramatirtha – Indian saint

Swami Vivekananda – Indian saint who introduced the western world to Vedanta; a famous disciple of Paramahamsa Ramakrishna

Swaroopa – one's own form

Swastika – a symbol of good or auspicious existence, of the Sun and light; a diagram worshipped as a symbol of Ganesh; often drawn at the holy places of pilgrimage, and on walls of temples

254

Tabla – a pair of drums used especially for classical Indian music

Taittiriya Aranyaka – a vedic text of philosophy

Taittiriya Brahmana – a vedic text of ritual

Tamas – one of the three gunas; quality of inertia, dullness or ignorance

Tambulam – betel nuts used in worship to represent Devi

Tantra – ancient universal science, philosophy and culture which deals with the way for human nature at the present mundane level of evolution and understanding to achieve transcendental knowledge, experience and awareness; process of expansion of mind and liberation of energy

Tapasvi – one who practices tapasya

Tapas/Tapasya – austerity; process of burning impurities

Tat Tvam Asi – Thou are That; one of the four mahavakyas, highest spiritual sayings

Tattwa – essence; the five elements are commonly listed as earth, water, fire, air and space or ether; true or real state

Teertha – sacred place of pilgrimage

Tika (tilak) – red paste applied on the forehead to symbolize and aid meditation on the third eye

Tirthgrahana – service or rite at the end of a pooja where the worshipper applies consecrated water to his head

Titiksha – endurance; one of the six fold virtues

Torah – Hebrew scripture

Tripurasaundari – deity of the Sri Yantra; form of the mother goddess

Tulasi vivaha – marriage ceremony of tulsi to shaligram

Tulsi bush – sacred basil plant; its leaves have medicinal qualities and are regarded as the prasad of Lord Rama and Lord Krishna

Tulsidas – famous Indian saint who wrote *Ramacharitamanasa*, the story of Lord Rama

Turiya – super consciousness; fourth state of consciousness

Tyaga – renunciation

Uddhava – devotee of Lord Krishna

Upachara(s) – materials used or services offered in ritual worship

Upanayan samskara – rite during which yajnopavita is performed, traditionally at the age of seven, when the child is taken to meet the guru for higher education

Upanishads – 'to sit close by and listen'; ancient Vedic texts, conveyed by rishis or seers inducing experiences and giving teachings on the ultimate reality

Uparati – turning away of the senses from the sensory objects

255

Upasaka – one who performs upasana, worship

Upasana – in the proximity of God; sitting near the Lord; personalized form of worship

Upasya – the object of upasana; that being worshipped

Upsarga – a disease, trouble; prefix

Urvashi – a celestial nymph

Uttara pooja – service or rite at the completion of pooja to dismiss the life force invoked into the temporary idol before commencement of worship

Utthana – to rise up or awake

Vaikuntha – heavenly abode of Lord Vishnu

Vaira bhava – feeling of enmity, e.g. feeling of Ravana towards Lord Rama

Vairagya – dispassion; indifference or non-attachment to sensual enjoyments

Vaishnava – tradition in which Lord Vishnu is worshipped as the supreme deity

Vaishnavites – worshippers of Vishnu and his incarnations as the ultimate form of God

Vaishyas – class of vedic society, engaged in trade, commerce and agriculture

Valmiki – rishi who wrote the *Valmiki Ramayana*

Vama marga – path following left hand ritual of the tantras

Vanaprastha ashrama – third stage of life from fifty to seventy-five years of age; retirement from worldly life in order to practice sadhana in relative seclusion

Vandana – prostration, prayer to God; sixth of the nine modes of upasana

Varnashrama – four ashramas or stages of life through which one moves

Varuna – god of water and the oceans

Vasana – seed or inherent desire

Vashishtha – celebrated seer, family priest of the solar race of kings and author of several Vedic hymns; guru of Rama

Vastra – cloth or garment

Vastu – substance

Vasudeva – a name of Krishna

Vatasavitri vrata – a ritual performed by married women in worship the of banyan tree

Vatsalya bhava – attitude of love between a parent and a child

Vedanta – 'end of perceivable knowledge'; one of the six darshanas or systems of Indian philosophy which deals with transcendental and manifest nature of consciousness; final teachings of the Vedas

Vedas – ancient scriptural texts of Sanatan or eternal dharma; revealed texts expressing the knowledge of the whole universe; the four Vedas are: Rik, Yajur, Sama and Arthava

Vibhooti – sacred ash given as prasad after worship; special siddhi

Videha mukti – beyond body consciousness

Vidhi – the correct process for pooja

Vidura – a great bhakta

Vigraha – form, e.g. form of Devi

Vijnanamaya kosha – sheath or body of intuitive awareness

Vinayaka – another name of Lord Ganesha

Vipassana – Buddhist meditation practice

Vira – hero; heroic

Virat – the universe; cosmic Vishnu

Virat Purusha – universal body of God

Visarjana – final act of worship when an idol is immersed into a tank or body of water

Vishad – unhappiness, dejection and despair

Vishnu – the aspect of the supreme concerned with maintenance or preservation often associated with water; second of the divine Hindu trinity; sustainer of the universe

Vishvas – belief

Vishwakarma pooja – ritual worship to sanctify tools of trade

Vishwakarma – engineer and architect of the gods

Vishwamitra – rishi who heard the Gayatri mantra in meditation; a kshatriya (warrior class) who became self-realized and a brahmarishi

Vivaha – marriage ceremony

Viveka – discrimination; right knowledge or understanding

Vrata – a vow prescribed by the scriptures and spiritual preceptors

Vrindavan – place where Lord Krishna played as a child expressing divine consciousness

Vritti – circle, pattern of the mind; mental modification

Vyasa – acclaimed author of the *Bhagavad Gita* and other scriptures

Yagyopaveet – sacred thread

Yajna – worship through sacrifice; sacrificial rite to gods or deities; a sacred ceremony, form of worship including offering oblations to fire; complete ritual of the fire ceremony performed for external and internal purification; education; any work which is beneficial to one and all

Yajna Purusha – where a Brahmin is regarded as sacrifice personified

Yama – social observances defined by Patanjali: non-violence, truth, honesty, sensual abstinence and non-possessiveness; god of death

Yamuna – sacred river of India

Yantra – geometric symbol designed for concentration to unleash the hidden potential within the consciousness; visual form of mantra which holds the essence of manifestation; a symbol of divinity

Yatra – pilgrimage; spiritual journey

Yatris – pilgrims

Yoga – union; from *yuj* to yoke; system of thought and practices leading to a state of union between two opposite poles, i.e. individual and universal awareness; one of the six classical Indian philosophies

Yoga Sutras – ancient authorive text on raja yoga by Patanjali

Yoni – source; womb; number of possible births, 84 lakh in number

Yuga – an age, epoch or cycle of earth and mankind, the four being satya yuga, treta yuga, dwapar yuga and the present kali yuga